SUPERTIPS 2

Moyra Bremner is the author of the hugely
popular bestseller, SUPERTIPS TO MAKE
LIFE EASY, and of PASTA FOR PLEASURE.
Having qualified both as an actress and a teacher,
she worked as a photographic model before
taking up a professional career in teaching. Later
she read Psychology at London University and
moved into journalism. Though she specialises in
business, science and medicine she has also
written on a wide range of other topics for such
publications as the *Sunday Times*, the *Guardian*,
Interiors, *Elle* and *New Scientist*. She was the first
woman presenter of the BBC's *Money
Programme* and is now a regular broadcaster. The
mother of three grown-up children, she combines
her career with running a house, car, garden, and
two cats, single-handed.

Supertips 2

Moyra Bremner

Illustrated by
Marie-Hélène Jeeves

CORONET BOOKS
Hodder and Stoughton

Copyright © 1985 by Moyra Bremner
First published in Great Britain in 1985
by André Deutsch Ltd

Coronet edition 1986

British Library C.I.P.

Bremner, Moyra
   Supertips 2.
   1. Home economics – Handbooks, manuals, etc.
   I. Title
   640   TX159

   ISBN 0-340-38312-7

Printed and bound in Great Britain for
Hodder and Stoughton Paperbacks, a
division of Hodder and Stoughton Ltd,
Mill Road, Dunton Green, Sevenoaks,
Kent (Editorial Office: 47 Bedford
Square, London, WC1 3DP) by
Hunt Barnard Printing Ltd, Aylesbury, Bucks.
Photoset by Rowland Phototypesetting Ltd,
Bury St Edmunds, Suffolk.

*To Dr Robert Shields and Joshua Fox
without whose encouragement I
might never have started writing.*

CONTENTS

INTRODUCTION

I introduced *Supertips to Make Life
Easy* by saying that it was 'shamelessly dedicated to making life easier'. So perhaps I should say this
book is shamelessly dedicated to
making it easier still. Once again,
my aim is to save time, money and energy by putting into
everyone's hands the tips, and wrinkles, short-cuts and bits
of expertise which I have collected from both experts and
ordinary people all over the country.

On hearing that I planned to write a sequel to *Supertips
to Make Life Easy*, a lot of people said, 'Is there anything
more to write?' My answer was a resounding 'yes'. The
problem with that first book had been not where to start,
but where to stop. I squeezed in as much as I could, but
there were entire chapters, and whole aspects of certain
topics, which I couldn't fit in. As my publishers pointed
out, I had no contract to write an encyclopedia.

Also, if you are an inveterate collector, you don't stop
collecting just because you have filled up a cabinet or – if
what you collect is ideas – a book. The first *Supertips*
hadn't even reached the printers before I was running
across new short-cuts, and new ways to do all kinds of
things just that little bit better and more easily. For

example, while reading *New Scientist*, I unexpectedly came across the only infallible way to crack a Brazil nut without breaking it. And while I was touring the television stations and being made up for cover photographs, I came across all kinds of new tips for applying make-up more effectively, which, added to those I had gained in my modelling days, formed the basis for a chapter on beauty.

Then friends – who have the mistaken idea that I'm well organized – badgered me into including a chapter on being organized and, knowing I can never resist passing on a good idea, threw in some of their own favourite tips to get me started. But most of all, I was inundated with marvellous hints and suggestions from readers and from people who had heard me on television and radio. As I went round the country, it was fascinating to discover that in certain areas – I particularly remember Leicester – people seem to be bursting with good ideas for saving time and money.

Finally, the readers of publications such as *Family Circle* and listeners to programmes such as 'Woman's Hour' sent in a splendidly imaginative and thoughtful selection of tips in response to 'Supertips' competitions, which the editors concerned have generously allowed me to use. What I liked most about so many of them was that they found practical and original ways of solving really basic problems.

In addition to all the information I received, there is also information I have been asked for. Writing the first book, I had to judge which pieces of information would be most useful on the basis of my own experience. In this one, I've been guided by the queries that people have come up with in letters and on radio phone-ins all over the country. Sometimes I knew the answers, but hadn't realized they'd be useful to other people; sometimes a problem was completely new to me, so I had to go away to get expert advice on how to solve it. This has meant that I've picked the brains of dry cleaners and furniture restorers, painters, decorators, professional gardeners, and a whole host of experts in companies up and down the country: in fact anyone who could give me the best possible answer to the problem in question. These solutions I've included in this book.

Some of the chapters may seem slightly unlikely for a book of this sort: the chapter on children, for example. But, as a mother of three children (now grown-up) and a teacher for many years, I felt that I could scarcely talk about saving energy without looking at the most energy-consuming element of any family. Of course child-rearing is a big subject, so this chapter doesn't pretend to be comprehensive; nonetheless it does something which is unusual in books on child-care: it starts from the parents' point of view. It may not be a complete survival course, but it does contain some hints which have helped other parents to draw breath.

This isn't a book just for women, even though it contains beauty hints; nor is it a book just for parents, even though it has a chapter on coping with children; nor is it a book just for gardeners, even though it has a large gardening section. It's designed for anyone who ever finds themselves short of time, or money or energy, and who would like to pick someone else's brains on some of the best ways to cope. My criteria for selecting a tip have been either that someone asked me to solve that particular problem or that the tip was one I wished I had known before. And, if anyone doesn't find the answer to their particular query in here, it is probably because it's in *Supertips to Make Life Easy*.

To make the information easier to find, the tips are in alphabetical order within each chapter and there is a comprehensive index. However, it is a book designed as much for browsing as for looking things up in an emergency. Most of the tips are strictly practical, but a few are included simply because they charmed and amused me; I hope they will do the same for my readers.

I want to thank the people all over the world, and particularly in Great Britain, who have not only sent me their favourite tips and shared their knowledge with me, but have also often trusted me with treasured family collections and old books. I also want to thank my friends and

acquaintances who have so often let me pick their brains
and given me so much help.

A special thank you is due to the staff of 'Woman's
Hour' and of *Family Circle*, to the *Nottingham Evening
Post* and the *Southern Evening Echo* and to BBC Radio
Cambridgeshire, BBC Radio Derby, BBC Radio Man-
chester and BBC Radio WM; and to all those who entered
their competitions.

I am also indebted to the following companies, organizations and individuals for letting me take up their time and
for sharing their expertise and giving me invaluable advice:

Addis Limited
The Automobile Association
The Boots Company PLC
Cadbury Limited
Cheseborough Pond's
  Limited
Coates UK Limited
Connolly Brothers
Dylon Limited
Evo-stik
Flint
G.E. Holloway and Sons
Imperial Chemical
  Industries
Dr J. Levin
Dr Linda Anderson

Made in Suede
The Meech Group
Polycell Products Limited
The Potato Marketing
  Board
Qualcast Limited
Tosh Reynolds
The Royal Horticultural
  Society
The Stove Shop
Superior Seals
Tate and Lyle
Thames Water
Tony Venison
James Walker Limited
Adam Wilcox

Without their generosity this book would not have been
possible, and it is in a sense their book as much as mine.
The verses by Lawrence Hills from his book *Grow Your
Own Fruit and Vegetables* are quoted by permission of
Faber & Faber.

My final thanks go to my family, who have eaten my
culinary experiments, trustingly allowed me to try out
stain-removal techniques on their clothes and uncomplain-
ingly picked their way round tests and experiments of every
sort; and to Diana Athill, the best editor any author could
hope for.

Your Plants

Seeding and Growing
Friends and Foes
Supporting and Tending
Pot Plants and Flowers

SEEDING AND GROWING

Grossly to adapt Shakespeare, 'Some are born gardeners, some hope to achieve gardening, and some have gardening thrust upon them.' The born gardeners are those who can be seen tidying their plants equally keenly in arctic wind and blistering heat. In the ranks of those who hope to achieve gardening, I count anyone who would, theoretically, like to garden if only it didn't involve more than reading the gardening columns and buying seeds on impulse; also those who genuinely enjoy planting, trimming and watering, but find that their work and the weather combine to prevent them doing so. Those who have gardening thrust upon them need no explanation.

This is mainly a chapter for those who hope to achieve gardening, or who have gardening thrust upon them. It contains some of my own favourite tips and a lot of hints from gardeners from all over the country: hints which make a difference, but seldom find their way into books. It combines the old know-how, which has traditionally been passed on from gardener to gardener, with ingenious ideas cooked up by individual gardeners and some of the latest ideas in professional horticulture.

Gardening is still an art rather than a science and many of the beliefs which gardeners have held for centuries – such as companion planting, in which problems are reduced or prevented by planting certain plants near each other – have never been thoroughly tested. So some of the ideas in this chapter are scientifically proven, some are not. Some go back centuries and some were born almost yesterday. What they have in common is that each was passed on to me because someone somewhere found it worked. Which is, after all, how gardening developed for all those years before science came along.

BULBS

The simple rule for planting bulbs of all kinds out of doors is to plant them at three times their own depth. If the planting is too shallow, they may flower well the first year but fail to get the necessary moisture and food to do well after that.

CABBAGES

Disease Prevention
The real curse of the cabbage tribe is club root, and the oldest method of preventing this is still the best. Allow at least two years before planting any member of this family on the same bit of soil – and meanwhile watch out for the weed Shepherd's Purse, which, though it doesn't look like it, belongs to the cabbage family. It could keep the disease active in the ground between one planting and the next. If there's a chance of club root being still in the ground, and you simply must plant cabbages, use the old gardeners' trick of popping a mothball down each hole where you plant a seedling. Or, better still, dress the land with hydrated lime the winter before.

Traditionally celery is meant to be a protective plant for cabbages and, when it's nearby, cabbages should be less prone to disease. Cabbages are also said to grow better near sage, rosemary, thyme, mint and potatoes. So there are plenty of companion plants to choose from, and sage in particular is said to keep away cabbage butterflies.

Extra Cabbages
When spring cabbages are doing well, you can trick the plants into producing extra cabbages for you. When you cut a cabbage for the table, strip the remaining leaves from

the stem and cut an X in the top of the stump. Then keep it well fed and watered and, since every plant needs leaves to survive, it will throw out new leaves on each section of the stump and produce three or four little cabbages for you.

CARRYING CUTTINGS

To carry a cutting safely from one garden to another, put it in a polythene bag, blow up the bag until it is really full of air, twist the top tightly and close it very firmly. With a nice cushion of slightly moist air all around it, the cutting won't dry out so easily, and it is protected from knocks.

CAULIFLOWERS

Towards the end of the season, cauliflowers are easily spoilt by frost and need to have their curds protected. The easy way to do this is to snap some of the longest leaves, without breaking them completely, and bend them over the top. Another easy way is to cover the curds with the inverted leaves from the base of a cut cauliflower.

CELERY

Cabbages are said to help celery just as much as celery helps cabbages. If they are grown as neighbours, celery is said to get less leaf miner. Celery is also meant to do better if dwarf beans are grown nearby – maybe it thrives on a sense of superiority.

CINDERS

At one time plants beloved by slugs used to have little heaps of cinders put over them in the autumn, after they had been cut down for the winter. The idea was to keep slugs off the new shoots the following spring. Some say that the undersides of slugs are so tough, and their appetites so demanding, that they'll climb over anything to get to a tasty shoot, but cinders seemed to work well in the gardens of my childhood and some people still swear by them.

Anyone who tries them should let the cinders stand outside in the rain for at least six months before they are used on plants. Fresh cinders contain chemicals which could be harmful.

COMPOST

It has become fashionable to regard composting as a science. Each compost heap is seen as a complex (but ecologically desirable) factory, which, given the right amount of air, activator, bacteria, moisture, heat and mumbo-jumbo, will produce nutrient-rich humus to make plants live happily ever after.

Of course no garden should be without compost and, if you do everything the compost experts tell you, a beautiful stack of humus will result. But the truth is, it probably will, even if you don't. Rotting is a natural process and it doesn't need a lot of help from man. As the old gardeners knew, all the heap needs is air – no problem; moisture – rain; bacteria – in the earth; and nitrogen – urine or sulphate of ammonia.

Anything which once lived can go on the heap, including egg-shells. Though it's wise to avoid anything which could breed flies, and such perennial weeds as couch grass and bindweed which may survive the heap.

Unless you actually *wash* your weeds before throwing them away there is no need to do as some suggest and add earth to provide bacteria. As far as activators are concerned, it's no coincidence that the compost heap and the privy often used to stand side by side. Slops were used on compost heaps for centuries before packets of activator, or sulphate of ammonia, came along, and garden scientists tell me that urine is probably the best activator of all. It has an established reputation. A manual entitled *Muck for the Many* published in the 1860s details the use of slops in the garden and reports that one correspondent grew an onion 18 inches in circumference on house slops alone –

though it does not say whether he ate it. I'm not suggesting
noisome heaps should sully the gardens of this green and
pleasant land, but if the activator does run out . . .

COUCH GRASS

Couch grass comes top of my personal list of garden
plagues. Once in a bed it behaves like the mythological
monster which grew two heads for each one which was cut
off. The golden rule, which I once arrogantly ignored, is
never to plant up a bed until this weed has been driven
from the spot, and never EVER to compost it. On bare
ground it can be eradicated by chemicals, but there's no
chance of using this easy way once it's happily entwined
with your plants.

Those who avoid chemicals at all costs say that a thick
planting of tomatoes, turnips or *Tagetes minuta* (see page
53) will kill it – though most gardening experts pour scorn
on the idea. There are also those who swear by getting a
pig to do the work: it seems it will pig the ground merrily
and munch up the dreaded roots – though it would take a
very thorough pig to get rid of all of them, and pigs, like
chemicals, would have to operate on bare ground. Those
who, like me, have it firmly ensconced in the garden must
resort to simply removing the grass the instant it shows
above the surface. After all, nothing lives for ever without
top growth – or so they say.

DEAD-HEADING

When I was a little girl I fell in love with pansies and
planted them everywhere. It was an elderly gardener who
taught me that I had to take off each flower as soon as it
wilted if I wanted the plants to keep on flowering. With
any flower it's easy to forget that their objective is to set
seed and so continue their species, and only if we frustrate
this purpose will they keep on producing flowers for us.

THE EIGHTY-TWENTY RULE

Businessmen in Manhattan talk of the 20 per cent rule –
20 per cent of the people in a company create 80 per cent
of the profits, 20 per cent of the people (a different 20 per
cent) cause 80 per cent of the problems and so on. It's
amazing how often the 80:20 ratio applies. It certainly
applies in gardens. If you want a garden that won't wear
you to the bone, no more than 20 per cent of the plants
should need regular attention and 80 per cent of them
should look after themselves, without pruning, tying up,
dead-heading, or any of those other time-consuming little
chores.

In Britain – where about 80 per cent of the weather is
poor and 20 per cent of it fine – it's worth remembering
that you'll be looking out at the garden from the windows
at least 80 per cent of the time. This affects the way you
design the garden and what plants you put in it. Ideally 80
per cent of the good bits (and no more than 20 per cent of
the bad bits) should be visible from the house. This sounds
obvious, but it's amazing how often people put incinerators
in full view and choice shrubs out of sight.

If you grow herbs, at least 80 per cent of them should
be in places where you can find them when it's dark and
raining, without ruining your shoes. For a well-known law
decrees that it's bound to be raining at least 20 per cent of
the times when you need them, and in my experience it's
dark for the other 80 per cent.

It's also a rule of nature that, however much we like to
think of plants in terms of their flowers, nothing, absolutely nothing, flowers for more than 20 per cent of the
year. (I do not count the daisies in the lawn.) So 80 per
cent of the pleasure in a garden has to come from the
shape of the plants and their leaves – so we pay a high
price for those seductive but ephemeral roses.

Opinions are divided on what proportion of a garden
should be evergreen, but, if more than 80 per cent of the
plants shed their leaves in winter, you can be sure the
garden will look pretty bleak for at least 20 per cent of

the year. But if 80 per cent of the plants are attractive evergreens, and 20 per cent of the plants have beautiful flowers, the garden will look good 100 per cent of the time. I just wish I'd known the 80–20 rule when I planted *my* garden.

FERTILIZER

Fertilizers are much cheaper if you mix them yourself and, if you can find a garden sundries supplier to give you what you require, it isn't hard. A good general fertilizer is composed of 3 parts superphosphate of lime, 2 parts sulphate of ammonia, and 1 part sulphate of potash, by weight. You need to use about 2–4 oz (60–120 g) per square yard (sq m). Be sure to transfer these garden chemicals to strong plastic bags and label them carefully. All too often old-style garden sundries suppliers use old-style paper bags which break at the first hint of damp weather.

GOURDS

Though they look so inviting on packets, ornamental gourds can be a great disappointment. They are not designed for temperate conditions and need constant greenhouse temperatures to be sure of germinating. If you can't offer them a greenhouse, start them on a warm window ledge, and try one of the old tricks for getting them going: some gardeners swear by holding the seeds in their mouths for a while before planting, to let the heat and wet work on the hard casing. Nowadays some seeds may be treated with chemicals, so it may be wiser to use another gardener's trick and cut a small nick in the edge of the seeds with a sharp knife and soak them for a little while in lukewarm water. This can also be tried on marrows and courgettes if you want to hurry them along.

HANGING BASKETS

The trouble with hanging baskets is that, if they are high enough to fill a gap, they are too high to water easily. However, I've been sent two rather neat solutions to this problem. One is to put the water in an empty, well-rinsed, washing-up-liquid bottle. Held at the right angle, and squeezed sharply, it will eject a neat arc of liquid which lands in the baskets – though maybe practice sessions should be done when nobody is passing, to get the aim right.

For sporting gardeners, there's the ice-cube basketball method in which ice cubes are lobbed into the baskets. Either way you can use a liquid fertilizer in the water – but, to avoid fertilizing your friends, ice-cubes containing fertilizer need to be very clearly labelled. I suggest cling film over the top and a label on the cling film – nobody will ever read the warning if you write it on the side of the ice-cube tray.

LAWNS

Cutting
First the good news. A recent study showed that the healthiest lawn is one which has the lawn clippings left on to fertilize it. So no more raking. The bad news is that this is only so if the lawn is mown very often. It is very short clippings which do the job: cutting out light and air with a quilting of hay is another matter.

Lawn Mowing for the Lazy
You may think that stories of circular lawns mown by a mower attached to a stake in the centre were pure mythology. Not so. A friend of mine has one and has devised a stake with a drum round it which exactly takes up the right amount of guide wire to allow the mower to go round and round, mowing a fresh piece of grass at each circuit. Meanwhile he just sits in the sun and watches it work. Any ingenious handyman could construct a similar service.

Weedkilling

You don't need an expensive branded weedkiller to remove weeds from a lawn. If you can find a good garden
sundries supplier, you need only buy the ingredients for
the following mixture: 1 part sulphate of iron, 3 parts
sulphate of ammonia and 20 parts sharp sand. Mix these
well together and, on a hot dry day – but not during a
drought – sprinkle the mixture on the lawn using about 4
oz (120 g) to a square yard (sq m). Three applications
during the summer should kill the weeds and make the
grass grow better. Don't worry if the grass turns black at
first; this is only temporary.

One of the good things about this lawn sand is that it
can be used just as well on individual weeds as on the
whole lawn, so it's useful to make a bit extra and keep it
for persistent ones.

Fertilizer

The old-fashioned mixtures for feeding lawns are also a
better buy than pricey packets. Old gardeners have many
recipes, but a simple one is 1 part sulphate of ammonia, 2
parts dried blood, 2 parts sulphate of potash, mixed with
20 parts sharp sand. The lawn will need a couple of applications in the spring, about a month apart, using 6 oz (180
g) to the square yard (sq m). Don't be alarmed that this
fertilizer has something in common with the weedkiller;
there is no mistake.

LEAF MOULD

Leaf mould is the easiest garden humus of all to make.
And the only leaves you mustn't compost are those from
diseased trees – which should be burnt immediately.
Leaves rot much faster than other compost and, provided
they are in a heap on their own, they'll be ready to dig
into the ground in a few months. Only a few trees have
leaves which take time to rot, among them are the plane
trees, horse chestnut, holly and laurel. But even these can
be dug into the soil within the year, and there's no need

to worry if they aren't fully rotted down; on clay soil or fine sand the coarseness of the leaves is a positive advantage and helps to improve the texture of the soil.

If there's no room in the garden for a special heap, push the leaves into one of the fine mesh nylon sacks which greengrocers throw away. This will hold them together and allow enough air for them to rot well. It also makes it splendidly easy to take the leaves to wherever you want to dig them in. But don't be tempted to put them in a plastic bag instead: without air, they will be broken down by a different set of bacteria and become a repellant stinking sludge instead of the crumbly humus which air-loving bacteria make.

LETTUCES

Varieties of lettuce which tend to trail their leaves in the dirt can be kept clean, and out of slugs' temptation, by planting them inside a ring cut from a bottle of washing-up liquid. Some people also swear by growing leeks and celery inside the cylinders from such bottles. Whatever the plants, this should be a shady practice, for in full sun the danger is that the plastic will overheat and 'cook' the vegetable it is meant to be protecting.

MANURE

Nowadays manure may not be all it appears to be. A lot of stables are using sawdust instead of straw. The trouble is that sawdust doesn't rot as easily as straw and if you put it on the garden before it has thoroughly rotted it will lock up large quantities of nitrogen which are needed by the plants, and make their diet poorer instead of richer. The solution is to stack sawdust-based manure in layers, with sulphate of ammonia in between to help it rot. Once rotted it will be as good as any other manure.

MARROWS

I remember as a child standing eye to eye with the great golden flowers of marrows which cottage gardeners had planted on their compost heaps. It is the ideal place for these greedy heat-loving plants and saves much space in the garden.

Unfortunately, the sex life of marrows is not what it might be, because, strangely, bees are not good at pollinating these inviting cornucopia. This means artificial insemination is needed to get a really good crop. When the flowers are well out, strip the petals off a male flower and push it gently into a female one – the female is the one with a tiny marrow shape at its base. After that, nature will do the rest.

NETTLES

Whether nettles are an excellent fertilizer or not is a matter of debate. Experts I've discussed it with say 'no', gardeners who use them say 'yes'. If you want to see for yourself, cut them and put them in an old dustbin full of water. When they begin to stink, they are ready. The liquid can be used as liquid fertilizer and the nettle sludge put on the compost heap.

There is just as much controversy over the best way to get rid of nettles. Some say that constantly cutting them kills them, other that it has the reverse effect and stimulates their growth. But since digging them out is impossible – there are always some of those thread-like roots left behind – the choice is between using a herbicide or cutting again and again and waiting to see if it works in your case.

PARSLEY

Tradition has it that if rosemary thrives in the garden, the woman of the house is the boss; it also says that whoever can make parsley grow wears the trousers. So a garden where both flourish under a woman's hand must surely be the sign of a hen-pecked husband.

Parsley certainly is tricky to get going, and old gardeners used to say that it went three times to the devil before it would germinate and various tricks were used to help it along. A popular one was to soak the seeds overnight in urine warm from the body. The fastidious may be relieved to hear that the modern way is to put the seeds overnight in a thermos of very hot water, or to pour boiling water along the row after it has been sown. Pouring boiling water along the row has the advantage that it will kill any weed seeds which are just starting to sprout, so the parsley gets off to a clean start. But in my experience the overnight soaking does more for its germination.

PEAS AND BEANS

All the leguminous vegetables – the pea and bean family – have nodules on their roots which put nitrogen into the soil. As nitrogen is just what many other plants need, growing them can be an effortless way to fertilize the ground. When the beans are over, don't pull them up. Cut them off at ground level, then the roots can be dug in to continue feeding the soil with nitrogen for the following year.

Cabbages in particular need nitrogen for their green leafy growth and traditionally cabbages are grown in ground where beans were sown the year before. Equally, if you are starting a new garden and plan to put in the shrubs and roses next year, it's a good idea to grow beans in the area where you'll be putting the roses. Nitrogen encourages roses to make vigorous shoots and leaves; this is just what you want in new plants at the start of the growing season. Though, by the same token, it's wise to avoid the temptation to plant a bean row behind the fledgeling roses, for too much nitrogen late in the season will make roses create leaves rather than blooms.

PICKING APPLES AND PEARS

It's tempting to pick apples and pears as soon as they look full and fat and can be pulled off the branch. In fact apples should only be taken from the tree if they separate when lifted and slightly twisted – though no apple should stay on a tree much after mid-October, ripe or not.

For pears the reverse is true. Only the early varieties ripen well on the tree, the rest should be picked as soon as they begin to ripen round the stem, then put in a cool place, nicely spaced so they do not touch each other. Like this they ripen better and are kept from marauding wasps which would invade at the first sign of ripeness.

POTATOES

I'm told that a crafty way to make new potatoes easier to dig up is to take short lengths of nylon netting and lay them in the potato trench – with their edges protruding on each side – then plant the potatoes on top of them. That way you can just lift up the netting to get at the potatoes and there's no risk of spearing them with a fork. Of course, a few may grow through the mesh and need to be forked up afterwards.

POTTING UP

Seeds
The cardboard centres of loo rolls and kitchen paper can provide free jiffy pots for seedlings which don't like to be disturbed. Just cut them in rings the right depth, stand them on a waterproof tray, fill them with earth and pop in the seeds. When the time comes to plant out the seedlings, just slide an old kitchen spatula underneath and slip the seedling, pot and all, into the hole. The cardboard will rot in the ground.

Plants
Plants in flowerpots need plenty of drainage, so broken

pottery flower pots and old china should be tucked away
for putting at the bottom of pots before they are filled with
earth.

PROPAGATION – THE COCA-COLA GREENHOUSE

It's amazing how many plants can be propagated in the
even heat of a sunny indoor windowsill, and there are all
kinds of expensive indoor propagators on the market.
Basically they are simply devices for keeping the plants
correctly watered, making a cosy light and draught-free
environment and preventing too much water escaping into
the atmosphere. Provided you get the watering right, you
can provide all these conditions by cutting the bottom off
a clear plastic fizzy drink bottle, removing the lid, and
popping it over the seeds or cuttings in an ordinary flowerpot.

RAMPANT GROWERS

Some plants are so invasive that they are introduced at
one's peril. Those which spread on the surface are manageable, if work-producing. Those with pervasive roots can
be a plague. Two major offenders are mint and horseradish. The traditional way to grow mint is in an old
bucket, pierced with drainage holes, sunk in the ground.
Cheaper and easier to pierce is one of the very large tins
professional painters buy their paint in – and they are
happy to give empty ones away. Horseradish may work its
way out of its container, so the only safe method is to grow
it in a tub standing on stone or concrete. Isolated in this
way, these plants are a boon not a curse.

ROSES

Feeding
Roses appear to have catholic tastes. Some gardeners say
their roses love a dose of Epsom Salts – a teaspoonful

each, watered into the base in spring to give good green growth. More, they say, makes them too leafy. Others say there is nothing they like more than a bit of fat under the roots, or a mulch of grass cuttings or tea leaves, or even banana skins. I personally suspect these blousy beauties just like attention of any sort, though there is one sort of attention I would hesitate to give them: an underplanting of French marigolds. This is said to keep away aphids – which makes me respect aphids. The colour combination would be too dreadful to live with.

If disease is a problem, some gardeners swear by an underplanting of chives or garlic to keep away black spot and mildew. And it seems the garlic will grow fatter if planted in October rather than in the spring – provided it survives the winter.

Pruning

Rose pruning is a contrary business – both easier and more difficult than many suppose. It's easy enough to cut out the dead wood and cut the stems at the right angle just above an eye, but the real skill lies in suiting the pruning to each particular rose. This isn't just a matter of pruning hybrid teas one way and floribundas another; some hybrid teas grow far more vigorously than others and each variety needs to be pruned to suit its vigour. This means getting to know your roses. After that, pruning should be the opposite of what you might think – pruning stimulates growth, so the more vigorous they are, the less hard you prune them.

RHUBARB

One of the peculiarities of rhubarb is that it needs to be plucked and not picked. To keep it pale and tender for the table, old-time gardeners used to cover each crown with a chimney pot, but anything of similar shape will do, and some gardeners force winter rhubarb by putting a large tub over the crown and heaping it with leaves and compost to keep the plants warm while they grow.

The leaves of rhubarb are an old-fashioned insecticide. You just steep them in boiling water for an hour or so and use the liquid as a greenfly spray. Let them do double duty; do the steeping in an aluminium saucepan which needs a good clean. The acid in the leaves will take the blackness from the aluminium, and all you have to do is wash it very well afterwards. As the chemicals in the rhubarb leaves are poisonous, the liquid should not be used on vegetables.

SEEDS

Longevity

When I first started gardening I was puzzled as to how long seeds would keep and still germinate reasonably well. Then, in Lawrence Hill's invaluable book *Grow Your Own Fruit and Vegetables*, I discovered the following rhyme created by him in the style of Thomas Tusser. Of course, it's only useful if you remember to date your seed packets when you buy them.

You have in your drawer since Candlemas Day,
All the seed packets you daren't throw away,
Seed Catalogue cometh as year it doth end,
But look in ye drawer before money you spend.

Throw out ye Parsnip, 'tis no good next year,
And Scorzonera if there's any there,
For these have a life which is gone with ye wynde
Unlike all ye seeds of ye cabbagy kinde.

Broccoli, Cauliflower, Sprouts, Cabbage and Kale,
Live long like a farmer who knoweth good ale;
Three years for certain, maybe five or four,
To sow in their seasons they stay in ye drawer.

Khol-Rabi lasts with them and so does Pei-Tsai,
The winter 'cos lettuce' to sow in July,
But short is the life of ye Turnips and Swedes
So next year, only enough for your needs.

Mustard and cress for when salads come round,
Sow for three seasons so buy half a pound,
Radish lasts four years, both round ones and long,
Sow thinly and often they're never too strong.

Last year's left Lettuce sows three summers more,
And Beetroot and Spinach-beet easily four,
But ordinary Spinach, both prickly and round,
Hath one summer left before gaps waste ye ground.

Leeks sow three Aprils and one hath gone past,
And this is as long as ye Carrot will last,
Onion seed keeps till four years have flown by,
But sets are so easy and dodge onion-fly.

Store Marrows and Cucumbers, best when they're
     old,
Full seven summers' sowing a packet can hold.
Six hath ye Celery that needs frost to taste,
So hath Celeriac before it goes to waste.

Broad Beans, French ones, Runner, sown in May,
Each hath a sowing left before you throw it away,
And short peas, tall Peas, fast ones and slow,
Parsley and Salsify have one more spring to sow.

Then fillen ye form that your seedsman doth send,
For novelties plentie, there's money to spend,
Good seed and good horses are worth the expense,
So pay them your poundies as I paid my pence.

Row Marking

The usual practice is to put seed packets on sticks at the
end of rows to show what is growing there, but they quickly
become sodden and blow away. If they are enclosed in a
lidded jam jar standing at the end of the row, they make
better markers and you can then slit open the packet and
note your comments on that particular variety on the
inside, and keep it for when you next order seeds. That

way you have a running file of the performance of everything you grow. If you think animals may knock the jars
over, you can always keep them in place with a stockade
of three sticks.

Saving

When plants are in full flower and you spot one which is
a bit special, it is easy to imagine you will remember exactly
which one it is when the time comes to collect seeds. In
my experience, by the time late summer comes, it has
blended in with the rest. The best plan is to tie a piece of
brightly coloured ribbon or wool to the plant – preferably
to match the flower – and make a note of which ribbons
you tied to which plants. Then in autumn you know exactly
which seeds you are taking. Once gathered they keep best
in paper bags.

Sowing Methods

It is almost impossible to sow very fine seeds without
spreading them too thickly unless you use a few tricks.

If you are planting individual seeds in trays for forcing,
spread the seeds on a plate and make a series of small
holes in the earth with the tip of a pencil. Then dip the tip
of the pencil in water, touch it to a seed to pick it up,
thrust the pencil tip into one of the holes, and twist slightly
to brush the seed off against the earth.

For sowing seeds in rows, the old trick is to mix them
with a handful of fine silver sand. A more modern method
is to mix a thin paste of flour and water, stir the seeds in
evenly, and put the mixture into an icing bag. All you have
to do then is to squeeze a line of seeded paste out along
your row as you might squeeze toothpaste on to a brush,
and the seeds get off to a good start in a nice damp
environment.

A tip a friend of mine recommends is to sow seeds in a
section of 4 in (10 cm) round gutter, instead of the usual
seed trays. For planting out, the gutter end can be removed
and they can be slid out into position with a minimum of
disturbance.

Trays for Seeds

To raise seeds outside, one needs neither expensive seed boxes nor a greenhouse. Greengrocers give away shallow wooden boxes. It doesn't matter that their slats are too far apart; just line them with polythene in which you've pierced drainage holes.

If you have some good loamy soil, you can use that instead of potting compost, provided you mix it with a little sand or peat – say, 6 parts of soil to 1 part each of peat and sharp sand.

When the seeds are planted and watered and the boxes put in a sunny position, a piece of glass laid across each box will create a miniature cold frame. It doesn't have to be new glass, so it can usually be found when buildings are being refurbished, or sometimes on skips.

If you live near a wholesale fish market, and have a garden large enough to hide a slight eyesore, you can create small cold frames from the large heavy-duty poly-styrene boxes which fish is sold in. They are usually thrown away in great stacks when the market closes.

SOOT

Soot is one of the oldest fertilizers, and it usefully doubles as a soil fumigant and an insecticide. Used fresh, the sulphur compounds it contains are fatal to plants, so they will usefully fumigate soil and kill weeds on bare land. If you want to use it as a fertilizer, it needs to be stored for 6 months in a bone dry, airy place to allow the sulphur to disperse. After that it can be put straight on the ground or you can put 2–3 lb (1–1 ½ kg) in a sack and suspend it in a dustbin of water. When the water is a deep golden brown, it can be sprayed on foliage plants which would benefit from nitrogen. The liquid acts both as a fertilizer and an insecticide.

SHRUB MOVING

The greatest enemy to successfully moving established shrubs is that transplanted roots take a little while to establish themselves and draw up the normal amount of water, but the leaves go on releasing moisture as if nothing had happened – so the poor shrub just dries out. Now there is a product which will coat the leaves without harming them and prevent a lot of the water loss. This gives shrubs a better chance. It's Wilt Pruf S 600, the same pine oil extract that can be sprayed on Christmas trees (p. 56), but if you have a lot of foliage to cover it may be more economical to buy the concentrate which is sold to commercial growers and dilute it yourself, rather than use a spray can. It can be obtained direct from the manufacturers. (See page 305.)

SWEETCORN

People often have trouble getting a good crop from sweetcorn. The pollen from its golden tassles is carried on the wind, so only when it's grown in a block, not a row, will you get good fertilization whichever way the wind blows. To make sure it reaches the fertilization stage, plant the seeds in peat pots: for it hates to be transplanted.

TEA FERTILIZER

According to my grandmother, tea was a favourite Victorian fertilizer for aspidistras, though how much good it did she couldn't recall. The Victorians were right in thinking it was good for plants: tea contains nitrogen. The only snag is that the tannin in tea tends to lock up the nitrogen and it is released very slowly, so tea leaves are best used in general compost or under trees where they can work away over several years. Plants can also find goodness in the tea you don't drink, so pour it on the flower bed.

TOMATOES

If you want to bring on the odd truss of tomatoes, one way to do it is to slip the truss into a plastic bag, make a few holes at the lower end to let any condensation run out, and close the upper end with a clothes peg. This mini-greenhouse will bring them on nicely, but don't be tempted to over-use the method – the bag can provide a cosy breeding ground for disease.

TREE PLANTING

People often make the same mistake with trees that they make with puppies and kittens: they forget they will grow into something much larger with quite different needs. All too often, beautiful young trees are planted so close together that some will certainly have to be chopped down before they reach maturity – and, as trees are never cheap, it is a huge waste of money. The trouble is that most catalogues give the height of a tree but not its width. The proportions of trees vary, but the rule of thumb is that, on average, the total width of a mature tree will be the same as its height.

When planting a tree in a small garden, you need to think about the size of its roots just as much as its branches – or maybe even more. The roots may be far wider. In many trees the root run IN EACH DIRECTION is the same as the height. And when a tree is to be planted in clay soil or near a house, this root width is the most important point to bear in mind, especially if the tree is a heavy drinker like a willow. Thirsty roots can draw so much water from soil that the ground shrinks and subsides – taking the house with it. And that isn't all: if a tree which has been taking lots of moisture from the soil is removed, the ground may expand with the unaccustomed moisture and lift the house.

As roots have built-in water sensors, another hazard is that they are attracted to drains. There is no stopping a determined root in search of water, so it may force its way through any pipe joint it finds and block the drain disastrously – and if your tree damages your neighbour's house or drains, you are very likely to be held responsible. So buying the right-sized tree for the situation and allowing it enough room to grow to its full beauty is money-wise as well as good gardening.

WALNUT TREES

There is an old saying, 'A woman, a dog, and a walnut tree, the more you beat them the better they be.' Untrue though this is of women and dogs, there may be some truth in it where walnuts are concerned. There are reports of them fruiting better after a beating with a stave and, I'm told, this used to be the practice in some parts of Britain. One possible reason why it works is that the beating breaks off old and rotten branches and gives the good branches more breathing space.

WATERING

'I do not think that, in the whole range of a gardener's duties, there is anything requiring so much care as the application of water to the roots of plants,' wrote a gardening journalist a hundred years ago. He was right. It is so simple one does it without thinking, but it's easy to get it wrong. Waving the spray about, creating a light shower, as children often do when asked to help with the watering, is just plant-teasing. It encourages their roots to come to the surface – which is just where they shouldn't be if the plants are to survive. Plants need a good soaking which will reach right down to their deepest roots, and they should be watered when the sun isn't on them.

WEED SIGNS

People will say their soil is clay, or sand, or sweet or acid, but soil can have unexpected seams left by nature or a builder's bulldozer. One of the simplest ways to spot such patches, or keep an eye on the condition of your soil, is to read the story told by the weeds. For weeds are surprisingly choosy about where they live. Dock, for example, likes wet acid soil, while chickweed only thrives on well-drained fertile soil. Both grow in different parts of a large flower bed I have and, sure enough, when one digs the soil, each part is totally different.

Groundsel tells you the soil is in good condition, for it likes an even richer diet than chickweed, while Fat Hen develops purple tips if lime is short. Looking for such signs, especially in a new garden, allows you to diagnose problems and treat them; it also saves you wasting money by planting expensive plants in patches of soil where they have no hope of thriving. I have a spit of poor soil in a position where I'd dearly like to grow delphiniums; but, until chickweed will thrive there, I know they would only die, though they will grow happily six feet away, where I don't want them.

WOOD ASH

In the days when nothing was wasted, the contents of the burnt-out incinerator went first to the fruit trees. The potash in the ash is just what they need for a good crop. In spring first turn should go to the gooseberries – the ash holds back the germination of weeds which are so difficult to get at under those low-slung, spike-covered branches. After them come the other soft fruits and then the apples and pears.

Supporting and Tending

BEAN POLES

A gardener I know says he finds the cheapest and most attractive way to grow runner beans in a flower bed is to plant each next to a giant sunflower. The two plants keep pace with one another and the bean twines neatly round the sunflower – though a few leaves may have to be snipped off as the bean grows. The sunflower may need staking, but at least you save the cost of a second stake for the bean.

The disadvantage of the sunflower method is that you have two plants competing for the same patch of nourishment and moisture. But competition can also have advantages: in dry summers some gardeners find that bean plants grow better in a circle, with all their poles meeting at the top like a wigwam, which keeps the sun off the ground in the centre and prevents it from drying out.

BROKEN PLANTS

If the main stem of a plant breaks but doesn't sever completely, it can sometimes be made to knit together again like a broken bone. Splint the break with a straight twig, or a wooden cocktail stick. Tie the stick on firmly with string or one of the wire ties used to close freezer bags, and support the whole stem so it doesn't wave about. I find this works excellently with houseplants and plants in sheltered positions, but it won't stand up to a buffeting by the wind. And, of course, some types of plants are much better at healing themselves than others.

EDGING AND TRIMMING

Sheep shears, being extra sharp, are sometimes better for edging than garden shears and, as you can operate them with one hand, you have the other free to pull overhanging plants aside or yank at a stray tussock.

FUNNEL IMPROVISING

To improvise a funnel, all you need do is cut the upper section off a plastic bottle and turn it upside down. You can make small funnels from the tops of washing-up liquid bottles and large ones from the big clear plastic bottles of fizzy drinks. Improvised funnels like this are particularly useful when transferring things like garden chemicals, where it is safer to throw the funnel away afterwards than to wash it up in the sink.

GARDEN KNEELER

The easiest way to make kneeling in the garden comfortable is to put an old cushion in a plastic carrier bag. Then you can carry it around the garden easily and the plastic protects the cushion from the damp. A double layer of carrier bags is best if the plastic is flimsy.

LAWN MOWER OILING

To last well, lawn mowers need a bit of care, especially at the end of the season. Before being put away, the blades should be thoroughly cleaned, and oiled with an average multigrade oil to keep them in good condition during the damp of the winter. The engine of a petrol-driven mower should be wiped down and suitably oiled, then covered with a large paper sack to keep it free of dirt and dust.

When oiling lawn mower blades with a cloth, it is all too easy to catch one's fingers in them if they rotate unexpectedly. A safer way to do it is to put the oil on an old-fashioned cotton dishmop. It slides in between the blades far more easily than a cloth, and one's fingers are out of the way.

During the winter, the engine of the mower should be started a couple of times, and run for a minute or two, to allow the lubricants to work on it and prevent it seizing up before the spring.

PATHS

If a path, such as that down the side of a house, is free of plants on both sides, a scrub with a fairly strong solution of household bleach will kill the algae which turn it green. But it will need a very good rinse indeed to avoid the risk of pale, bleached footprints ruining the carpet when you walk in. A heavy dressing of ordinary salt is another way to kill algae, but both salt and bleach will harm plants. Near plants it is safer to dress the path with superphosphate of lime, which should do no harm unless the plants are lime haters. Another rather surprising way to kill algae is to use a degreasant called Easy Cleen. Its manufacturers assure me that it will kill algae without harming any neighbouring plants.

Whatever you use, you may find the dead algae cling just as greenly to the path as when they were thriving – to remove them you need a very stiff scrubbing brush or a very fierce jet of water; if they are a regular problem it may be worth buying one of those metal-bristled brushes that butchers clean their blocks with and giving the path a fierce scrub.

PLANT SUPPORTS

Plants such as oriental poppies, and certain geraniums, look splendid in the early days but, just as they come into flower, fall outwards from the centre and drag their petals on the ground. The conventional way to tie them up is to use expensive metal rings or a ring of stakes with twine wound between them. Quicker and cheaper than either of these is to save the strong nylon mesh bags in which fruit and vegetables are sold in many supermarkets and cut the top and bottom so you have a mesh tube. All you need do is thread a stake down through the mesh in three places and push the stakes well into the earth around the plant. It will then grow up through the tube and be well supported. This is a job to be done early, so the leaves can grow through and hide the tube. Choose dark mesh bags which will blend with their background.

SHRINKING TUBS

Glycerine is able to hold moisture in all kinds of fibres. So natural wood tubs will be less likely to shrink and crack, through drying out, if they are painted inside with glycerine before being filled with earth. Or, for economy's sake, with glycerine and water.

SOFTWOOD POSTS

Softwood – which is the wood used for most garden posts and fences – rapidly takes up water and will rot unless some kind of preservative is used on it. If you are in no hurry, the cheapest and easiest treatment is to stand the posts in a tin of old sump oil for a month or two. Garages will usually give you the sump oil for nothing. Handling it will do you no harm at all, whereas recently there have been queries as to whether some other wood preservatives are a health risk.

TREE TIES

Most tree ties are expensive and some of them are liable to rub the bark off trees when they sway in the wind. Cheaper and better ties can be made with old nylon stockings, lengths of heavy-duty plastic, plaits of the lighter kind of plastic, rings sliced from a tyre inner tube, or even the tops of worn-out wellington boots. The best method with stocking and strips of plastic is to wind them around the tree and the stake in a figure 8. That way they hold it in place and stop it rubbing against the post at the same time. Rings of tyre or wellington should be slipped over the tree before you plant it, then over the post. Bind the ring together between tree and post to get a snug fit.

TROUGHS FROM SINKS

For years I kept a dreadful old glazed kitchen sink in my garden in the belief that sooner or later I'd discover some way to turn it into an attractive trough for alpines. My optimism was rewarded when Percy Thrower gave the method in his column in the *Daily Mail*. He recommends that you first paint the sink with Unibond, then spread on an inch-deep mixture of 3 parts sand, 2 parts peat and 1 part cement, mixed with just enough moisture to make it tacky. Leave it to dry. He adds that you need to wear rubber gloves as it's bad for the hands.

WALL SUPPORTS

Putting vine-eyes and masonry nails into walls is always harder than it sounds, so an ingenious friend has devised a way of cutting the number you need to support a plant to the bare minimum. You take a square of trellis made of plastic netting, or plastic-covered wire, and thread a long strong stake in and out down each side. Then stick the base of each stake firmly in the earth approximately 1 ft (30 cm) from the wall and lash the top of each to a single vine-eye or masonry nail. That way you only need two nails, or vine-eyes, to support a whole plant and there is plenty of air between the plant and the wall – which is what climbers like.

WHEELING BARROWS

Some of the best tips are the simplest. It was an old gardener who told me, 'Always put down an empty wheel barrow so it faces the way you want to go once it's loaded' – such a simple ploy, but one which saves an immense amount of back strain from turning loaded barrows.

FRIENDS AND FOES

It's only a little while since gardeners believed that the answer to every pest could be found in a packet or canister of all-powerful insecticide. But in the last twenty years we've seen more and more strains of pest becoming resistant to those 'all-powerful' chemicals and the growing plagues of snails in some gardens bear witness to the death of the song birds which once kept down their numbers. Killed, ironically, by the poisons in the pests they preyed on.

Now the experts who once recommended the chemical sprays are turning back to traditional ways of gardening and examining the benefits of less drastic, but perhaps more lasting, ways of keeping the gardener's foes in check. This chapter is about some of them. I'm not suggesting that such methods are always best or always appropriate; but I've chosen them because chemical sprays are on sale everywhere and advice on them is plentiful, whereas some of the old ways are hard to find in gardening books and may need explaining. It's no good pretending that a return to the old-fashioned methods is an easy answer, but even commercial growers are finding some of them have a place in the scheme of things. And for the amateur gardener, many of these methods have the advantage of being simple and inexpensive, and of posing no hazard to pets or children. Which in itself makes it worth giving them at least a try.

APHID DETERRENT

Aphids seem to dislike rue. Plants growing near rue are almost invariably clear of them and a strong tea of rue can be used as an aphid spray. Though I suspect it may drive them away rather than kill them.

In medieval times the bitter scent of rue was thought to be a great protection against insects and the plague. The French so believed in its power to keep moths away they even called it *garde robe*. In England they put it in tussie-mussies, the bouquets carried against the plague which came in time to be messages in flowers, such as that which Ophelia gave Hamlet.

BEES

Nobody needs to be told that bees are friends well worth cultivating, and there are many plants which will attract bees to the garden. Most of all they like the old cottage flowers – borage, forget-me-nots, alyssum, and Michaelmas daisies – planted in large drifts. Double flowers and those standing by themselves are far less likely to seduce them.

Since the Greeks, it has been believed that bees have a special love of lemon balm. Balm is sometimes rubbed inside a new hive when bees are transferred to it and lemon balm should be planted near the hive. According to Pliny, 'when bees have been away it guides them home', and the other name for balm is melissa, the Greek for honey bee.

A curious old custom is the burning of a puffball near a hive of bees before handling them. The smoke from the puffball is said to be so soporific that the bees become drowsy and docile. Apparently the same is true of humans, for at one time a puffball would be put on the cottage fire last thing at night as a cure for insomnia.

If a bee needs to be captured and removed from the house, half open an empty matchbox, place it over the bee, and slide it shut.

BIOLOGICAL CONTROLS

At one time biological control simply happened. That was before the pest predators began to be destroyed by insecticides. The old days weren't as idyllic as they may sound; it was a matter of chance whether the balance of nature was for or against the gardener. Now predators are on sale commercially and it's becoming easier to get back to nature yet tip the scales firmly in the gardener's favour. What is more, predators will gobble up creatures which can no longer be killed by sprays. Whitefly and red spider, for example, have both become highly resistant to chemicals, but both will succumb to the right predators.

Whitefly in a greenhouse can be controlled by introducing the chalcid wasp (*Encarsia formosa*), and several types of parasitic wasp can be used against leaf miners, especially on chrysanthemums. A little mite with the outsized name of *Phytoseiulus persimilis* can be put in greenhouses to prey on red spiders, and an Australian ladybird (*Cryptolaemus montrouzeri*) can be introduced to tackle mealy bugs and perhaps munch up the odd scale insect or two when it feels like a bit of variety in its diet (see page 304).

The snag is that, although professionals are using these predators very successfully, amateurs may not always be so lucky. Some of the predators are fussy about the temperatures at which they will live and breed and may not thrive on the fluctuations in a domestic greenhouse. The matter of breeding is important, for the predators have to build up their numbers before they can cope with quantities of pests. This also means that the time to introduce them is before there is a serious problem, and precautions need to be taken to make sure they don't escape into the garden where they will do no good. And, of course, even when gorging themselves to capacity they won't kill every single one of the pests they live on: simple creatures are too canny to wipe out their own breakfast, even if man isn't.

Slightly more sinister forms of biological control are also on the market now. There is a fungus which can be used in the greenhouse against aphids and whitefly, and a bacterium which attacks leaf-feeding caterpillars. As the bacterium only attacks the caterpillars of cabbage butterflies and moths and does no harm to other insects or to mammals, it can be sprayed on vegetables which might be attacked by caterpillars. However, one can only guess at its possible long-term effects on the population of butterflies and moths which don't attack vegetables, and on the birds which live off caterpillars. So this is one biological control it might be best to avoid.

BIRD DETERRENTS

Birds seem to dislike sawdust, so sawdust sprinkled over a patch of newly sown grass seed will generally keep them away. I also know of someone who keeps birds away from her seeds by sticking children's plastic 'windmills' in the ground near them. But the most popular method is to tie black cotton between sticks stuck in the ground.

BROAD BEANS AND BLACKFLY

There are several cottage remedies for blackfly on broadbeans. Tradition has it that dill grown nearby will keep the blackfly away, and so will a spray with the liquid from fermented nettles.

In many old cottage gardens summer savory (*Satureia hortensis*) was grown beside broad beans to ward off blackfly. It was doubly useful, since summer savory cooked with broad beans improves their flavour, and it was ready to hand for the pot. Such partnerships may not be as effective as pesticides, but they have a roll to play.

CABBAGE ROOT FLY

Paraffin is an unlikely, but good, insecticide, because many flies are attracted to vegetables by their smell, and there isn't much that even a fly can smell through the odour of paraffin. The way to use it against cabbage root fly is to soak wood shavings or old tea leaves in it and sprinkle a thin layer of them alongside the row of seeds after sowing. Then sprinkle on some more when the seedlings are a few inches high as an added precaution. Some gardeners also hang paraffin-soaked rags on a string over the bed to keep cabbage butterflies away. If it's to be any use, this needs to be done early, before any eggs have been laid on the leaves.

When using paraffin on cabbages great care has to be taken not to taint other vegetables. Carrots in particular will take up the taste.

CAT SCARING

I was told that those who wanted to keep neighbouring cats out of their gardens could do so by painting a length of hose green – like a snake – and laying it near the places they walk in by. But the hose has to be moved regularly or the cats learn that it isn't a snake. It seemed a charming idea, but, having no wish to scare my own cats, I didn't try it. My editor did, and has come to the conclusion that only neurotic cats are scared of green hose-pipes, for those which plague her garden just walk by with their tails in the air. So, if your garden suffers from neurotic cats . . .

GARDENER'S FRIENDS

Finding Friends
The most restful way to control garden pests is to let nature do most of the work for you, through natural predators. But it can be hard to tell friends from foes in the insect world. a rule much advocated by gardening experts is that if it moves fast it's a friend, if it moves slowly it's a foe. That condemns too many friendly creatures such as aphid-eating ladybirds, for my liking. I prefer the rule that if you like the look of it, it's a friend; it not, it's a foe. But looks, even in insects, are a matter of taste – and fortunately I happen to like spiders, slow worms, lizards, centipedes and quite a few other creatures which might not appeal to everyone but are definitely friends of the gardener.

Free Caterpillar Control

No easy rule works with birds. Bullfinches are undoubtedly bud-eating enemies. However tits, which look as if they are eating buds, are in fact winkling out pests. Analysis of their stomachs has shown the voracious little creatures do gardeners a tremendous service. A single nest of tits has been known to eat as many as 500 caterpillars in a day (which makes one glad not to be a parent tit), so a nest box is an excellent investment.

Another way to attract tits is to plant teazles. Tits adore them and, if you put the teazles where you can see them at breakfast time, the tits will give you the bonus of a dazzling display of acrobatics as they rootle out the seeds in the early morning.

The Aphid Eater

Harmless and much misunderstood hoverflies are often killed by people who, seeing their striped livery, take them for small hovering wasps. They deserve to be cherished, for their larvae are great aphid eaters. Like bees they are attracted to gardens by bell- and daisy-shaped flowers, though strangely, their favourite plant is said to be buckwheat.

INSECTICIDE

Those who don't want to kill friendly bees should leave the spraying of insecticide until the evening. By then the bees will have finished their day's work and be out of harm's way.

MOLES

It isn't easy to get rid of moles, nuisance though they are. Not long ago there was a long correspondence in the press as to whether caper spurge (*Euphorbia lathyrus*) planted in strategic places did or did not keep out moles. Opinions were sharply divided. Other anti-mole measures which have been recommended include putting mothballs, cloves of garlic or slices of lemon down their holes. All these are very much pleasanter – though probably less effective – than the old and dangerous method of dipping earthworms in strychnine and tucking them in the mole runs as a deadly breakfast.

NASTURTIUMS

There are two schools of thought about nasturtiums. Old gardening lore, which some swear by, says they act as a decoy, attracting blackfly to themselves and away from other plants. Others say they act as a magnet, drawing blackfly into a garden when they might otherwise not be there. It is all a question of what you want to believe. What is certain is that they are a great bonus in other ways: they will thrive in the poorest soil and their leaves, flowers and seeds are all edible. They provide a delicious piquancy to salads which no other plant can give, and there is no quicker and easier way to make a green salad look spectacular than to throw on a few nasturtium flowers.

ONION FLY AND CARROT FLY

An old gardener once told me, 'Mind you be planting carrots by they onions 'cos carrot fly don' like onion fly and vicey versey.' His advice has some truth in it, but not because of some war between opposing flies. The fact is that a strong-smelling plant near the one they like confuses the scent trail for the flies – and to these flies both carrots and onions have a strong scent. The smell of creosote stretched on lines above the rows has the same effect.

The dangerous time for attracting these flies is when thinning releases the scent into the air. So it's safer to keep thinning to a minimum by mixing the seed with sand to give a less dense row and, if you have to thin, kill the scent by watering the row very soon after. Another precaution is to plant the carrots a little late. There are three generations of carrot fly in a season; so planting after the beginning of June should mean one down and only two to go. And when the year ends, be sure to remove every scrap of carrot from the ground or some of the flies will happily over-winter in the bed and be all ready to greet next year's planting. As a final precaution, put some paraffin-soaked sand alongside the row – but not too close, for carrots easily pick up the taste.

If, despite everything, flies are a big problem one year, guard against them by putting mothballs on the land in the autumn.

PEA SEED PROTECTION

Pea seeds are notoriously popular with mice. But if you want to keep scrounging rodents from your rows, the answer is to tuck a few prickly holly leaves or gorse sprigs round each seed as you sow it. Mice don't like getting their sensitive noses pricked and will keep away. If there is no holly or gorse to be had, another good method is to sprinkle the row with naked naphthaline or soot; alternatively the seeds can be soaked in paraffin for a few hours. In the old days gardeners would soak them in paraffin and then shake them in red lead, to give the mice a really nasty mouthful; however, paraffin alone should be enough, unless you have starving mice. The same protection can be given to those other mouse delicacies – beans, sweet peas and crocuses.

RABBITS

There is not a lot which will deter a determined rabbit, but an old way of keeping them out of a garden, which some find successful, is to plant onions all round the edge of the ground. If they are chewing the bark of trees, a wire guard is the only effective solution, though some believe that rubbing the bark with carbolic soap keeps them off.

SLUGS AND SNAILS

It has been known for a long time that slugs have alcoholic tendencies. Normally they make a beeline for any saucer of beer left out for them, slither in and die in ecstasy. But recently there have been disquieting stories of slugs which appear to have taken the pledge and refuse to go near the beer. If that is so in your garden, take comfort in the fact that bran is irresistible to both slugs and snails. Put it under cabbage leaves, or other vegetable waste which will afford them a night's shelter, and collect and destroy them in the morning. If you can't bear to squash them, drop them in a solution of strong washing soda – though it will probably be a nastier death for them.

Whether you trap them with bran or with beer slops (which are usually free from the local pub), there should be plenty of traps. There is a limit to how far they will travel without pausing for a snack of young shoots.

Though I did hear of an intoxicated slug-eating hedgehog rolling its way down a Hertfordshire garden, the great advantage of both these methods is that they do no harm to the birds which prey on slugs and snails. And there is the bonus that the beer attracts and kills some of the moths with destructive caterpillars.

SOIL PESTS

When I first started gardening, I thought the emphasis on autumn digging was some kind of masochism, or a penance for the joys of summer gardening. I was, of course, quite wrong. It is turning over the soil which reveals buried soil pests to hungry winter birds and, though the balance of nature may not be as much in the gardener's favour as one would like, it is amazing how much the birds will eat given the chance. There's also the bonus that during the winter the frost can get down into the soil and break it up ready for spring planting.

SOFT FRUIT AND VEGETABLE PROTECTION

The classic way to protect soft fruit is to stretch black cotton so it zigzags between the branches. It is pleasantly invisible and, although birds do sometimes fly into it, it will break and release them if they struggle. In contrast, nylon thread, which is sometimes sold for this purpose, should never be used: it will ensnare them and leave them hanging there to die.

If the fruit bushes are out of sight, a quicker and even safer way is to throw an old net curtain over the bushes while the fruit is still ripening. This has the advantage that it can easily be lifted off while you're picking, whereas black cotton gets in the way.

If bushes are protected by nets the easiest supports are simply canes with inverted jam jars on the top.

Where deer are the problem, it has to be admitted that there is little one can do to keep a determined deer out, but black threads hung with disks of silver paper do seem to act as a slight deterrent.

WHITEFLY

French marigolds (*Tagetes*) have a considerable reputation for keeping whitefly out of a greenhouse. Many gardeners find them invaluable next to tomato plants to protect them; to be effective you need one of the strong-smelling old varieties, not one of the modern ones.

WIREWORMS

My favourite advice on ridding a garden of wireworms comes from a nineteenth-century magazine. It said, 'Tormenting the insect by digging, scarifying, and rolling the land will have good results.' Apart from 'scarifying' your wire worms, you can always plant *Tagetes minuta*.

Deceptively named, this is a vast plant with minute flowers, not the little French marigold usually found in gardens. Recent experiments have shown that its reputation for preventing wireworms is justified. Unfortunately it only affects some types of wireworm: the British potato pest (*Heterodera rostochiensis*) is not among them. In a totally organic garden, traps can be laid for them by burying halves of potato below the surface of the soil, marking them regularly and digging them up and destroying the traps – but it will be an energetic gardener who kills them faster than they can breed.

WOOLLY APHIS

An old way to get through the woolly covering of this pest, which causes so much damage to apple trees, is to brush the area with methylated spirits several times during the year. This is also a good treatment against scale insects, so both can be attacked at once.

As woolly aphis move from one tree to another by walking up the trunk, an old-fashioned grease band, put on each tree trunk in early September and left until spring, will catch them as they move. But the band needs to be kept free from debris and may need re-greasing during that time.

In some countries an aphid parasite (*Aphelinus mali*) is available as a way of controlling woolly aphis; in Britain the natural predator is the hoverfly. Its larvae eat vast numbers of this insect, so a very practical measure is to plant flowers which attract hoverflies round apple trees.

POT PLANTS AND FLOWERS

A lot has been said about the value of talking to plants and telling them how beautiful they are and how you love them. The fact is that plants may be dumb, but they're not stupid. As with people, it's not so much what you *say* to them that counts, it's how you treat them. That means not so much talking to them – though you can do that too if you like – as following the old gardener's ways of 'listening' to them and learning to understand the ways that they signal their needs. For what would be pampering to a cactus would be rank cruelty to an azalea.

Happily plants are sensible creatures and will respond just as well to thrifty treatment as to luxury and there are quite a few ways of saving time and money in their care.

AFRICAN VIOLETS

It's not surprising that African violets should have a penchant for east windows – many plants have strong preferences about the way they face – nor that they also seem particularly happy in steamy bathrooms and kitchens.

But what is odd is that many people find these flowers do best when grouped with members of their own family – not just other African violets, but cuttings from the same plant.

AZALEAS

The rule for azaleas as houseplants is 'Don't water them, dunk them.' They are inordinately thirsty, especially when in flower, so the whole pot should be put in water up to the surface of the soil for an hour or so. It should then be allowed to drain before going back in its saucer. An azalea will need this every day or so, depending on the weather, the type of pot, the position it is in. It is worth taking this trouble for, whether it is in the house or the garden, an azalea doesn't easily recover from drying out – the leaves fall, never to be replaced, and the bud formation for the following year may stop entirely. They need lime-free or distilled water to thrive.

CHRISTMAS TREES

The best container in which to carry a largish Christmas tree home without breaking its branches is a sleeping bag. Put the root end in a carrier bag (if it's dirty or rough). Then put the root at the foot of the bag and zip it up, pushing the branches carefully upwards as you go. You can then carry it home without a prickle.

There is an aerosol spray on the market which is meant to ensure that the needles stay on a Christmas tree. Though I haven't tried it yet it is called Wilt Pruf S600, and marketed under the name Spray and Save. As it's an organic extract of pine oil, it's quite safe to have in the house and it's designed to cut down 80 per cent of the water loss from the leaves of the tree. People find it most effective. The best way to use it is to spray it on before you bring the tree into the house. At this stage it will look whitish; but don't worry, it dries clear. Then re-spray the tree from different angles so it's well coated, before you bring it in. It doesn't matter whether the tree has or has not got roots, but obviously the sooner the spraying is done the better. If you have to do the spraying in the house and some gets on the furniture, it should wipe off with warm water.

Another way to avoid the bane of Christmas tree needles on the floor is to buy a tree with roots (if you can find one), plant it in earth, and keep it well watered.

If you have to make do with a stump, and are too late to buy Spray and Save, there are still ways you can reduce the fall-out. If you want the tree to look good for Christmas itself, keep it out of doors until as close to Christmas as possible. Then, before you bring it in, spray the tree thoroughly with a firm-hold hair lacquer. Its base needs to be wedged in a container which will hold damp paper without leaking on to the carpet and, once you've wedged the tree with bricks (or whatever you normally use), surround it with as much damp newspaper as the container will hold, and remember to keep moistening the paper while the tree is in the house. The moist atmosphere from the paper will stop the tree drying out so fast.

To minimize the needle shower, when Christmas is over envelope it completely in a sheet before you try to take it out of the house.

CLEANING

It's easy to forget that the leaves of indoor plants can become just as clogged with dirt as our faces would if we never washed them. Wiping dark shiny hairless leaves with equal proportions of milk and water cleans them and adds gloss to the leaves. Brighter green hairless leaves like an occasional shower under cool, not cold, water. A very hairy or spiky cactus should have a wash-and-brush-up with clear water and an old-fashioned shaving brush – but its soil needs to be closely covered with polythene first.

The only plants which need to be dry cleaned are those with hairy leaves, and these should just be brushed gently with a small dry paint brush.

CYCLAMEN

These temperamental ballerinas are notoriously difficult to keep, until you understand them. Cyclamen are like people – they don't mind having their feet in water but they object to sitting in it. They object so strongly that if their corm gets wet they will quickly die. Therefore the surface of the cyclamen pot must never be wet, or even really damp. To avoid this, water them little and often, and put the water into the saucer and never into the pot. The water should, ideally, be distilled water, for they hate lime, just as they hate being in a room with gas.

This sounds fussy, but if you keep them happy they will last for years, especially if they can spend the summer months outside with their pot just tucked in the earth – though beware of them drying out in too much sun or becoming sodden in a wet summer.

FEEDING

There is really no need to buy those tiny, overpriced bottles of houseplant fertilizer. A far cheaper way to keep your plants happy is to put a few drops from a big inexpensive bottle of general-purpose garden plant food in their water. But work out carefully how much should be used per pint (500 ml) and give the plants no more than the suggested dosage – too much could burn their roots, and you would kill them with kindness.

HEAT

Houseplants usually have to put up with the temperature *we* like, whether they like it or not. By and large then *do* like it or they wouldn't be sold as houseplants, but they don't like to be too close to the sources of heat. One of the fastest ways to kill a plant is to steam its roots by putting it above a radiator or heater, or to stand it on a television set. A rival killer is the practice of drawing a curtain across plants and leaving them trapped in the chilly

space between the glass and the curtain on a winter's
night. Some plants are also intolerant of gas as a form of
heating.

HYDRANGEAS

It is thought that the name hydrangea, which means water
vessel in Greek, came about because of the shape of the
seeds. But I can't help thinking it really comes from their
need for water. They can't stand being dried out and, like
violets, they drink through their flowers as well as their
roots, so they are grateful for an occasional spray.

People have asked me how hydrangeas cut from the
garden can be prevented from hanging their heads. The
secret is to give them a big drink as soon as you bring them
in. To do this you need to submerge them – stem, leaf,
and flower – in cool water overnight. After this treatment
they will stay fresh for several days, especially if you spray
the heads occasionally or cover them with a damp tissue
at night.

LEAVING PLANTS ALONE

There are now some nifty gadgets to keep plants watered
while one goes away. But even without them, keeping
plants healthy and happy while you are away isn't as
difficult as it might seem. In summer they last longest if
they are moved into a cool relatively shady room – although
flowering plants shouldn't be too far from the light. A
bathroom is often ideal and the bath provides an easy way
to keep them watered. First, water them in the normal
way. Then, put a thick layer of wet newspaper or bath
towels in the bottom of the bath and sit the plants on
this. (Remember to put a sheet of polythene under the
newspapers so the print doesn't stain your bath.) Most
plants should then last a couple of weeks without further
attention.

If you don't want to fill the bath, another method is to
stand each pot inside another one, several sizes larger, and

fill the space underneath and around with well-moistened peat. This is more costly and more time-consuming, but it does mean the plants can stay put. They should remain moist for much the same length of time.

LIGHT

The secret of giving houseplants the right amount of light, if there is no instruction label to help you, is to look at the leaves. Coloured leaves usually mean the plant needs a very light position; hairy or variegated leaves tell the same story. Cactus plants and plants which flower also like a sunny position. Bright green foliage, such as you find on ferns, indicates that the plant probably dislikes strong sunlight – though it won't like too dark a place either. While dark green leaves show that a plant will live happily with relatively little light – which is why rubber plants are planted inside so many large office buildings. When deciding where to put a plant, bear in mind that you are simply trying to give it the conditions it chooses in the wild, so it helps to know where it comes from.

The ledge of an east window is ideal for plants which like a lot of light – they get the light without being scorched by the midday sun, as they might be at other windows. It's also good to turn each plant a little whenever you water it, then all the sides are evenly exposed to the light and it grows evenly. Even so, flowering plants, especially African violets, will also need plenty of artificial light in the evenings to do well, for most are used to longer days than we have in Britain.

PESTS ON HOUSEPLANTS

Pests aren't a great problem on most houseplants. However, if you find unidentified leaf munchers have been at work, they probably operate in the dark and are most easily caught if you do a surprise inspection after the lights have been turned off for a while. If you think something may be getting at the roots, try putting a piece of apple or potato on the soil. After a while, you may find the creatures on the underside and be able to identify them.

Pests on leaves need to be removed as fast as possible, for if they are prepared to live indoors at all they will breed rapidly. The most basic remedial measure is to put something firmly over the earth, to hold it in, and swish the plant, upside down, through cool soapy water until all the creatures have come off. Then rinse the leaves in clear water to remove the soap. Only pure soap should be used for this, as plants don't like detergents.

Woolly aphis – easily recognized by the little mounds like white polystyrene with which they surround themselves – are particularly tenacious and may resist the soapy water. Dabbing their white mounds with a cotton bud soaked in methylated spirits will kill them, but you need to repeat this attack at frequent intervals to kill the succeeding generations. Plants seem to tolerate meths remarkably well, but before using it on anything expensive and precious it would be wise to check with the original grower.

POINSETTIAS

Poinsettias like moist air and do best if their pot is set inside another filled with damp peat. But, now that poinsettias are selling in hundreds of thousands every Christmas, an annual question is how to get them to turn red the following year. A nurseryman in one of Britain's top nurseries says the secret is to let growth slow down in the middle part of the year. Then, from September to Christmas, allow the plant light ONLY during the hours of daylight. This light regulation isn't really as easy to get right as it sounds, even if you rigorously avoid switching on the lights in their room, and the ideal conditions are even more complex; however, it is worth a try.

Some people also swear by cutting the stems by half in March; but it takes a lot of confidence, or optimism, to cut off those beautiful red rosettes with no more than a chance that they will return next year as a result.

POT HOLDERS

One day I did a quick calculation on how much I would
have spent if I had bought pot holders for all my
houseplants: it came to as much as a meal in a good
restaurant. Luckily I didn't buy all of them; I used the
upturned lids from big plastic sweet jars – begged from my
local sweet shop. They come in dayglow orange, livid green
and a discreet matt black, according to the type of sweets.
So you can decide whether you want to be garish or discreet
and pick your lids accordingly. Of course they only take
fairly small pots, but even small plant saucers are a silly
price.

POTTING

To tell whether a plant needs repotting, look at its roots.
If they protrude from the drainage holes in the bottom of
the pot or show on the surface, it needs more room. Other
signs are that it wilts easily and only makes small leaves.
If so, give it a pot one or two sizes larger – where pot room
is concerned, enough is better than a feast.

PROLONGING LIFE

I was talking to an elderly gardener in Cambridge recently
who told me that an undertaker friend of his had an
excellent tip for making cut flowers keep longer – he added
a dash of embalming fluid to the water. Embalming fluid
may not be on every kitchen shelf, but the principle of
killing off the bacteria which make flowers like chrysanthemums rot under water still holds good, and a few drops
of bleach will do the job; or you can use a little 5 per cent
chlorhexidine from a chemist. Be careful to keep both of
these off your skin.

WATERING

Nursery gardeners say that more houseplants drown than
ever die of thirst, but it's seldom realized that too much

water is just as bad as too little. In general, plants need less water in winter than in summer, but if they are in flower they need extra water whatever the season. Most plants prefer to become slightly dry before being watered but, as they don't like cold baths any more than we do, the water should be at room temperature.

You'd think that if a plant wilted it was safe to assume it lacked water. Not so. It could just as easily be an insect attacking the roots. Leaves turning yellow aren't a sure sign either; they could be caused by too much water, or too little. But green scum on the soil always means the soil is too wet and the roots are probably rotting as a result.

Professional gardeners often check if a plant needs watering by picking up the pot. With a little practice you will notice quite small differences in the weight of each pot and know how much water is in the soil. This method is far more exact than looking at the soil on top or simply watering by rote. But, of course, you are looking for the right amount of water for that particular plant, taking into account the type of soil and the pot that it's in. Water evaporates far more quickly from porous pottery pots than from impermeable plastic ones.

It's normally recommended that the water should be put into the top of the pot. The snag is that though most plants accept this very happily, some can't stand it. On the other hand, I've never met a plant which objected to having water put in its saucer – so this can be a safer method if you aren't sure of a plant's tastes. However, as standing in water is death to all but swamp plants, the success of the method depends on emptying out any water that is still left in the saucer after half an hour.

Azaleas, blue hydrangeas, cyclamen and heathers all need special care. They are lime-haters (though pink hydrangeas aren't) and will only thrive on lime-free water. Pure rainwater, if the rain in your area is pure, is ideal. Failing that, distilled water will do. There's no need to buy it specially, just save all the water which drips off when you thaw the refrigerator.

DUST AND FLUFF

'There is . . . but an hour in one whole day between a housewife and a slut,' said an eighteenth-century writer. I suspect that most of us have the inclinations of a housewife, but the available time of a slut. So this chapter is about getting housewifely results in a slut's time. I covered the major cleaning jobs in *Supertips to Make Life Easy*, but I couldn't cover everything. In every household there are small, irritating, time-consuming jobs which can be done very much faster and better if one knows just exactly how to do them. Those are the ones I cover here. The tips are all designed to cut the time and money you spend on cleaning to a minimum, or help you make a better job of it when you want to do things thoroughly.

I have nothing against branded products if they work well, and as a woman who does all her own cleaning, while involved in a full-time career, I have no time for quaint old-fashioned methods for their own sake. But the interesting thing is that very often the branded products don't do the job nearly as well as something very basic which is sitting on the kitchen shelf. That's why in this chapter you'll find old-fashioned chemicals like washing soda side by side with the very latest scientific developments. I'm in favour of *any* method which works quickly and easily, and costs no more than it needs to.

ADHESIVES

In *Supertips to Make Life Easy* I said that if adhesive was left behind after the removal of sticky-backed labels, it could be removed with methylated spirits. I still think meths is the most effective but, if you don't have any, white spirit or oil of eucalyptus will also do the job. If the adhesive is on fabric use oil of eucalyptus as it's least likely to affect the dye.

ANTI-STATIC

What have televisions, artificial flowers, computers, nylon carpets and record players got in common? The answer is, of course, a problem with dust caused by static electricity. The solution to keeping all of them a good deal cleaner is to use an anti-static spray such as Croxtine. You can spray it directly on to flowers and carpets without harming them. With hard surfaces you can clean and de-static in one go by spraying a clean cloth and then wiping them over with it. The kind of charge built up by televisions and computers means that you will need to repeat the process every week or so, but on the others the treatment works for much longer.

With computers it's worth wiping all the surfaces, keys included, and not just the screen, as a lot of the dust which is drawn to the outside of the keyboard eventually finds its way inside. It's a precaution some of the major computer companies take.

BLU-TACK

If Blu-Tack and similar substances are reasonably fresh and soft, they will come off the wall without leaving a trace; if a bit stays on, you can usually get it off by dabbing it with a larger lump. If it has gone dry, this doesn't work. The way to get it off then is to rub it gently with the sticky side of a piece of masking tape.

BOLTS

Bolts on french windows can get very stiff if they are unused all through the winter. A few drops of penetrating oil put into them in autumn will make sure you don't have to do battle to get them moving in the spring.

BREAD BINS

Bread bins which have begun to smell musty, and in which bread goes mouldy quickly, can be cured if they are washed and dried, then wiped out with neat vinegar, and the vinegar simply allowed to dry off in the air. In fact it's worth remembering that vinegar seems to be lethal to quite a number of moulds.

CANDLE WAX ON WOOD

If candle wax falls on polished wood, flake any lumps off gently with a fingernail, then very carefully rub it smooth with OO or OOO wire wool. If the wax has fallen on a french-polished or polyurethaned surface and won't flake off safely with a fingernail, warm it very gently with a hair dryer until it is JUST soft enough to wipe off with a tissue.

CANE

If cane has become yellowed with time, scrub it over with a solution of oxalic acid and let it dry naturally. You need about ½ teaspoon of oxalic acid to 1 pint (500 ml) of water. But keep the solution away from pets and children, and off your skin.

CARPETS, RUGS AND COVERS

When a carpet is laid or a chair is covered, it's always worth keeping a few scraps. Then if anything is spilt, you can spill the same thing on one of the scraps and test the various stain-removers to see if they affect the dye. As carpet dyes are especially fragile, this is the only sure way to avoid making a mark worse, not better.

If you buy ready-covered furniture it's a good idea to write to the manufacturer for cleaning instructions straight away. By the time it needs cleaning you may have lost the documents with the address on, or the company may have closed down.

It may not be very economical, but to make life really easy one needs two vacuum cleaners – a normal 'beats as it sweeps as it cleans' type for the main areas of carpet, and one of those tubby little vacuum cleaners, like a big tin can on coasters, for the odd jobs. The tubby tin can suck up water as easily as fluff, tackle dust and leafy porches with equal ease, and has enough suck to get the edges of a carpet really clean, where the other kind of cleaner misses it. It is also invaluable for cleaning up after DIY jobs.

If you have only the standard vacuum cleaner, by far the easiest and most effective way to clean the edges of the carpet is to put on a pair of rubber gloves (the ones that feel like an india rubber, not the shiny sort) and rub your fingers firmly round the carpet. Though it sounds like hard work, it takes much less effort than brushing the edge with a hand brush and, surprisingly, gets up more fluff without raising nearly so much dust.

To get rugs really clean when spring cleaning, vacuum the surface, then turn them over and vacuum or beat the back, to judder clean the back and also judder dirt out of the roots of the pile. Then re-vacuum the right side.

The old-fashioned way of 'washing' delicate rugs is to take a clean cloth and put it in hot water containing a few drops of ammonia, then wring it out VERY WELL and wipe the rug vigorously all over with it. It's important that the cloth is well rung out as the colours in patterned rugs may run if they become wet and this applies particularly to valuable hand-made rugs.

CHAMOIS LEATHER

Chamois leather, for cleaning windows, needs to be kept clean by washing in pure soap flakes rather than detergent. To make sure it remains soft and pliable rub and stretch it gently in all directions from time to time as it dries. If you let it just hang out it may dry as hard as a board. But don't try to stop it becoming hard by putting it in a plastic bag – moulds and bacteria love the conditions in plastic bags and they will eat into it and weaken it.

CIGARETTE ASH

Among the detritus of modern living cigarette ash must rank with the nastiest: touch it with water and the rank, morning-after odour rises distastefully to the nostrils while the ash sticks resolutely to its container. But in a cafe in Assisi I discovered the perfect solution. They had a dry pastry brush hanging behind the bar with which they simply brushed out the ashtrays each time they needed emptying. In a jiffy it removed every trace of ash without a hint of the usual smell. I wondered if they had something special on the brush, but found they didn't: an ordinary pastry brush worked just as well when I got home. Though, of course, you can't use the brush for pastry afterwards.

COAL AND COKE STOVES

As slow combustion stoves with doors are far more economical to run than normal fires, they're becoming more and more popular. They need to be treated gently – cast iron is far less robust than you'd suppose and slamming a lid or a door could crack it. Cleaning, however, is simple. The great thing to avoid is using water on cast iron. Though the outside may look better for it, any trickles which slip through to the inside will rust it in places where you can't see the damage which is being done.

If a stove coated in vitreous enamel becomes grimy, you can clean it with OO or OOO wire wool – but don't use this on the panes in the door. If the finish is what used to be called 'black lead', you need a graphite paste such as Zebrite (made by Reckitt in Hull). But don't try to apply the paste as it comes out of the tube. You will get a far better finish, and make it last longer, if you mix a little of the paste to the consistency of cream with some white spirit. You then paint this evenly on with a small paint brush (choose a cheap one – you'll never be able to use it for anything else) and leave it to dry for 24 hours before buffing it up to a good shine with a soft shoe brush.

The panes of the doors should keep clean if you just wipe them with a cloth, but if wood is used in the stove and a tarry deposit gets on them, a little oil of eucalyptus will usually remove it.

Any bright metal on an old stove is likely to be nickel plate and needs ordinary metal polish; and if the door hinge is stiff, don't oil it. The oil will only vaporize when the fire is lit: instead puff in some graphite powder from a locksmith. Apart from that the fires need only an annual check over to see that the inside is still sound.

After riddling a stove, remember to cover the ash drawer with an old damp cloth as you remove it, then the dust won't waft all over the rest of the room as you take it out to empty it.

CONDENSATION

Washing-up liquid wiped, neat, across glass virtually eliminates condensation on bathroom mirrors and the insides of car windscreens. It doesn't last forever and it can look a bit smeary for the first few minutes, but it is still worth using when condensation is a problem.

COOKER CLEANING

Glass Doors
Paint stripper and brush softeners contain methylene chloride which is rather good for getting the splashes off the glass doors of ovens. But avoid getting them on the enamel

of the oven – they may not seem to do any harm, but they could cause long-term damage.

Having got the glass clean, wipe it over with a little neat washing-up liquid. This will make it easier to wipe the splashes off next time.

Grill Pans
I'm not sure whether putting foil in a grill pan is more trouble than the cleaning it saves, or less, but it's an idea to think about if you want to avoid scrubbing greasy metal. A boil-up with washing soda will take burnt-on debris off the grid – but don't boil it up in an aluminium pan because prolonged contact with washing soda pits aluminium.

Ovens
On seeing my remarks in *Supertips to Make Life Easy* about hanging bat-like upside down to clean an oven-roof, a reader wrote to tell me that she saved herself a twisted neck by putting an old mirror in the bottom of the oven so she could see if the top was clean. Her idea certainly works – but don't use a precious mirror or the oven cleaner may damage it, and keep taking it out while you do the actual cleaning or the drips will make it too dirty to see in.

I have tried standing a saucer of ammonia in the bottom of the oven after I turn it off in the hope that it would be easier to clean the next morning, and frankly it hasn't made any difference. But I know people who swear that it helps considerably – maybe it will work for you.

I still find the easiest way to clean an oven is the method recommended in my previous book, but if you haven't got the chemicals try wiping the oven with a strong solution of biological washing powder and leaving it to soak in. This does seem to make it slightly easier to get the dirt off – though it won't do much for burnt-on dirt.

Shelves
A soak in a sink full of hot water containing washing-up liquid and a good dash of bleach makes oven shelves much easier to clean.

Spills

If something boils over in the oven, sprinkle salt very
thickly on the drips as soon as you see them. This will stop
them burning on and it will be quite easy to wipe the oven
clean later.

Some people also find that if salt is sprinkled thickly on
the top of the stove it makes it much easier to wipe off
food that might get burnt on. It does make a difference,
but it is more effective with some foods than others.
Another preventive measure is to put foil all round the
burners. It can be a bother, but is worth doing when
cooking jams, which may bubble over and burn on.

Switches

It's easy to forget that the backs of switches on gas cookers
need a clean, but if they aren't cleaned they can sometimes
jam completely. Slip a bit of button-hole twist or dental
floss behind each when you spring clean and pull it to and
fro. I know of someone who even managed to bring a
defunct timer back to life that way.

COPPER

Wiping copper with a mixture of detergent and lemon juice
is a quick way to give it a shine. It won't bring it up as
brightly as metal polish, but it will rapidly remove surface
tarnish. The only snag is that detergents may change and
it could cease to work or even become harmful. And,
unlike brass, copper doesn't respond to lemon juice alone.

CURTAIN RAILS

Plastic rails which loose their 'slip' are usually sticking
because they need a good wash with soap and water. If
they still stick after that, put a drop of any fine oil, such
as penetrating oil, on a tissue and wipe the rail with it. Oil
spreads with particular ease on plastic, so only a minute
amount is needed – too much will clog up the rail and
attract dust, making the runners stick once again.

CURTAINS

Even washable curtains need gentle treatment as sunlight may have weakened the threads. A washing machine may seem ideal, but unless the material is obviously very strong it may be wiser to stick to hand washing – I have seen curtains go into a machine whole and come out in shreds. Start by giving them an overnight soak in cold water. It's amazing how much dirt comes out with this simple treatment. Then wash them in soap powder rather than a detergent, pressing the dirt out rather than rubbing at it. An easy way to do this is to walk up and down on them in the bath. Having rinsed them, press out as much water as possible and lift them out without letting any one part take the weight. You can then use a spin dryer to get rid of most of the water before hanging them over – not from – the line.

When washing terylene net curtains, some people find that a bit of washing soda dissolved in the water with the soap powder makes the curtains come up cleaner, and some smokers find the curtains come up best with a denture-cleaning tablet in the water.

DECANTERS

Reading the section on decanter-cleaning in my previous book, my mother expressed surprise that I hadn't mentioned that lead shot shaken about in the bottom of a decanter removes the stains. Lead shot being somewhat hard to come by, I have not tested this, but she assures me that it works.

If you can't get lead shot, try crushing the shells of several eggs quite finely – you don't want a powder but the pieces mustn't be too big to come out easily – and putting them to soak in the decanter with some water. Then move the decanter so they swirl around and scrape off the sediment. This old method of cleaning glass can also be extremely good for cleaning out vacuum flasks and vases, and if the flask has become smelly the egg-shells do double duty and leave it smelling sweet again.

DELICATE ORNAMENTS

The safest way to clean fragile ornaments is to put on a pair of old cotton gloves and dust the ornaments carefully with one's fingers, without using a duster. That way you can feel your way into every nook and cranny. Chemists often sell cheap cotton gloves which can be used for this.

DOORS

When doors are veneered with dark wood and left un-painted, bringing them up to a shine with polish is a mammoth task. Instead of using polish, wipe them regularly with a small amount of boiled linseed oil. It should sink into the wood as you work, not lie on the surface. After a few coats the oil should form a coat which will gradually begin to shine, without you having to do any rubbing. It should also be satiny smooth. But if you've overdone the oil and the surface is rough to touch or has little runs of oil, just go over it with OOO wire wool, working *with* the grain, and then give it the lightest possible smear of oil afterwards.

If you want the finish which comes only with a wax polish, the linseed oil base will make it far easier to get a polish quickly on the rather porous wood with which modern doors are veneered.

DRAINS – PREVENTING BLOCKS

Where a pipe flows into a drain above ground and regularly disgorges water containing bits and pieces which could cause a blockage, some people save on drain-cleaning by covering the end of the pipe with the foot of a nylon stocking, held in place with a rubber band, to collect the bits. If you find changing the nylon stocking less distasteful than drain-cleaning, this is the method for you – but be warned: if the stocking isn't changed often enough it will become full of rubbish and could stop the water flowing out. So if the water comes from a washing machine, and the stocking prevents it from draining, there could be damage to your machine or your washing or both. This method is only for those with a firm grasp on routine.

DUSTBINS

Some dustbin lids can easily be knocked off by rummaging animals. To deter such nocturnal raiders, put a few drops of ammonia in the dustbin. The eye-watering smell is not one they will want to return to.

To clean metal dustbins thoroughly, all you need do is to put a few crumpled newspapers in and set light to them. The fire will clean up the bin and remove any smell. But this is not a trick to try with plastic bins.

EGG

Spilt on Floors
One of the more repellent household jobs is trying to clear up an egg which has broken on the floor. If you can bear to leave it, just sprinkle it with masses of salt. In a few hours the salt will have taken up the egg and made it really easy to wipe up.

Stains on Silver
It is curious the way nature produces her own solutions. If you eat a boiled egg with a silver spoon, the sulphur in the egg quickly makes greeny-blue marks on the silver. These stains aren't easy to get off with silver polish, but if you drop the teaspoon in the water in which the egg boiled, the stains usually vanish miraculously after a short while. What I haven't been able to check is whether the egg water does any harm to silver plate. It seems unlikely, but I always believe in caution where plate is concerned.

ELECTRIC FOOD MIXERS

To get the most out of liquidizers and food processors, scrape them out, then switch on once again – the blades will fling the last scraps of food on to the sides where they can be scraped off easily. After that, liquidizers and food processors will almost clean themselves if they are switched on with hot water and a dash of washing-up liquid in them, but don't over fill them or the suds will overflow.

FINGER MARKS

The usual way to remove finger marks is, of course, with hot water and washing soda and/or ammonia. That's certainly best for a thorough wash. But if you're in a hurry to remove grubby fingermarks from gloss paint, white spirit on kitchen roll makes short work of them. It's especially good in the kitchen where grease is likely to be the cause of most of the marks.

FLOOR MOPS

Sponge floor mops often 'die' long before they've had a good run for your money simply because the grease and dirt on them has provided a feast for bacteria, which destroy the cellulose they are made of. To keep the bacteria at bay and make the mops last rather longer, rinse them in water containing a household disinfectant of the phenolic type, such as Dettol, or Boots Pine Disinfectant. But avoid bleach or anything containing chlorine, as these will be as bad for the cellulose as they are for the bacteria.

FLOORS

I was testing the effects of biological washing powder on the inside of an oven when a pool of it formed on the kitchen floor. When it was wiped up some while later the area where it had been was decidedly cleaner than the rest of the floor. That was odd because the floor had just been washed. At first I thought I'd found a new magic mixture for washing floors. A series of tests revealed something rather better: like washing powder on clothes, anything used to wash a floor works better if it has a chance to soak into the dirt. So leaving pools of ANY washing solution on the floor and mopping it up half an hour later is the easiest way to get a floor really clean – provided the flooring won't be harmed by that much water, of course.

If it has small dents, impossible to wash clean, these can be filled. Scrape the dents clean with a knife point, then drip a little candle wax into them, quickly smoothing the soft wax with your finger and scraping off the surplus with the flat of a knife before it set hard. Choose a candle which matches your floor, or colour the wax with scraps of children's wax crayons.

FRENCH POLISH

I have been taken to task by readers of my previous book for not mentioning that an oily Brazil nut or metal wadding are both good for taking the white heat and moisture rings out of French polish. In *Supertips to Make Life Easy* I suggested using cigarette ash and cooking oil, rather than either of these, because this method is more effective than the Brazil nut and cheaper than buying metal wadding. However, if the latter are what you have to hand, they can certainly be used, and so can camphorated oil. Brazil nuts are probably the least effective. And none of these methods work on anything other than French polish.

FRIARS' BALSAM

Don't try to wash Friars' Balsam off a spoon – it will stick faster than glue. Just wipe the spoon clean and THEN wash it and there's no problem.

GREASE ON POROUS STONE

When porous stone absorbs grease you may be able to get some of it out by covering it with a heap of fuller's earth (from a chemist) or grinding some cat litter firmly into it with your foot. Either will draw out the grease better if it is warmed first. Leave it on for at least a day, but don't

expect all the grease to come out that way: the next step
is a good scrub with a stiff brush using washing soda
dissolved in hot water. It's better not to use soap or
washing-up liquid – porous stone will absorb these and
become slippery when wet, which can be dangerous.

LEATHER-COVERED FURNITURE

Broadly speaking there are three different finishes which
can be used on leather for chairs and sofas – suede, an
aniline finish; and a pigmented finish. An aniline finish
looks and feels soft and pliable and is scarcely shinier than
your own skin. Because both this finish and suede lack any
outer coating to seal them, they are very vulnerable to
water and to every kind of stain, and certainly not ideal if
you have children in the house. It may be possible to
protect them with one of the silicone sprays sold for preventing dirt from penetrating suede shoes; however, it is
strongly advisable to check with the manufacturer of the
furniture before using such a spray. If the furniture does
get dirty or stained, it is really a job for the experts (see
page 304), but at your own risk you could try the methods
given for leather clothing with these finishes.

Pigmented leather usually feels firmer to touch and has
a definite shine to it; it is a far tougher material than the
other two. But there is also a semi-aniline finish which
could be confused with it. To test which you have, damp
a white tissue and press it against a part of the furniture
which won't show (but not near a seam). If it produces a
dark patch you have some sort of aniline finish which needs
careful handling.

To keep pigmented leather clean, all you need do is dust
it and occasionally wipe it over with a cloth which has been
well wrung out in warm water and pure soap flakes (not
detergent). It's important *not* to use a wet cloth or trickles
of water may seep through the stitching, and if the back
of the leather gets wet it may shrink and crack, and be
ruined. Professionals sometimes find that dabbing milk
carefully into a grease mark on pigmented leather reduces

the mark, but this needs to be done with great care or the stain could be increased rather than reduced. Dabbing on methylated spirits is another possibility, but it can harm the surface of the leather. So these are methods to use only when you can't get it to a professional and don't mind taking a risk.

If pigmented leather is in a particularly dry centrally heated atmosphere, go over it two or three times a year with hide food or the mixture given for leather book-bindings in *Supertips to Make Life Easy*.

MIRRORS AND GLASS

Mirrors which are marked with hair lacquer can easily be cleaned by wiping them with methylated spirits. In my previous book I recommended either methylated spirits or paraffin for cleaning glass, but you may prefer to use a mixture of equal parts water, methylated spirits and paraffin, shaken together in a bottle. Each removes a slightly different kind of mark from the glass.

RECORD PLAYER HEADS

If you saw a highly magnified picture of a well-used record stylus, you'd be amazed at the amount of dirt on it, and a dirty stylus can distort the sound and push dirt into the record grooves. The professional way to clean it is to use a fine artist's paint brush moistened with just two drops of cleaning fluid. The ideal cleaning fluid is equal parts of distilled water and isopropyl alcohol – which may sound like something any ordinary chemist would blench at, but mine produced it without batting an eyelid. You then brush the stylus very lightly FROM THE BACK TOWARDS THE FRONT – if you do it the other way, or from side to side, you could bend it. How often you do this depends on how much you use the stylus. But whatever you do be very careful not to get the isopropyl alcohol on anything – it could stain badly.

RECORDS

Cleaning

The whole business of cleaning gramophone records is riddled with pitfalls and misconceptions. It's easy to see why when you realize the extraordinary precision of the product we take so much for granted. The groove on a record can be up to half a mile long and isn't straight but is a series of minute zigzags, accurate to within a millionth of an inch. To negotiate these zigzags, the needle has to reach a greater acceleration than a rocket to the moon. And this exceedingly precise 'instrument' is made in a plastic which can be seriously damaged by alcohol and by many basic household chemicals. It can even be harmed by water. And, contrary to current folk wisdom, the shellac of the old 78s is even more vulnerable.

So it's not surprising that the first rule for clean records is don't get them dirty in the first place. There are three pitfalls: touching the grooves so they absorb dirt and body chemicals from the fingers, and leaving the record uncovered to gather dust are two of them. But the commonest of all is simply taking the record carelessly out of its sleeve. The friction from just pulling a disc out of a sleeve will charge it with enough static electricity to draw dust on to the surface like a magnet. So the sleeve needs to be pulled open slightly to keep it clear of the record as you take it out.

If the record is already charged with static, and dirty to boot, DON'T succumb to the temptation to give it a good wipe with a damp cloth or even an anti-static cloth; and DON'T – this is even more important – wash it. If the label gets wet, it may warp the record and invisible traces of dye running on to the tracks can ruin them and in some cases create a sound rather like gunfire when you try to play them. Even a recommended anti-static cloth used too heavily can rub dirt into the tracks like mud into a tyre groove. Don't be misled by the fact that some of these methods can make a record sound better at first; they will still ruin it in the long term.

The best cleaner of all is an expensive anti-static gun which, in true space-age fashion, cleans the record by shooting out a stream of positive and negative ions. Next best is an anti-static cloth used the professional way: let the record rotate on the turntable while you hold over it the very slightly damp cloth, so that it JUST touches the surface. This cleans the record without pressing the dirt in. Dry cloths should be moistened like the handkerchief in the following paragraph.

If you don't have an anti-static cloth, keep a clean, well-washed lawn handkerchief in a box, near – but not touching – some well-damped tissues. The slight moisture which forms in the handkerchief will have evaporated out of the tissues and distilled on the box before being absorbed by the handkerchief. Hold the handkerchief, which is moist with this distilled water, over the record, just like the anti-static cloth. It will do the job perfectly well, but the effects won't last so long.

SILVER

When a silversmith I know of is on holiday, she always cleans her silver jewellery with toothpaste and a toothbrush. Toothpaste also works beautifully on small intricately patterned silver boxes and it is far easier and less messy than other methods. But choose a soft toothbrush or it could scratch the silver.

SQUEEZY BOTTLES

The nozzles of squeezy bottles of thick bath cleaner tend to get blocked by dried-up lumps of the cleaner. To avoid this frustration don't put on the lid but stick a matchstick in the hole instead. If you look inside when the bottle is 'empty' you'll usually find a thick sediment in the bottom. Add a little water (and a dash of ammonia or washing soda, if you have them) and it will often keep going for a week or more.

STAINLESS STEEL

A friend swears there's not much you can't clean with washing-up liquid and a dash of bleach, but even so she sometimes gets better results than she expects. She accidentally dropped a stainless steel teaspoon in the mixture. When it fell in it was dull from years of use and the deposits left by her washing-up machine. It emerged gleaming like new: so she threw in all her stainless steel cutlery and brought a shine to the whole lot. I find you need a couple of tablespoons of bleach in a pint of water to get a good result; if the stainless steel is really dull, it needs a good soak in the solution to loosen the deposits and a quick brush over to bring up a really good shine.

STICKY SPILLS

If you don't have time to clean up a sticky patch on a hard floor, sprinkle it with talc. It won't be clean but it won't feel sticky to walk on either. This works beautifully on dry sticky patches such as those from jammy bread, but don't be tempted to try it on wet ones – all you get is the talcum powder version of a mud pie.

TAPE RECORDER HEADS

These may not be on everyone's cleaning itinerary, but if tapes are to sound good the heads of any tape machine need regular cleaning to remove the deposits left by the tape itself. The BBC's technical experts recommend methylated spirits on a cotton bud and say it is just as good as a pricey cleaning kit. And if you dislike the smell of meths, you can use surgical spirit instead – any chemist sells it.

TILES

When a housewife in Cheshire wrote to tell me that her mother always used soapy water and ash from the fire for cleaning the blackened glazed tiles round a fire, I was inclined to dismiss the idea as being much too much like hard work. When I tried it, I had to revise my opinion. Soapy water alone wouldn't make any impression on the dirt on my fire tiles, but adding a bit of ash had them clean in a trice. One word of caution, though – I used wood ash, but ash containing bits of rough clinker could scratch the tiles and damage them permanently.

TOOTHBRUSH MAINTENANCE

I'm told there really are people who don't save their old toothbrushes and use them to clean in awkward places – like the backs of taps. Personally I can't recommend them too highly; nothing else gets into awkward places so well, and you can use nylon brushes on tough surfaces and bristle brushes on delicate ones such as silver.

TORTOISESHELL

When tortoiseshell becomes clouded by water or sunlight, the experts say there is no cure except expert burnishing. However, a reader wrote to tell me that rubbing in a product called Vitapointe, which is designed to treat dry hair, would cure clouding. I found it cured slightly clouded tortoiseshell and made some improvement even when it was very clouded. This isn't really too surprising: tortoiseshell (which is actually turtle shell) and hair evolved in very similar ways; both contain keratin. In fact one of the ways in which imports are tested by Customs and Excise to see whether they are made of genuine tortoiseshell is by burning a little piece. Real tortoiseshell gives off an unmistakable smell like burning hair.

Before using an unconventional treatment like Vitapoint, do remember that it hasn't been recommended by tortoiseshell experts, nor have I been able to find what its long-term effects may be, if any.

TURNING THE UNTURNABLE

Screws and Nuts

When a nut or screw won't budge, the important thing is to get it moving – even if it's in the wrong direction. If it refuses to turn the way you want it to go, stop struggling and try turning it the opposite way: it will often turn quite easily. After that it should go the way you want without too much effort.

If that fails drop penetrating oil on the jammed area and give it time to work its way in before you try again. This also gives your arms a rest so you can then assail the job with more attack than if you just kept trying and trying.

Stopcocks

When a stopcock needs to be turned it's often an emergency. If it's seldom used it may be locked solid but, if water is leaking everywhere, there won't be time to sit around letting penetrating oil work into it. The answer is a bit of leverage. Don't let the shape of the handle fool you. It should be possible to clamp a long handled Mole wrench onto one side of it, and the extra leverage this gives should enable you to get the handle turning.

TYPEWRITER ROLLERS

Left to their own devices, the rollers of typewriters become dirty and hard, but watch a thorough service engineer working on a typewriter and you'll find he or she rubs the rollers with methylated spirits. This is a job one can do oneself at much less cost, but it's wise to check with the manufacturer of the typewriter that the meths will do no harm – the materials used to make technical equipment are changing all the time and using an unsuitable cleaner could be a costly mistake.

WALL BRUSHING

If you need to dust down the walls, but lack a trunk-style vacuum cleaner, you can always tie a clean towel round the head of a broom and brush the walls down with it. It's harder work, but it does a good job.

WALLPAPER

Even non-washable wallpaper may need to be cleaned in places where it gets particularly grubby, as it does round light switches. The dirt will usually come off quite easily if you give it a gentle wipe with a clean white tissue dipped in neat ammonia. But do test the fastness of the wallpaper dyes in an inconspicuous place first and be careful that you don't rub so hard you take the surface off the paper.

If the problem is a grease mark, try a spray-on dry cleaner. But, once again, do a test patch on a hidden, or left-over, piece of wallpaper before using it where it shows. Another method of drawing grease out of paper is to apply a paste made of oil of eucalyptus and fuller's earth. Let it draw out the grease for twenty-four hours and then brush it off gently. Before trying this, do a test patch as for the spray-on dry cleaner – what works well on one paper may stain another.

WASHING LINES

A washing line can be an eyesore which dominates a small garden. A keen gardener I know of found a way round this. He bought two strong posts, of the sort used to build rustic arches, screwed a vine-eye near the top of each, placed them where they improved the look of the garden and had a good span of clear ground between them. He then grew a plant up each and attached dog clips to each end of the washing line, so it could be clipped to each post and easily removed afterwards.

WASHING UP

Burnt-on Dirt
When glass oven dishes get burnt rims, try rubbing the burnt part off with a damp cloth dipped in salt; if that isn't sufficient, soak them overnight in a strong salt solution.

Cutlery Draining
If it's been well washed and thoroughly rinsed, most cutlery
will drain itself dry and spotless, provided it's standing on
end, not lying down. In a country-style kitchen one of the
nicest and cheapest cutlery drainers is a simple terracotta
flowerpot.

Egg
The easy way to remove runny egg from a plate, or from
cutlery, is to rinse it off in cold water before washing the
plate. Hot water just cooks the egg and makes it set more
firmly on the china.

Glass
When washing up fine glasses or glass ornaments, there'll
be less risk of a breakage if you take four precautions. Put
a folded towel in the bottom of the sink, in case something
slips. Use water which isn't too hot, as thick glass may
crack in very hot water because the part closest to the
water expands faster than the part furthest away. Wash
each piece singly with nothing else in the sink, to prevent
accidental bumps.. Make sure any central tap is turned
away, so you can't knock the glass on it.
    Any gilding on glass could be damaged by soda, so the
safest cleaner to use for gilded glass is a pure soap.
    As vinegar counteracts soap, glasses have a better shine
if you put a good dash of vinegar in the rinsing water.

Milk
Anything which has had milk in it cleans better if it is
rinsed out in cold water first – heat sets the albumen in the
milk and makes it harder to clean off.

WASTE BINS

It's a lot easier to keep wastepaper baskets clean if you
line the bottom with paper or, if it won't be seen, a surplus
carrier bag, each time you empty it. This is one of the
trivial details of life which may not seem worth bothering

with, let alone worth mentioning in a book, but I can't be the only person who got it wrong in their first home and wasted time cleaning out dirty bins as a result.

WATER DEPOSITS

In *Supertips to Make Life Easy* I mentioned that a mixture of salt and vinegar – or, even better, salt and hot vinegar – would take hard water deposits off baths and basins. Since then people have written to point out that the mixture also removes deposits from shower coils and the bottoms of irons. Happily the mixture will work on water deposits wherever they are found, provided the surface you are using it on will not be damaged by either the salt or the vinegar. Before using it on irons, check with the manufacturer. And don't leave the mixture on any longer than is necessary to make the deposit loose enough to rub off.

PAINT AND PASTE

When I wrote the do-it-yourself chapter for *Supertips to Make Life Easy*, I thought that I had covered the bulk of the tips which would be useful to the average enthusiast. But in the past couple of years I've been sent or have come across a whole lot more. In fact I've come to the conclusion that this is one field where there are always new tips to discover and better ways to do almost everything. So in compiling a chapter like this, the problem isn't where to start – it's where to stop. As in my previous book, I've concentrated on the basic jobs which anyone, male or female, might find themselves doing in order to save money or to cope with a crisis. I have omitted the big projects – such as building a garage or making furniture – which only the fairly expert are likely to attempt. My purpose isn't to turn anyone into an expert, but simply to smooth the paths of those who, like me, have to do such jobs themselves, and to give them the satisfaction of doing the job that little bit better, or faster, or more cheaply.

BALLCOCK SUPPORTING

Years of camping holidays, and no father around to fix things, have taught my children to improvise. One of my sons greeted me on my return from a filming trip by announcing that the main water tank had been overflowing but he'd solved the problem without calling the plumber. Through old age, the ballcock, which floats on the surface of the cold water tank and shuts off the supply when it's full, had ceased to float properly. So the valve stayed open and water had kept on coming in. Seeing that this was the cause of the overflow, he'd found one of the inflatable armbands with which he had learnt to swim as a toddler, put it round the ball, blown it up, and the ball had floated again and shut off the water. As armbands slowly deflate, this isn't a permanent solution, but it gives you time to find a plumber at leisure instead of paying premium rates at the weekend. For sod's law decrees that such problems always occur on Saturdays and Sundays.

BATH GAP FILLER

The silicone pastes designed to fill the gap between a bath and the wall can give an excellent finish if properly handled, but they look a mess if they aren't – I made a dreadful job of them until I got some tips from the manufacturers.

The first secret is to wipe the area thoroughly with methylated spirits to remove any soapy film that may be on it. Soap and dirt prevent the filler sticking properly. Then put masking tape very exactly along any area where you don't want the filler to go – it may look easy to wipe off, but it isn't (so don't be tempted to do a bit of filling in an odd moment, wearing decent clothes). Make sure you remove the masking tape *as soon as* the filler has been smoothed into place.

If you have a very big gap to fill, stuff it with tissues and apply the filler in two separate coats, leaving time for each to dry in between.

Finally, remember that the filler sets very rapidly. So

choose a time when you won't be interrupted and take the phone off the hook. Apply it in a continuous stream and IMMEDIATELY remove any excess, smoothing each section by wiping it with a finger dipped in washing-up liquid. The washing-up liquid acts as a smoothing fluid and prevents the paste sticking to your finger. Keep some cling film handy and if you are unavoidably called away in the middle of applying the filler, cover it with cling film. The filler cures and forms a skin by absorbing moisture from the air, so excluding air with the film slows down the setting process quite considerably.

There isn't yet a solvent to get rid of old silicone filler – or new silicone filler which you've botched up. You just have to cut it out. So it really does pay to get it right the first time.

BATHROOM WALLS

It's usually assumed that bathrooms must be either tiled or covered in a washable paint or paper. But really it is only the areas round the bath and behind the basin which are liable to get wet. This means any paper can be used in a bathroom, and the vulnerable areas can be protected with transparent stick-on plastic or by screwing sheets of transparent acrylic over the paper. To cut the acrylic to shape, use a very fine saw and smooth off any curves with a file.

Another solution is to surround just the bath with tiles. If you don't want the permanency of ceramic tiles, mirror tiles, though a nuisance to clean, do have the advantage of doubling as a shaving mirror and are a decided incentive to slimming.

CARPET LAYING

Carpet Pattern Taking
In laying a carpet, the crunch comes when you have to cut round tricky shapes, such as the door lintel or the pipes of a radiator. There are various tricks for making it easier.

It's not necessary, or even very helpful, to make a pattern of the whole room you intend to carpet. Just put it in place and tack the centre of each side in position then work away from these tacks. However, it is useful to make small patterns to show how you need to cut round awkward places. Use newspaper for this, cutting slashes down into the newspaper on the curves and corners until you can fold the surplus back to get a perfect fit. Professional carpet layers don't do it this way, but making a pattern does two things: it shows you the shape you must aim for; and it allows you to practise the slashing process – to see, for example, how close together the slashes need to be to produce a smooth curve – before you cut into the carpet itself.

Cutting

If you've taken paper patterns of awkward places, you can mark them out with chalk on the surface of the carpet. This provides a ROUGH guideline of the shape you are trying to achieve – but it will be only a rough guide, because carpet is far thicker than paper and this alters the position of the fold.

When you start cutting the carpet DON'T CUT ROUND the shape you've marked, cut slashes GOING TOWARDS IT, BUT NOT UP TO IT, so the slashes point towards places where the line changes direction. Use a Stanley knife with a new blade – trying to use scissors will wreck both them and

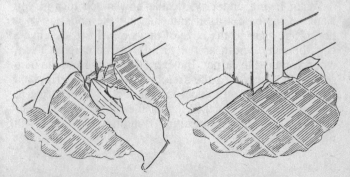

your hands. Don't cut too deeply at first and keep turning the carpet in and seeing how well it's fitting before cutting a little bit deeper. Only when you have a really good fit when you turn the surplus in can you afford to trim it to the same width as the rest of your turn-in.

Preventing Fraying

The job of cutting round awkward places is made twice as hard if the carpet starts fraying as you cut it. It's easy to avoid this: just paint a fairly thick coating of a rubberized adhesive, such as Copydex or Evo-stik, on the back of the area you will be cutting into, and let it dry before you start cutting. If you're a quick worker, you may find that when you fold in the surplus carpet the glue is just tacky enough to stick to itself and the fold will lie flatter than it normally would. But this is a bonus. You don't HAVE to work quickly. Unfortunately the rubberized coating makes the carpet harder to cut, so use a very sharp blade.

Underlay

Professional carpet layers often put large sheets of thin cardboard under the underlay to smooth out ridges from the floorboards. If the floor is reasonably flat, this isn't essential, but it's quite a good idea to use several layers of newspaper to provide some padding and to prevent the dust and cold air rising between the cracks in the boards.

When laying underlay, decide how much turn-in you want on the carpet itself and then cut the underlay so it doesn't go right to the edge of the room. Instead, leave a gap the same width as the turn-in of the carpet. Then, when you lay the carpet, the extra thickness from the hem should fit neatly into the area between the underlay and the wall, giving you a nice smooth edge. If you forget to do this, the carpet at the edge of the room will be higher than the rest and any furniture standing near a wall will tilt slightly forward.

Waste Carpet

It's a good idea to keep the larger off-cuts of any carpet you lay, or have laid for you. It has a number of uses. Carpet dyes are particularly fragile, so stain removers should be tested on off-cuts. When a stain can't be removed, you may be able to use the off-cuts to put in a patch. If the carpet is in the hall and the part in front of the door is taking too much wear and tear, you can use an off-cut to make a matching mat to protect it. In a small hall a mat which matches gives a greater impression of space than a contrasting mat which catches the eye – and, of course, the off-cut is free and a mat isn't.

CASTOR CREATION

If you want furniture to slide better but don't want to raise it up on castors, a set of buttons may be the answer. Try putting a largish button under each leg. You need the sort of large plastic buttons which have a nice smooth curve on the underside and you fix them with the curve towards the carpet. Put them on with adhesive tape first and, if they work well, glue them firmly. They work better with light pieces of furniture than with heavy ones.

CHIPBOARD

Chipboard may crumble if you screw directly into it. The solution is to drill a hole just a FRACTION larger than the screw you want to use. Then firmly glue in a wood-fibre Rawlplug and, when the glue is fully set, you can insert the screw with no problems.

CISTERNS

If a lavatory cistern starts to overfill so that water comes out of the overflow pipe, there are two likely causes. The first possibility is that the ballcock, which should rise and shut off the water, has stopped working properly. Usually this is because of some obstruction like a build-up of deposits from hard water near the point at which it pivots. If the ballcock is hanging down and not moving freely, a careful scrape with the end of a screwdriver round the pivot area should cure the problem.

The other possible cause of overfilling is that the washer in the cistern needs replacing. There are a lot of different designs of cistern. Some washers can be replaced by simply uncoupling the inflow pipes, just inside the cistern, but to get at others you virtually have to take the whole cistern to pieces. On the whole, it's a job for professionals, but, if you attempt it yourself, remember to turn off the water leading to the cistern before you start.

DENT MASKING

If a piece of wood furniture has the kind of dent which is made by dropping a small sharp object on to it, you can easily mask it. Over very hot water (but OFF direct heat) melt together a small piece of beeswax (from a good ironmonger) with enough shoe polish to tint it to match the piece of furniture. Mix the two well together and drop the wax into the hole. Let it cool slightly before you rub off the excess, then polish it up when it's dry. Remember that beeswax is highly inflammable and should not be put over a flame or allowed to overheat.

DOOR TRIMMING

When you saw the bottom off a door after fitting a carpet it's all too easy to leave the door a fraction of an inch too long. But it's well nigh impossible to saw off a fraction of an inch, and if the door is veneered you can't take it off with a plane either. Instead, put a large sheet of coarse sandpaper under the part which rubs the carpet, stand on the ends of the sandpaper and swing the door to and fro over it until enough door has been rubbed off. As the paper presses the pile down slightly, you'll gradually need to slip other sheets of paper under the sandpaper so that you can sand enough off the door for it to clear the carpet.

DOUBLE GLAZING

It is a good idea to have some silica in the gap between the two panes of a double-glazed window. The silica absorbs the moisture which would otherwise steam up the glass. The easy way to do this is to make a tiny sausage of silica by putting it in a very small tubular bandage. The sausage can then lie tidily along the gap between the two windows.

DRILLING

Equal Holes
If several holes have to be drilled to the same depth, the easy way is to decide how deep the holes need to be, then measure that length up the bit of the drill, from the tip. Then wind a piece of adhesive tape round the bit at that point, so that its lower edge marks the length that needs to be drilled. Then you know precisely how far to go in, and don't have to keep on taking the drill out to check the hole.

Matching Holes
If you need to drill matching holes on the inside of two different pieces of wood, all you need do to mark the place is to put a ball-bearing in the right position on one, put the other in place on top and give it a sharp tap with a hammer to indent the ball-bearing into both.

Safety
There is always a temptation to change the attachment on a drill without unplugging it. But if the starter switch is accidentally pressed while someone's hand is holding the attachment in place, there could be an accident. To avoid this risk, tie a short string to the chuck key and attach it firmly, with adhesive tape, to the plug end of the cable. It will then be really inconvenient to use the chuck without unplugging the drill. The bonus is that the chuck won't go missing when you need it.

FILLING GAPS

When filling gaps in walls it is tempting to bash on regardless and leave the smoothing till later. But it's really much quicker and easier to do it as you go along. Scrape any lumps and bumps off immediately and keep an old paint brush handy in a jar of water; brush the filler over as soon as you've applied it. The brush leaves a smooth finish and is much less rough on the hands than smoothing down with a cloth. With care, you may have a finish which can be painted as soon as it's dry, but, if any roughness remains, a quick rub with glasspaper will smooth it down.

FUSE REPAIRS

There are two kinds of fuse: those which control the supply of electricity to your premises, and those which are incorporated within an appliance. The wisdom of women and gullibility – or gallantry – of men is well demonstrated by the way that repairing either has been designated a man's job. Nothing could be easier, but houses and flats often have their fuse-boxes in inconvenient places, and who wants to poke about in inconvenient places if they can persuade someone else that performing this mundane task is proof of skill and courage? However, a knight errant is not always at hand when needed.

Fuses in Appliances

A very capable producer at the BBC came to work one morning fuming. Her washing machine had stopped working. She'd immediately suspected the fuse and had changed it, but the machine still wouldn't work so she arranged a service call. The man had been round that morning and had repaired the machine in an instant – by changing the fuse. She had learnt the expensive way that any fuse being put into an appliance should be tested first. The best way is to try it in the plug of a light and see if the light will go on. Only when a WORKING fuse has been fitted, and has failed, do you need to call someone in. Changing the fuse is just a matter of swapping one cartridge for another, but it is vital to use the right amp for the particular appliance, so if you are in any doubt, consult an expert.

For all repairs to electrical equipment, UNPLUG THE APPLIANCE. Do not neglect this golden rule: switching it off at the wall is not good enough.

House Fuses

When no one else can be persuaded to do it, this is the procedure for repairing a house fuse. TURN THE ELECTRICITY OFF AT THE CIRCUIT BOARD and (by the light of a torch if necessary) take the fuses out (and put them back) one by one until you find one in which the metal wire, which runs from end to end, is broken. If it's a cartridge fuse, you replace the cartridge with a new one of equivalent power. If it's the old-fashioned kind in which a piece of wire is screwed to a porcelain gadget, remove the broken wire, slip the new wire in through the hole at one end and out at the other, wind it round the screw at each end, slightly tighten the screw, and trim off any excess. Don't make the wire too taut, because, if you do, it will break as soon as you put current through it.

GLUE REMOVAL

Ideally one should always ask manufacturers what solvent to use to remove their glues, but if you don't know who made the glue it's a matter of trial and error. Apart from well-known glue removers like methylated spirits, it's also worth trying some less obvious ones. Some glues respond to acetone and others even respond to hot vinegar.

GROUTING

Plain white tiles are the cheapest to buy, and to make them more interesting you don't need to buy pricey pots of grouting tint. If you've an eye for colour you can mix powder paints with the grouting to make any colour you wish, though the white in the grouting means you won't get really strong shades. Just be careful to measure exactly the proportions you use – so you will be able to get a good match each time – and to mix them very evenly into the grouting – otherwise the results will be streaky.

HAMMERING

When hammering in a short or very fine nail, fingers and tempers may be saved by holding the nail with a pair of eyebrow tweezers, or sticking it through a piece of polystyrene (the offcut from a ceiling tile for example).

LADDERS

Ladders need to be used with care. The safe distance from the base of a ladder to the wall it leans on is not less than a quarter of the height of the ladder. And if the base of the ladder needs to rest on soft earth, put a plank underneath so it stands on a firm base.

LAVATORY BLOCKAGE

If a lavatory becomes blocked there's a chance that the obstruction is only just round the bend, in which case you may be able to clear it yourself – if you can bear to. The least distasteful method is to try to force it right down the drain. To do this, you need to take a couple of buckets of water and pour them, simultaneously, into the lavatory pan from as great a height as possible. But watch out: if the method fails and you have too much water in the buckets, the lavatory will overflow.

The alternative method is to bail out the lavatory pan and then, preferably with rubber gloves on, reach round the bend and pull out the obstruction. If you can't reach it, a piece of thick wire, suitably bent into a hook, and if necessary filed to a point, can be pushed round the bend to hook the object out. But do be careful not to scratch the glaze of the lavatory pan with the wire.

NAIL REMOVING

Levering a nail out of wood can leave dreadful marks where whatever tool you used pressed into it. To avoid this, just slip the end of a wallpaper scraper or a kitchen spatula under the pliers before you lever.

NEW BRICKS

The glaring newness of the bricks on an extension to an old house sometimes spoils the appearance of the whole building. But I'm told that new bricks age faster if you brush them over with milk: then all the brick-aging elements in the air have something to work on.

PAINTING

Brush Cleaning
To have enough paint brush cleaner to come right up the bristles of a brush uses up a lot of cleaner. A more economical method is to put the cleaner in the corner of a strong plastic bag. This has the added advantage that you can do up the bag round the handle and stop the cleaner evaporating, or air getting to the upper part of the bristles and drying them. You can also work the cleaner into the bristles, with your fingers, through the bag.

Clothing
It's not by chance that painters wear cotton overalls: if, when painting, you wear a fluffy fabric, or even a wool jumper, little pieces of fluff will get into the air and stick to the paint. These pieces are particularly noticeable on gloss paint.

Emulsion over Gloss
Water-based emulsion paints don't take well over gloss paint and after a while you can get flaking. Unfortunately there isn't a short cut to making the two key together. You have to wash the gloss paint well, then sand it down

thoroughly with fine sandpaper so the emulsion has a good surface to cling to, then wipe off the dust with a rag moistened with white spirit.

Emulsion on Polystyrene

To prevent emulsion paint sinking into polystyrene, brush the surface over with wallpaper paste before painting. Choose a paste which is designed for hanging polystyrene, so it will bond well to it, and allow rather more time than usual for it to dry. It needs to be absolutely dry before the paint is applied.

Emulsion Splashes

Splashes of emulsion paint on a skirting will sometimes come off with methylated spirits when nothing else will shift them.

Flaky Paint

When paint flakes, it's very seldom the paint which is at fault. The culprit is usually the surface it was applied to. A hint of moisture, a little grease, or even left-over detergent can all stop the paint sticking fast to the surface. And though it may look fine when it's applied, those things are a built-in time bomb which will cause it to lift sooner or later.

The correct treatment for flaky paint is to remove it entirely so you get to a clean sound surface. If you've taken the worst off and really can't bear to go on you could try painting the walls with a PVA adhesive as for 'Plaster' (p. 105). This is a last-ditch measure. Nobody would guarantee the results, but there's at least a chance that you can then paint or paper the walls without trouble. How smooth a surface you will get is another matter.

Gloss

Gloss paint shows every fleck of dust. For a good finish, you need to wipe the surface down with a clean rag immediately before painting and make sure the room itself isn't dusty. It's a good idea to damp the rag with white spirit, so that you kill two birds with one stone and remove any traces of grease or detergent which may still be on the surface after washing and rinsing.

Masking

An absolutely invaluable tool when painting goes by the name of 'George'. George is a sheet of metal curved to fit over the edge of carpets, so you can protect them when painting skirtings, and with a straight edge to place against the ceiling if you are doing the walls a different colour. Most good hardware stores have them.

Over Nicotine

Nicotine is a stain which has extraordinary powers of penetration. It will not only sink right into the paint it lands on, it will also come right through any new paint which is put on top. This makes it one of the most difficult stains to cover. To get good results with a badly stained ceiling, you need to scrub it as clean as possible with Sugar Soap, and rinse it very well. Then, to stop the remaining nicotine seeping through, it needs to be sealed with alkali resisting primer. This is sold to the trade by builder's merchants but isn't generally available at DIY shops, so you may need to get the name of your nearest stockist from Dulux. On top of the primer, use an oil-based paint such as a silthane silk rather than a water-based emulsion.

Over Screws and Nails

Strictly speaking, screws should always be removed before painting, but sometimes a screw won't come out, and some nails (such as those keeping ceiling boards in place!) need to stay. If you paint over them with a water-based paint, they will rust and show through. To avoid this, just paint the ends with gloss paint – or even clear nail varnish. When dry, give it a quick rub with fine sandpaper to provide a slightly rough surface for the emulsion.

Overnight Breaks

If you want to stop painting overnight, you don't have to

go to the bother of cleaning your brush. Just drop it in enough water to immerse the paint-covered end of the bristles and the paint will stay pliable whether it's oil-based or water-based. Don't let the water cover the metal band round the top of the bristles. If it does, the wood will swell with the wet and when it shrinks the brush will start shedding its bristles.

Spectacle Protection

Those who wear spectacles have to be very tidy workers if they are to avoid specks of paint getting on the lenses – in this situation prevention is very much better than cure. Smooth cling film tightly over the lenses before you start work and you can be as messy as you like without worrying.

Stencils

One of the least expensive and most attractive ways to make a painted room look a bit different is by using stencils, and some very attractive ones are now available. It takes a little practice to get really good results, but there are a few professional tricks which help.

Although the wall may be painted in emulsion, some of the top professionals in decorative finishes use cans of spray-on car paint for stencils. Sprayed on very very finely, these allow you to get subtle blends of colour which look nothing like the same-all-over colour of a car. Experiment and you'll find the combinations which work.

Coat the back of the stencil with the spray-on adhesive used for mounting photographs. Let it dry; then spray on another coat. That gives the stencil a tacky backing which allows you to position it firmly yet move it easily – provided the wall you are working on is thoroughly dry. If you rush things, and the paint is still drying, you are courting disaster.

Position your stencil and then mask the area around it very thoroughly with newspapers. Sprays always cover a larger area than you expect.

When the stencil is finished and dry, you can create the illusion that it is in, rather than on, the paint by watering down a little of the emulsion paint you used as the basic wall colour until it is very thin and milky and just dabbing it over the stencil with a soft cloth.

Tinting

If you have some white paint and want to tint it slightly, you may be able to produce the shade you need, really cheaply, by mixing in part of a little matchpot of a suitable colour. How good the result is will depend on whether you have a good eye for colour, and how judiciously you mix the two together. It can work very well, but make sure the two paints are the same type. Also, be careful to make enough of it. If you run out before a job is finished, it may be impossible to mix an exact match.

PLASTER

Painting Over

New plaster can't be painted until it's dry, and even when it seems dry there will be some moisture in it. This means it can only take a water-based paint. If, after a while, a powdery white deposit comes out on the paint surface, it is the salts in the plaster coming through as it dries. Don't wash this off – rewetting the plaster will only increase the problem. Instead brush it off with a soft cloth.

Occasionally damp can cause the alkali in plaster to come through in white patches even when it's well established. The solution here is to wipe it over with water and vinegar mixed in equal amounts until you can hear it fizz slightly as the acid and alkali interact.

Plastering

If you want to plaster a wall after a major alteration, like removing a fireplace, you may find that the surface of the wall is so dusty that the plaster can't get a good grip. The way to create a good bond is to paint the area with a PVA adhesive, such as Evo-bond, first. This sticks the dust to the wall and you then have a firm surface on to which you can apply the plaster.

Plaster also attaches more firmly to non-porous surfaces like gloss paint if you coat the surface with a PVA adhesive first. But if you are repairing a porous surface, such as old plaster, you get the best results by brushing on a coat of dilute adhesive before you plaster. Check the dilution with the makers of whatever brand you are using.

PLASTIC WOOD

If you need plastic wood, but don't have any, a good substitute is woodwork adhesive mixed with sawdust. If you want to be really thorough, you may even be able to tint it with a wood stain.

POINTING

When pointing becomes dry and crumbles away, it's difficult for the new pointing to get a good hold. Once you've brushed out the loose pointing and dust, you can give the new mortar better holding power by adding PVA adhesive. When you mix the mortar, a good basic ratio is to add adhesive and water in equal amounts. You then use it just like ordinary mortar.

When pointing, the essential thing is to get the moisture balance right – too dry and it's too crumbly to use, too wet and it runs down the wall bearing permanent witness to your amateur status in this line of work. It should look rather like sand when the tide has just gone out – moist if you press it, but not wet.

The easiest way to get a smooth finish to mortar is to brush the surface with an old paint brush as soon as you've applied it.

POLYURETHANE

When polyurethane varnish becomes old and flaky, the only way to remove it is with a varnish stripper or paint remover, or by sanding it off. Sanding it off is extremely hard work and strippers and paint removers may bleach and damage the wood itself. So it's worth thinking carefully before applying polyurethane in the first place. It should never be applied to anything which stands the faintest chance of having value as an antique.

PUTTY

Painting over wet putty is normally impossible – the paint brush just drags at the putty. But if you need to paint in a hurry, you can give fresh putty a firm smooth skin by brushing it over with a wet paint brush. You'll find paint can be applied next day without problems, and the putty will dry quite happily through the paint.

RADIATORS

If a radiator is cold, while all the others in the system are hot, it almost certainly has air in it. As air rises to the top of radiators all you need do is slip a radiator key into the little square socket at one end of the top of the radiator. Now watch out; the screw which stops up this hole is quite short and if you open it too far it will fall out; once out it will be a tricky job to get it in against the pressure of the water. So turn it very gently, anti-clockwise, a LITTLE bit, and you should hear a slight hiss as the air comes out. As soon as the first drop of water follows it, you should shut the valve again by turning the key clockwise. The radiator should then become hot.

REFRIGERATOR

If the rubber seal round the door of a refrigerator loses its bounce and begins to let in air, you can make it seal properly again by running a strip of sticky-backed foam insulation tape round the door under the flap of the rubber seal.

WALLPAPER

Bubbles

It sometimes happens that bubbles develop in wallpaper. There are two possible reasons for them – either you forgot to put glue on that bit of paper, or there is a bubble of air caught under the paper. Either way, it is easily cured. Just take an ordinary medical syringe with a fairly large needle (you can buy them at a chemist), push the needle gently into the bubble, with the plunger down, at a point in the pattern where a small hole won't show, and pull up the plunger to suck the air out as you smooth the paper down. If the paper bounces up, you know it needs gluing. Just draw a little, rather thin paste into the syringe, push the needle through the hole again and squirt in enough glue to fix the paper in place when you smooth it down.

Hanging

If you are hanging wallpaper straight on to a wall, without cross-lining it, it's a good idea to coat the walls with a solution of wallpaper paste before you apply paste to the paper. Having paste on both surfaces makes it much easier to manoeuvre the wallpaper against the wall and match the pattern perfectly; it also gives a far better bond when it dries.

Marks

If off-cuts of wallpaper are kept after it's hung, you can use them to try out stain removers if the paper gets marked, without putting the wallpaper itself at risk.

If a boldly patterned wallpaper gets marks on it which can't be removed, but is still generally clean, the marks can sometimes be concealed by making an appliqué from a left-over piece of the paper. Find the section of the pattern which exactly matches the area where the stain is, then very carefully cut round the edge of the pattern and stick it over the place with wallpaper paste. It won't be totally invisible, but it should look a lot better than a splash of wine or a toddler's scribble.

WASHER CHANGING

Washer changing is easy. All you really need to know is that there are two main types of tap, ordinary ones and Supataps. Supataps are the ones which have a curving tube rising from the basin, from which the tap mechanism hangs over the bowl. In ordinary taps the mechanism sits above the 'shelf' part of the basin and the spout protrudes over the bowl. The distinction is important because the types of washer they use are different; also you don't have to turn off the water supply when changing a washer on a Supatap, but you do for an ordinary tap.

Ordinary taps

TURN OFF THE WATER SUPPLY AT THE STOPCOCK. With modern taps you then have to remove the tap knob by undoing the screw at its top. With older taps you need to hold the tap firmly with one wrench (to prevent any pressure on the basin) while you undo the nut-like section of the body of the tap with another (put a cloth over it, so that you don't scratch the chrome). Once the body of the tap is off, you should be able to see the washer as a contrasting ring. Then all you need to do is undo the nuts to get at it. If you think you might forget the order in which to put them back, make a sketch before you start. Replace the old washer with a new one of the same size and put the tap together again.

It is important that washers should conform to Water Board standards. Currently, all those sold IN taps have to meet these standards, but replacement washers do not. When you have new plumbing installed, be on the safe side and write to the manufacturers for some spare washers of the type fitted in your taps. That is the only way you can be sure of fitting safe washers.

Supataps

Turn the tap slightly and use a spanner to undo the nut at its top. Continue to turn the tap and it will fall off. Press the bottom of the tap and the washer unit inside should

come free. Then lever out the washer, which looks like a
flat-headed spinning top, and pop in the new one. Put it
back by reversing the procedure.

WOOD STAINING

If a wood stain is too light, you can always go over it with
a darker one, so if you are staining wood for the first time,
and have no off-cuts on which to experiment, err on the
side of lightness. The secret of applying it evenly is not to
go over the same piece of wood twice: easy to avoid if you
apply the stain with a small oblong paint pad. But for a
large area the quickest and easiest way is to hire a spray
gun and spray it on.

ODDS AND ENDS

This is a section full of tips and short-cuts which make it easier to do those odd jobs around the home which are neither to do with cleaning nor with do-it-yourself.

ANT SCARING

In *Supertips to Make Life Easy* I recommended peppermint as an ant deterrent. A reader wrote to tell me that ants depart not only at the smell of peppermint but also at the smell of orange peel, which he scattered down after being given the tip by a neighbour. As my ants haven't returned since I zapped them with peppermint, I haven't been able to test this; but it could be worth a try. Ants do seem to have an aversion to certain smells. I'm told cucumber is another they dislike.

APPLIANCE MOVING

Some appliances, like washing machines, have remarkably rough feet which are liable to plough a furrow in the surface of the floor when they are pulled out for servicing.

To prevent this, keep a piece of hardboard, large enough to pull them out on to. And, if it can be managed without the hardboard showing, have them standing on another piece of the same thickness – pulling them out is easier if they start at the same level as the hardboard on to which they are being moved.

BLANKET LENGTHENING

A blanket too short to tuck in properly is a nuisance, but you don't have to lengthen it with another bit of blanket. Any fabric which can be washed at the same temperature will do – after all, it is only going to be tucked in.

CARS

Battery Care
The positive and negative terminals of a car battery sometimes get corroded. The manual of my Japanese car says an easy way to remove this is to wash them with a mixture of water and baking soda. Few European manufacturers make such thrifty suggestions.

Starting
In *Supertips to Make Life Easy* I pointed out that when a car had damp points and wouldn't start, even though the battery was live, drying the points with a hairdryer would often do the trick. If, instead, the problem is a car past its first youth, with a tired engine, try pulling the choke right out and then easing it in as you try to start it. This will often get a car to start when keeping the choke at a single position leaves the engine dead; but you may need to do it several times to get a really tired car to go. In some a touch of accelerator at the same time helps too.

CAT SMELLS

If you are unlucky enough to have a male cat spray its distinctive smell indoors, it can be very hard indeed to get rid of. While you are working on it, burn a sandlewood joss-stick in the room. They are very effective for masking unpleasant smells.

DUVET COVERING

In Austria, where duvets have been used for far longer than they have been in Britain, they have an excellent way of getting the covers on easily. They wash and hang them up inside out – which, incidentally, saves them from fading in the sun. Then, to put the cover on the duvet, they leave it inside out, put a hand down into each corner, catch hold of the corners of the duvet through the cover, lift it, and shake the duvet cover down over it. Which is easier done than said!

FIRE LIGHTING

Fire lighters cost money, but all kinds of things can be found in any house which will help a fire to get going. A thrifty Welsh barrister I know uses the waxed cartons in which Welsh milk is delivered. Any wax will help, whether candle ends or waxed paper cups. Fat is equally good but can make a greasy layer in the chimney which could catch fire, so it is strictly for outdoor fires. And dried peel from citrus fruits contains oils which burn beautifully and give a lovely aroma.

FURNITURE CARE

Moving a Long Case Clock
If you ever have occasion to move such a thing, it is worth knowing the furniture trade's golden rule – 'weights, pendulum, pendulum, weights'. Which means that you first take out the weights, then take out the pendulum; and you put them back in reverse order. If you took out the pendulum before the weights, the action could be damaged.

Party Precautions
When slightly merry, friends can be less than careful.
You can protect your french-polished furniture from their
dripping glasses by covering it discreetly with cling film. If
it is well smoothed out and the lights are not too high, it
should be invisible.

Writing Marks
It takes only a moment for the pressure of a biro through
a single sheet of paper to ruin the surface of a piece of
good furniture. There should always be padding underneath before you start writing.

HEADBOARDS

Wooden supports for headboards often damage the wallpaper they rub against and make it impossible to change
the position of the bed without redecorating the room.
The damage can easily be prevented by gluing a small
chunk of fairly firm foam rubber to the most prominent
parts of the back of the headboard.

HOUSE SELLING

All kinds of impressions combine to make a house desirable, but some of them may be registered quite uncon-
sciously. Some estate agents say that a house sells best if
it has an atmosphere of homeliness and welcome. Nothing
is more homely than the smell of baking. So an old and
proven ruse to give a house the smell of baking, but without
the work, is to sprinkle powdered cinnamon and sugar on
a baking tray and put it in a hot oven until the aroma fills
the house. Flowers and house plants also make a house
seem more homely.

KNOTS

I was preparing some props for an appearance on 'Pebble
Mill at One' when I noticed a very bright researcher

struggling desperately to tie a knot which would stay tied. When I showed her how to tie a reef knot she said it was the best of all my tips. Having been a Girl Guide I've always taken knot-tying for granted but for those who, like her, find it difficult to tie a secure knot the rule is this.

Left over right and under.
Right over left and under.

In other words you take one end of the string in each hand, place the left string over the right, tuck the end of it round the right hand string and up again the other side, and then do the same with the end of string which is now to the right, and pull the knot tight. Incidentally don't try to keep rigidly hold of the ends of string in the process – it's not which hand you're holding the string in that counts, it's the position of the string itself. It should give you a really firm knot, provided all the string is the *same* thickness.

To join two pieces of string of *different* thicknesses you need to use the sheetbend illustrated below. To make it you just fold the end of the thicker string into a loop and then thread the thinner string through it as illustrated and pull the knot tight.

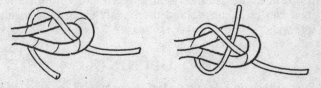

LABEL REMOVING

If a container such as a plastic box or a jam jar has a label on it with a self-adhesive backing, don't try to get it off by putting it in water. That will just make the paper go mushy but leave the glue where it is. Instead, fill the container with the hottest water it can stand. Then leave it a few minutes for the heat to soften the glue and you should find that the label will peel of easily, leaving no trace behind. If that fails, the label is probably secured with a water-based glue and you should be able to get it off in water.

LAVATORY SMELLS

Brief
To banish a temporary smell, try striking a match. I didn't believe the person who told me that it worked, but she was right – it's remarkably effective.

Lingering
If a lavatory smells all the time, the lavatory basin itself and the floor are the most likely culprits. Try brushing the lavatory round with about half a cup of bleach – making sure the brush takes it up under the rim – and leave it overnight. Bleach is an excellent smell killer, so if that doesn't work the chances are that the culprit is the floor. Carpets in a loo are a snare and delusion – every man deludes himself that he doesn't drip. A good carpet shampoo MAY do the trick, but, once a lavatory carpet starts to smell, the only way to get rid of the smell could be to get rid of the carpet. When laying carpet in a lavatory, it could be wise to choose a washable one and, instead of nailing it down, fix it with heavy-duty velcro all round the edge, so it can be taken up and thoroughly cleaned at regular intervals.

LID OPENING

Some press-on lids can be ridiculously hard to open – one old lady I know of actually broke her ribs opening a tin of instant coffee. Anyone who finds such lids hard to lever up may prefer to tie a large knot in one end of a piece of thin ribbon and drop the knotted end into the tin, leaving the rest hanging over the side. The lid then goes on as usual, but to get it off you only need to jerk the ribbon up. Those with arthritis may find it easier to pull on the ribbon if it has a large loop sewn in the end.

Small screw-top lids can be a devil to get off, but one solution is to hold them in a pair of nutcrackers. Another method – which can be used on screw-tops of any size – is to hold them through a piece of coarse sandpaper, to get a better grip with less effort.

MATCH LENGTHENER

A friend of mine who has been in a wheelchair for thirty years has a splendid device. It's a long wooden rod which her husband devised so it would hold a match. He simply drilled a hole, slightly smaller than a match, down the centre of some stout dowelling, and then sawed a slit down the dowelling through the hole. When you push a match into the hole, the slit allows it to open just enough to hold the match firmly. My friend says this very simple device has made all the difference to lighting the oven, as well as fires and candles.

Your Sewing And Knitting

Making and Mending
Plain and Purl

MAKING AND MENDING

Sewing is second nature to anyone who grows up, as I did, in a household where almost every garment and item of soft furnishing is home-made. Before I was even in my teens my mother had taught me all kinds of easy ways and short-cuts which never get into the pattern instructions. Mind you, they did cause me problems – the ultra-conformist French mistress who taught sewing at school would shake with fury when she saw me taking half the expected time to make a garment, and would growl, 'Ah, Moyra, you are so slap-dash!' Which was quite untrue, because I've always felt that the only short-cuts worth taking were ones which both reduced the work AND improved the look of the finished garment. If one's going to make something badly, one might as well not make it at all – but whoever saw a tailor working slowly?

This section is for those to whom sewing is not second

nature. It collects together some of the tricks my mother taught me, some that people have sent me, and others that I have picked up from experts. All of them make sewing and mending just that little bit easier, and help to give a more professional look to the finished job. For the gap between the amateur and the professional isn't a great gulf, it's just a tiny bit of know-how.

BIAS STRIPS

There is a rather neat trick for avoiding the tedious job of sewing lots of tiny seams to make a bias strip. Cut a fairly long rectangle of fabric on the straight, and seam the two longer edges together, to make a long tube. Then, starting at the bottom, cut diagonally across ONE layer of this at an angle of forty-five degrees (you can find this angle by just folding the fabric, as in the illustration, and marking the fold). Continue, cutting round and round the 'tube' of fabric, until you reach the other end. Like one of those

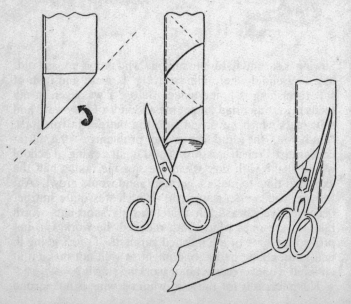

conjuring tricks with folded paper, it will open out as a bias strip which can be cut to the width you need.

It's easier done than said, but experiment first with newspaper to see how large the tube must be to give you the right amount of bias.

BLOODY SEWING

Small drops of blood from a pricked finger can easily be removed with just cotton and spit. Immediately the blood gets on the fabric, chew a length of white cotton thread into a small ball, and when it is thoroughly wet dab it carefully on the blood. It should come off without leaving a trace. The only exception to this would be a fabric which couldn't take moisture of any kind.

Tradition has it that the trick only works with one's own saliva on one's own blood. Having been loath to go round pricking my friends in order to try my saliva on their blood stains, I haven't tested the truth of that.

BUTTON SEWING

Buttons on Thin Air
Sometimes, especially in playgrounds, buttons are pulled off, taking whole chunks of cloth with them. It may look impossible to sew a button on the same place without tedious patching, but it isn't. Sew the button in the centre of a piece of strong straight tape, then push the button through the hole in the garment, from the back, position it correctly and just sew the tape firmly in place on the inside.

Buttons on Wool
Wool does not stand up well to the constant pulling from buttons. One way to support it is to sew two buttons on at the same time – one on the inside and one on the outside with the same thread passing through both of them. Another way is to cut button-sized circles from an old kid glove, preferably the same colour as the wool, place these

on the inside of the garment and sew through them when you put on the button. Either way, the strain is taken off the wool.

Heavy-duty Buttons
Putting an inner button on coats takes the pull off the fabric, but it must be sewn on with the outer one. This means that, as the needle comes out on the inside of the garment, it passes through a hole of the inner button. Then it goes back through the next hole, through the fabric and out through the outer button – and so on. That way none of the pull from the outer button is ever taken by the fabric of the coat itself. This may sound a pernickety detail, but tailoring traditions like this grew up to keep clothes looking good for longer, and that is just what this achieves.

Keeping
It sounds crazy to start mending a new garment as soon as you get it home, but very few clothes have buttons which are securely sewn on and it takes much less time to add a few secure stitches to each one than to search the shops for matching buttons once one is lost.

Secure Buttons
Some mothers I know have become so tired of sewing buttons on school blazers they now attach them with fishing twine. I'm told they never break off – the trouble is, if they are pulled really hard they just rip a chunk from the blazer.

Shank Making
A friend once complained that her husband – an eminent and meticulous lawyer – was for ever yanking the buttons off his clothes. It seemed so out of character for him that I asked to see how she sewed them on – and sure enough she had done them without a shank. On a heavy garment, there must always be enough room for the thickness of the buttonhole side of the garment to sit comfortably between the button and the cloth. Some people like to allow for

the shank by placing a matchstick under the button while they are sewing it on. This works well for a shirt but leaves too short a shank for the thickness of a coat or suit. I find it easier to rest the button on the first two fingers of the left hand and sew between them. It feels odd at first, but it's easy to get the knack. Having left a 'stalk' of threads between button and cloth, bring the thread back through the cloth, wind it firmly round 'stalk' from bottom to top, pass needle back through cloth and secure it finally on under-side.

Stronger Thread

For centuries tailers have rubbed their button thread over a block of beeswax to make it stronger. Do this when you sew buttons on coats and suits and they will stay on twice as long – provided you've made a proper shank. The beeswax can be bought at hardware stores and haberdashers.

Uppercrust Buttons

The quick way to tell a hand-tailored suit from a mass-produced one is to look at the buttons. A machine sews in parallel lines, whereas tailors make an X with the thread. Of course, in resewing buttons on a machine-made suit you can always cheat and use the tailor's method.

CURTAINS

Making

When calculating the amount of fabric needed for curtains, remember that ideally curtains should be at least twice the width of the window, but with some types of heading you can get away with one and a half times.

The longer the curtains, the more hem you need, for extra length means extra potential for shrinkage. It is worth writing to the fabric manufacturers and asking how much shrinkage to allow on the particular fabric you are buying. Then add a bit to what they say, and keep your letter and theirs. Then, if the fabric shrinks more than they said it

would, you have a better chance of getting compensation.
It is also wise to hand sew the hems, then, if any shrinkage
is expected, the curtains can easily be let down BEFORE
washing or cleaning, so the hem fold can be properly
washed out; moreover, if the curtains shrink unexpectedly
and have to be let down after washing, there will be no
ugly machine line.

Shortening
If curtains need to be shortened, it is often very much
easier to cut off the top and machine on a new heading
tape than to re-sew the hems. But you do need to measure
the length very carefully before you cut and, if the curtains
are lined, run a very firm row of tacking stitches below the
cutting line to secure the lining and interlining to the
curtain itself. Otherwise they will be all at sixes and sevens
when you need to put on the new header tape.

DARNING

Darning went out of fashion a while ago, but the way
clothes prices are rising it could be due for a come-back.

Avoiding Darning
On home-made jumpers, it is often possible to double the
life of the sleeves, and avoid having to darn them, by
taking the sleeves out and swopping them over. That brings
the thin part from under the elbow to the top. Some people
find this easier than darning, though personally I'd rather
do a Dutch darn anytime.

Conventional Darning
There are only five things anyone needs to know to darn
well. First of all, the needle should be round-ended, so it
doesn't cut the threads. Secondly, the hole is much easier
to mend when stretched over a curved surface. Thirdly,
you are basically weaving, so you need a set of threads
very close together going in one direction, then you weave
in and out of them in the other direction. Fourthly, you

need to leave a small loop of spare wool at the end of each row, in order to give a little stretch. Finally, the darn needs to be quite a bit bigger than the hole itself, as the end stitches must go into the strong parts of the fabric.

Dutch Darning

Lazy menders and perfectionists alike will find it quicker and more satisfactory to do an old-fashioned Dutch darn before the hole appears. If you are lucky enough to find matching wool, it is completely invisible.

This is how you do it. Using a blunt-ended tapestry needle, attach the mending wool to the inside of one end of the thin patch, and slip the needle through to the right side. Stretch the thin area over a darning mushroom, or other curved shiny surface, and take a good look at the way a single strand of wool in the knitting meanders to and fro in a series of loops. Take the darning wool along exactly the same path, by slipping it through one pair of loops after another, until you get to the far edge of the thin patch. Keep going, for a few stitches, into the strong section of the garment; then turn round and meander back along the row below, making sure your thread passes through both the stitches of the original knitting and the stitches you've just made. Repeat this until the whole of the thin area has been strengthened.

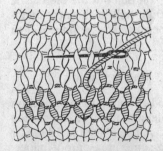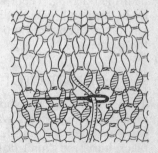

It's difficult to describe but remarkably easy to do, and it's the only darning which doesn't spoil the look of a garment. But, to be easy, it does need to be done BEFORE a hole appears. When a hole is there you need to run a suitable size of knitting needle through the stitches of the same row to either side of it. You then make new stitches, where the hole is, by looping the wool round the needle and then going back down into the row below – which requires a little skill.

Wool Shrinking
Its always safer to shrink darning wool before using it. Either steam it in a steamer for 10 minutes or hold it in the steam from a kettle – but mind your hands if you use the latter method, as a steam scald is particularly nasty.

DROPPED PINS

At one time magnets were always kept in sewing baskets so that if the pins were spilt they could be quickly picked up again. It is still by far the quickest way to pick them up.

ELASTIC REPLACING

The quick way to replace perished elastic is to safety pin, or sew, one end of the new elastic to the old one. Then safety pin the other end of the new elastic to the garment, near the opening. Then, when you pull out the old elastic by its free end, you automatically pull in the new one – and it can't come out too far because you've pinned it to the garment.

EMBROIDERY PATTERNS

There's no need for anybody to be limited to the selection of embroidery patterns available in the shops. Any design can be copied and transferred. All you need is a blue or black biro (red won't do) and some greaseproof paper. Trace the design on the greaseproof paper, position the paper, ink side down, wherever you want to embroider the design, pin it in place and iron with a hot iron. The pattern should be as clear as it is with transfer ink. There is just one snag: biro does not come off with washing as easily as transfer ink, so this is not very suitable for pale embroidery, and you need to make sure that you sew just OVER the line, not just inside it, or the transfer will show.

FABRIC KEEPING

Most dressmakers sooner or later go mad and buy more fabric than they can sew. When this happens the fabric will remain new looking if you beg a long cardboard roll from a fabric department and roll it round that – if it's folded up for long it will be badly creased. It's also wise to keep dust and insects from it by putting it in a plastic bag and closing it tightly.

FEATHERS

Feather-proofing

Good ticking should be so closely woven that no feathers can get through it, but, if there is any risk of feathers poking through, the fabric can be made a little more feather-proof by the old trick of rubbing it very well with beeswax on the inside.

Transferring Feathers

If you try to pull feathers out of an old eiderdown or cushion to stuff a new one, both you and the room are likely to end up feather-coated. There are several ways to avoid this.

If you are transferring feathers from one cushion to another of very similar size, the traditional method is to leave a fist-sized opening in one seam of the new cushion, and make a slit the same size in a seam of the old cushion. Then sew the two openings together – mouth to mouth, as it were. By pushing from the outside of the old cushion, you can work the feathers through the joined slits into the new one. Push the feathers well down before you unpick the place where they are sewn together, and sew up the slit.

An ingenious modern way of transferring feathers was given to me by the manageress of a bookshop where I was signing copies of *Supertips to Make Life Easy*. If you have a vacuum cleaner which takes simple disposable bags and has an extension, you can do it like this. Remove the old vacuum cleaner bag, attach a new one; clean out the inside of the machine by running the machine while it sits on a clean sheet of paper, and remove the bag. Now fix the cushion or pillow which you want to fill firmly where the bag normally goes. Then push the plainest nozzle of the vacuum cleaner extension through a slit in the seam of the old cushion and suck out the feathers, straight into the attached cushion.

FINE FABRICS

Fine fabrics like chiffon, tulle and even mohair can make nonsense of the advantages of machining rather than hand sewing: they catch or pucker on a machine and make it impossible to sew evenly. The way to avoid this is to give them the paper treatment.

When machining, put a strip of newspaper under the fabric along the seam line. There should then be no problem in machining the fabric and the paper tears off cleanly afterwards. Very tricky fabrics may need paper on top as well as below. If they do, cut a strip of paper an inch or so wide and fold it in half down its length. Then pin it in place so the fold falls exactly on the seam line, and use the fold in the paper to guide you in sewing a straight seam.

Bear in mind that newsprint will come off on fabric; so if you are sewing pale colours it is safer to use a couple of layers of white tissue paper, or even fine typing paper.

GATHERING

People often find it hard to distribute gathering evenly. The trick is to divide both the material you are gathering, and whatever you are attaching it to, into even sections (halves, quarters and so on), mark these divisions on both lots of material, and match the markings. The shorter the distances between the marks, the easier it is to distribute the gathering evenly. Small lengths may only need to be marked at the quarter, half and three-quarter points, but long ones may need to be marked into eights and even sixteenths; this is easily achieved if you do it by folding rather than by measuring.

It's far easier to draw up a short gathering thread than a long one. So, once the material is marked off in sections, run a separate gathering thread round each section. But overlap the threads slightly where one section meets another, then you won't get a flat area where the sections meet.

The other trick with gathering is always to run two parallel lines of gathering thread, not one. It makes the gathering more even and if one thread breaks you don't have to start again.

HEMS

Curved Hems

When hemming round a SLIGHT curve, the extra fullness can be disposed of almost imperceptibly if the needle is pulled slightly to the right as you sew. You then make the next stitch slightly to the right of the natural point. (A left-hander would pull to the left.) This has the effect of making a tiny gather at each stitch, which can be shrunk to nothing in pressing.

A deep hem or a large curve needs more gathering than this method gives. In those cases, run a series of gathering threads round the bottom of the garment before turning it up to hem it. Use a different thread for each panel of the skirt – it's easier to pull up the gathering and, if you happen to pull too hard and break the thread, you only have a small section to re-sew.

Hems on the Bias

Any garment which is cut on the cross – and this includes skirts which are so full that parts are on the cross – will usually sag slightly. To avoid an uneven hem on a dress or skirt, you need to hang the garment up for several days to let it drop before turning the hem up. Then wear the garment, and the shoes you'll wear with it, and get someone to mark the hem line by measuring carefully from the ground UP to the hem at frequent intervals. That way you will remove any unevenness where the material dropped.

Removing Hem Lines

When thick fabrics are let down, the old hem line may remain as an unsightly hump. I was struggling with this problem when a tailor's wife showed me the solution. With the right side uppermost, put a thick piece of old-fashioned white cotton twine (coloured twine may run) exactly along the hump of the old hem; cover it with a damp cloth and press it with a fairly hot iron. Then remove the cloth, cover the area with a block of 2 by 4 in (5 by 10 cm) unvarnished pine and, when the fabric is cool, remove the string, brush up the nap and move on to the next section of the hem. This method normally removes the hump completely. What it can't cure is a wear line which may have been rubbed into the nap where it was folded.

If all that remains is a shiny fold line on a fabric without a nap, the shine may come off if you sponge it with equal parts white vinegar and water – but check that the colour won't be affected by the mixture before using it on anything as conspicuous as the hem line.

Thick Hems

If material is very thick, turning a hem in, or even using a normal hemming stitch on a flat hem, will pull the edge of the hem too close to the garment and make a ridge show through. To avoid this, whip the raw edge of the hem so it won't fray and pin up the hem in the normal way, but don't put the pins too close to the top. Then fold down the top ¼ in (5 mm) TOWARDS you, with your fingers, and treat the folded edge as if it were the edge of a normal hem. That way, when you let go, the stitches fall between the two layers of material and the flat hem makes the least line possible.

Like all hems, it needs to be pressed after sewing but great care must be taken not to press the upper edge of the hem into the fabric – if necessary, slide a piece of cardboard under the upper edge before you press that part of the skirt.

JERSEY FABRICS

The risk with jersey fabrics is that a thread will break and run, producing a ladder. Any normal needle can cut through the thread of a jersey fabric and produce runs, so use only ball-ended needles for both hand and machine sewing.

It's one thing to buy ball-ended needles in the shops, but it can be quite another matter to find them in a sewing box when you need them, as they look almost identical to other needles. To make it easy to find them again, as soon as you buy them put a dab of nail varnish or paint on the shaft of each needle, just below where it fixes into the machine (and let it dry well before using it). Then you'll also know at once whether you've got one in the machine.

To sew jersey fabric on a machine, you need to use a fairly long stitch, with the machine set to give a VERY SLIGHT zigzag. The zigzag isn't enough to prevent you making a straight seam, but it will give the same elasticity to the stitch that the fabric has in its structure. This prevents the thread breaking when the garment is worn.

LEATHER

The sort of leather used for garments is as easy to sew as most fabrics, and rather less work in many ways. For a start, you don't have to finish off any edges to stop them fraying and hems can be glued, if you choose a suitable glue. There are just a few things you need to know.

Cutting Out

The first thing to watch is that all the pieces are cut out with the nap running in the same direction – on leather it should run down the body.

If the skin has any flaws in it, cut out with the right side up, so you can skirt round them. And when cutting out don't pin the pattern on – pin marks remain forever – but stick it on the leather using very small pieces of sellotape and marking the outline with a piece of ordinary school chalk (tailor's chalk contains grease) before you cut the piece out. That way it won't matter if you cut through the sellotape as you go round. If you need a really clear guide to keep you on the straight and narrow, you can switch the paper to the wrong side and mark the sewing lines in biro afterwards.

Pattern Choosing

As leather only comes in skin-shaped pieces, you either have to put in extra seams where you need to join skins together, or choose a pattern which only has pattern pieces which will fit on the size of a skin. If you need to create joins, they should be carefully planned and marked on the pattern, so they will match up when fronts and backs are joined.

You can't unpick and re-sew leather if it doesn't fit; the row of holes where you first sewed it will reveal your mistake, so any alterations must be done on the pattern before it is cut out. If you are using expensive skins, it can be worth making a test garment in calico first, to check that the pattern fits perfectly.

Sewing

As leather can't be pinned together without leaving marks, the best way to hold the sections to be machined is with paperclips, clothes pegs or small bulldog clips – but keep even these to the selvages, so as not to mark the leather.

To sew even the softest skins, by hand or by machine, you need a longish stitch and a special three-sided leather needle. Leather clings to an ordinary needle and makes it almost impossible to pull through, but a three-sided needle will slip through with ease. They come in a variety of sizes and in general you should use the smallest one which suits the job you are doing, as holes in leather do not close up as they do on fabric.

Darts need to be slit up to the point and opened up like seams after sewing. Then seams, darts and hems can all be held flat with a light smear of a rubberized adhesive on the inside.

MACHINE THREADING

The quick way to switch from one colour to another on a sewing machine is to break off the old thread near the reel and tie it to the new one. Then you just pull the old thread out, and the new one is automatically pulled into place, right up to the needle.

MARKING

All kinds of sophisticated equipment is sold for marking the sewing points on garments and most dressmaking classes recommend putting in long threads to mark each point – which take almost as long to pull out of the finished machining as they do to put in. It is far, far easier to use light pencil marks on the wrong side of fabrics like cotton, and chalk marks on fabrics like wool. The secret is to leave the pattern pinned to the pieces until you are ready to sew them, then mark and sew them immediately; that way there's no time for soft chalk marks to rub off. Having said that, I have to admit there are times when marker threads are the only way – on chiffon for example, or where you need marks on the right side.

MOHAIR

Mohair is difficult stuff to get through a machine evenly and needs to be sewn through paper, as described in 'Fine Fabrics' on p. 130.

MOYGASHEL AND LINEN

The looseness of the weave of these fabrics makes them fray very easily indeed. It's a laborious job, but it is advisable to hand whip all the seams before you start sewing. However, before you whip the seams, work out the places where you will have to trim them, or you will end up cutting through your careful whipping.

NAP

If fabric has a nap, it should be cut out so that it can be smoothed by stroking the hand down the body. The only exceptions to this are velvet and corduroy, which should be cut so the nap runs UP the body.

NEEDLEPOINT

When doing needlepoint or tapestry work, it is easy to push the needle down into the canvas, but much harder to pull the thick wool through after it. As the pulling is harder than the pushing a rubber finger stall is often far more help than the traditional thimble. The sort of finger stall they once used for counting money in banks is the kind you need; office stationers still stock them.

If you are using several different colours in little patches near each other, you can avoid constant re-threading by using a different needle for each. The trick for not getting them tangled is to leave all the spare threads at the FRONT of the canvas where you can keep an eye on them. Then, when you want to bring the next colour into play, you just slip it through to the back and run it in and out through the existing stitches to get the place where you need it – provided that place is less than ¾ of an inch (2 cm) away. It it's more, anchor the thread, snip it and start again.

NEEDLES

One of the sayings I dislike most is that a bad workman blames his tools. I've so often seen people struggling to sew well with needles which would have defied the skill of an archangel (for I assume archangels are good at such things). The commonest fault is using needles which are too large. To sew finely, you need the smallest needle which can do the job; and if you're hemming, a needle which is fine enough to curve slightly as you sew will make it far easier to pick up minute amounts of fabric.

It is far easier to thread the oblong eyes of crewel needles than the short round eyes of other needles; for most purposes the shape of the eye makes no difference at all to the sewing you do.

Tradition has it that because of the way sewing thread is twisted, it will be less likely to tangle in knots if you thread the needle with the end nearest to the reel with cotton and furthest from the reel with silk. The manufacturers tell me this rule is probably just an old wives' tale and that the direction of the twist is now varied. However, if you do find your thread twisting and knotting, try breaking it off and threading it from the other end – there may be no firm rules, but the principle still holds.

Those who find needle-threading hard on their eyes can buy a special needle-threader – a loop of very fine wire which can be pushed through the eye, threaded with the cotton and then pulled back through the eye taking the cotton with it. But on all but the finest needles a diamond-shaped loop of 5 amp fuse wire will do the job just as well.

A trick for threading wool is to fold the end of the wool over the needle. Then, holding the wool pulled tight over the needle with your left hand, pinch the fold with your right finger and thumb and slide it off the point of the needle (reverse this if you're left-handed). You then have the flat section of fold to push through the eye. If that fails, slip a loop of cotton through the eye, thread the wool through the cotton and the cotton will pull back through the eye, bringing the wool with it.

PATCHING KNEES

If you need a matching patch for the knees of a pair of trousers you can usually find a suitable square of material under a pocket. Then you can either sew up the pocket or mend the hole with some other material.

PATCHWORK

If any of the material you plan to use in a patchwork is new and unwashed, it's a good plan to soak it in the hottest water it can safely stand before you start the patchwork. It only takes a little shrinkage in a finished patchwork to ruin it utterly. For that reason a sheet which has seen better days is one of the best backings for a patchwork once it's completed.

PATTERN FITTING

I once had a dress which measured exactly 33 inches round the hips. I was slim but not anorexic and had reasoned that, as I was 33 inches round the hips, the dress should be too. So in making it I carefully removed all the 'ease' which had been allowed to make the dress hang properly. The result was a sausage skin into which I squeezed myself uncomfortably for the next year or two – it was expensive material.

It was only when I learnt professional pattern cutting that I discovered that even on fairly close-fitting garments an average-sized skirt should be 3 in (7.5 cm) larger than the actual hip size, a sleeve 2 in (5 cm) larger than the upper arm, and that 4 in (10 cm) should be allowed round the bust. This amount of ease may sound a lot, but, if you work it out, an extra 3 in (7.5 cm) on the circumference of a skirt adds very little to the radius, and skims the body by less than half an inch. So large sizes need to add slightly more – and very small sizes perhaps a touch less.

Of course such allowances are not hard and fast. A strapless bodice would fall down with that much allowance and a baggy style look as if it had shrunk in the wash. But such rules do provide guidelines by which to decide if something IS baggy or IS tight. Once you know that, you can make the right adjustments to the pattern.

Uneven Shoulders

Very few people are symmetrical, but one of the trickiest adjustments in the whole of pattern cutting is allowing for one shoulder being lower than the other. You can't alter the height of a shoulder without re-cutting the entire armhole and altering the head of the sleeve and these are adjustments which take a lot of experience. The easy way to solve the problem is to put in a small shoulder pad on one side to compensate for the lower shoulder.

PERFECT STRIPES (AND CHECKS AND PATTERNS)

When making a garment, stripes and checks need to be perfectly matched at the seams. It sounds hard, but it's just a matter of careful planning before you cut the fabric and a few simple tricks to make it easy.

Adjusting the Pattern

If the fabric has a design (horizontal stripes for example) which needs to be matched, you should check that the paper pattern fits you perfectly before you cut it out. If you try to improve the fit by taking in the garment after it's cut out, you may throw all your careful matching out of true.

Buying Enough Material

With fabric, as with wallpaper, you need to allow extra material on horizontal stripes, or very striking patterns, so you can move the pattern pieces around until they match. There are no hard and fast rules for how much extra to allow: it depends on both the fabric and the pattern; but the bigger the design, the more fabric you will need. Good patterns should give rough guidance on the back, but remember it's only rough.

Cutting Out

The trick here is to ignore instructions which suggest you cut the pattern pieces with the fabric on the double – however carefully you pin the two layers together the stripes always wriggle out of true somewhere. Cut each piece out singly. But leave the first half of the front (back, or whatever) pinned to the paper pattern when you position it for cutting the other half – then you can see precisely how the stripes match up and position it for a perfect match.

If you lay your pattern piece on the wrong side of the fabric for cutting the first half, and on the right side of the fabric to cut the second, you will end up with the two layers pinned together and positioned for marking just as they would have been if you'd worked with the cloth on the double.

Sometimes it's impossible to get all of the design matching all the way down the seam; the shape of the pattern pieces may prevent it. When this happens, take a look at the garment and decide which bits will hit the eye when it's worn. Then get the design to match at these points, and let the rest of that seam more or less take care of itself.

Making Up

There is a certain pleasure in rule-breaking, especially when it produces better results. The time to break rules about tacking seams is whenever there are checks or horizontal stripes. Because tacking is loose, it allows the stripes to move out of true. So, the secret of perfectly matched stripes (assuming you've cut the pattern out so they CAN be matched!) is simply to pin the seams and not bother to tack them at all. Use long, fine, tailoring pins and put them in so they run ACROSS, not down, the sewing line and are positioned so they hold the stripes in the two layers of fabric perfectly matched together.

When pinning up, don't start at the top of the seam.

Start at the points which will catch the eye when the garment is worn. Get everything matching perfectly at those points and then do the rest of the seam.

Once a seam is pinned – and with pinning you need to pin and stitch in quick succession – you can machine down the seam line with the pins still in place. They should be fine enough for the machine to ride right over, unless the stitch is exceptionally small.

PIPING

The white cotton cord sold for piping cushions and covers usually shrinks in the wash. To avoid disaster when it's in the covers, drop it in boiling hot water for 10 minutes to pre-shrink it and dry it thoroughly before use.

PLASTIC

Plastics do not like going through sewing machines. Heavy plastic, such as PVC-coated cotton, tends to stick to the machine as you work. To avoid this, brush the plastic down the sewing line with a thin layer of fine oil. Any light oil will do; the cheapest is usually clean cooking oil. Sponge it off afterwards with a little soap, for oil left on plastic hardens it.

Light plastic, with no fabric backing, simply puckers up as you sew. The answer here is to put newspaper above and below the seam as recommended in 'Fine Fabrics', p. 130. Remember that plastic is weakened with every perforation, so it needs a fairly long stitch and as much support from backing tape as the job you're doing will allow.

PROFESSIONAL FINISHING

When I first learnt tailoring I discovered, to my surprise, that meticulous pressing, rather than amazing sewing, was the key to garments looking professional instead of amateur. Amateurs tend to make up a garment and then press

it: professionals press each seam, dart or tuck as soon as
it is sewn and only when it is lying perfectly do they sew
it to the next section of the garment. It is so EASY to do it
that way and the garment looks 100 per cent better. But
remember, shiny iron marks can ruin a garment. Even if
you have a steam iron, many fabrics need to be pressed
from the wrong side and through a damp cloth. In fact, in
my experience, a damp cloth gives better results than even
the best steam iron.

But have a care – some fabrics, such as velvet, must not
be pressed in the ordinary way and others react to damp.
So if in doubt check what treatment a fabric will take
before you even buy it.

Pressing Folded Seams

Wherever a facing is attached to a garment and folded
back on itself, the easy way to get a perfect edge is to sew
the straight edge first, and then press the seam OPEN, just
as you would a side seam. Even if you then have to fold it
back the other way for a while (to sew another part of the
facing round a curve, perhaps), you have the basis for a
perfectly sharp edge.

Pressing Heavy Fabrics

Fine fabrics are easy to press well, but the secret of perfect
pressing on heavy ones is a 'banger'. This is a block of
untreated pine about 2 in by 4 in (5 cm by 10 cm) and
some 6–l2 in (15–30 cm) long. When you press heavy fabric
with an iron, the steam in the fabric makes it spring up
slightly the moment you remove the iron and the pressing
is never as flat as it needs to be. To deal with this, all
you need do is remove the iron and the damp cloth and
immediately place the banger lightly on the section you've
just pressed. As it lies there the wood absorbs the steam
and holds the fabric in place as it cools: the result is a
perfectly flat seam. You don't, in fact, need to 'bang' at
all; you need to put pressure on the wood only at VERY
bulky spots – and, if you've trimmed it perfectly, there
shouldn't be many of those.

Trimming

Most patterns tell you to trim the seams in places where they will be concealed – for example, round the inside of a cuff, or the outer edge of a collar – before turning the fabric right side out. What they don't always tell you is that, if you cut the two sides of the seam to the same length, they sometimes make a solid ridge when folded together and pressed. For the best result of all, cut them so the one which will be nearest to the outside of the garment is longer than the inner one. This prevents that ridge.

QUILTING

When quilting fabric sew one row in one direction and the next in the other direction – then you won't find one fabric creeping against the other.

SHOESTRING STRAPS

It's extremely easy to make a rouleau belt or shoestring strap to match a garment when you know the string trick. Cut the strip of material twice the width you need the strap to be, plus seam allowances, and a couple of inches longer. Then fold it in half, down the length, with the wrong side out. Place a piece of strong white cotton string inside the whole length of the fold, so it sticks out at each end. Sew two rows across one end of the fabric so the string is firmly attached to it, and then sew up the whole length of the strip, leaving the other end open. Trim any surplus fabric down the long seam – bearing in mind that the right amount of fabric left on the selvages can give a rouleau a nicely rounded look. Then pull the loose end of string and ease the fabric down so it slips over the string and turns inside out, giving you a perfect rouleau. When you've finished, just snip off the end where the string is attached and pull the remainder out.

SNAP FASTENERS

To position the two halves of a snap fastener so they match
perfectly just sew on the male half first. Then rub its tip
with light chalk or a soft pencil lead (to contrast with the
fabric) and press it firmly in place where its other half
should go. Position the female half by inserting a pin into
its centre and pushing the pin through the chalk mark.

STOPPING AND TURNING

It's always wise to secure your stitches wherever the end
of a line of machining will take some strain – the tip of a
dart, the top of a seam below a zip opening and so on.
There are several ways of doing this but the easiest is to
machine exactly to the point you want to stop at. Stop and
rotate the wheel of the machine, by hand, until the needle
is well down into the fabric. Lift the foot of the machine
and turn the garment right round, so you can accurately
machine back down your sewing line for an inch. Then
you can safely cut off the threads close to the fabric.

To change direction when machining, and turn a corner,
you use the same technique of stopping and winding the
needle in by hand.

ZIPS

Inserting
To ensure that a zip is properly covered by the seam edges,
sew up the zip opening by hand, with rather short tacking
stitches, and press it open like a machined seam before
pinning in the zip. Remove the tacking only when the zip
has been sewn in. On some fabrics, adhesive tape may
then hold the zip in place for machining rather better than
pinning or tacking.

Mending
If a zip breaks when it's amply long, it may not need to be
replaced. Slip the detached side of the zip into the fastener

and pull it through so the two sides are level at the top. Zip it up, then sew or staple the bottom together, just above the broken part. Check that the zip slides properly and sew up the opening in the garment to conceal the break.

Mending Short-cut
However good you are at inserting a new zip, it is always a time consuming operation. If a garment with a broken zip is needed in a hurry, or if it belongs to a young child who will grow out of it before you have time to mend it, Velcro makes a good short-cut. Sew it down the length of the facing which lies just inside the zip, or, for an even shorter cut, use stick-on Velcro – but be warned: if you use this, it is well nigh impossible to sew if you feel it needs strengthening later.

PLAIN AND PURL

Knitting patterns always look as if they contain all the information one needs, but even the best work better for the experienced knitter than for the inexperienced. So I've picked the brains of some experienced knitters to find the tricks which they find useful, as well as including some of my own favourites.

CASTING OFF

Casting off almost always needs to be a little looser than the knitting itself. The easiest way to achieve this, and have the casting off perfectly even, is to change to a larger-sized needle for the final casting-off row. The larger it is, the looser the result, but one size larger is usually enough.

INCREASING AND DECREASING

Curiously, a lot of patterns tell you to increase and decrease on the last stitch of a row. Almost invariably you will get a better result if you ignore this and increase and decrease one or two rows in from the edge. This gives you a good straight edge to work with when you make up the garment.

If you are increasing or decreasing in conspicuous places,

such as on either side of a V-neck, you need to knit into the backs of the stitches to decrease on one side and into the fronts the other side; then both sides will slope away from the V.

LEFT-HANDERS

Learning
Left-handed people need to learn to knit by sitting FACING you, then their movements are just a mirror image of what you do. But even when a left-hander has mastered the basics of knitting, it is less easy to follow a pattern when working in reverse. For this reason it may be better for them to adopt the continental style of knitting, which gives far more work to the left hand but allows them to follow a normal pattern without confusion.

Problems
The twist of the wool is designed for use by right-handed people, so a left-handed movement tends to untwist it slightly, reducing its elasticity. Also left-handers need to remember that wherever knitting instructions say something should be done to the 'right', they need to substitute 'left'.

PLACE KEEPING

It's easy to lose one's place in a knitting pattern, especially if knitting is put away and not picked up for a few days. To keep a note of your row, slip a firm kirby grip or paperclip on to the edge of the pattern and keep sliding it down so it always points to the part of the pattern you are working on.

PRESSING KNITTING

A Word of Warning
Pressing is something which needs to be done with great caution. It only takes a second or two of heavy-handedness

with an iron to ruin all the work on raised patterns and cable stitch, and reduce chunky ribbing to a disappointing flatness.

Acrylics are especially vulnerable to losing their bounce when pressed – don't iron pure acrylics at all and treat mixtures with great care. (See 'Pressing without Pressing', below.)

Blocking
To do this, just lay the piece of knitting on a well-padded ironing board, smooth it to shape and insert pins diagonally into the board at frequent intervals all round the edge to hold it perfectly in place. The pins must go into the loop of the edge stitch, not into the wool itself, or they may cut it. To get a nice straight edge, put the pins very close together and don't stretch the knitting too much. Spaced pins or too much pulling will produce a scalloped edge.

To be sure that all your seams are the same length, ready for easy sewing up, measure all of them before you block the garment. Then, if one is a fraction smaller, you can pull it to the correct length when you block it out and make it match the others. But don't expect blocking to make good a BIG difference. Even if it did, you would just run into trouble when the garment was washed and that part sprang back to its old size.

Pressing without Pressing
One way round the problem of acrylics and raised patterns is to 'press' the pieces without using an iron. To do this you block them or simply smooth them into shape. Then you take a thick bath towel, put it in fairly hot water, wring it out very well and lay it smoothly on the knitting and leave it overnight. Remove the towel and let the knitting dry completely before you move it.

Another version of this system of pressing is to roll the pieces of knitting in the towel and leave them for an hour or so and then unroll them, block them out and leave them to dry. Both these techniques are suitable for acrylics and mixtures of acrylic and wool.

A 'Woman's Hour' listener wrote to tell me that you could press knitting by putting the pieces carefully between magazines and sitting on them. This may well work, but there is a certain lack of precision in the system. However, she added, 'Slim ladies can manage any lightweight garment but thick knits require a more rounded form' – so maybe you can tell what your friends think of your figure by the thickness of the jumper they ask you to sit on. But don't sit on acrylics.

Traditional Pressing
The traditional method of pressing is to put the piece of knitting on an ironing board, smooth it to shape and press it, with a fairly warm iron through a damp cloth, without pressing down with the weight of the iron. This undoubtedly works, but if you are heavy-handed with the iron a new piece of knitting can emerge looking tired and flat, and any garment with a raised design can be spoilt.

When to Press
With knitting, as with sewing, you get much better results by pressing the individual pieces before you sew them together. Some wools can be smoothed into shape by hand and pressed without more ado, others tend to curl up and need to be blocked into shape.

ROW MARKING

If you need to mark a particular row, or stitch, so you can come back to it, just tie in a piece of contrasting wool or fine string as a marker. Alternatively you can snap in a large snap fastener so it clamps the place you want to mark. Either way you can find it again instantly.

SETTING STITCHES ASIDE

When stitches have to be set aside for something else to be knitted on later, a nappy pin makes the most secure holder.

SEWING UP

The first tip is to think of the sewing up as a major part of the making. Having made the 'fabric', so to speak, knitters often spoil the result by feeling that the real job is over. Yet if they were sewing a fabric garment, they'd never feel the job was done when they'd bought the material.

Needle Choice

Wool needs to be sewn with a round-ended needle; a pointed one may cut the stitches. Ideally the sewing thread should be the same as the thread used to make the garment. If it is too thick to use and you want a perfect finish, cut a few lengths, divide each one into half the number of strands, damp the strands and twist them firmly together, then leave them to dry before you sew with them.

Stitch Choice

There are all kinds of stitches which can be used to sew up the seams. The firmest, and one of the neatest on a heavy garment, is backstitch. It is particularly good for large garments which may sag at the seams if a loose stitch is used, but beware of sewing so firmly that the seams are tighter than the body of the garment – it will just sag in the middle instead.

The loosest form of sewing up is when you place the two right sides face to face and whip the two pieces together

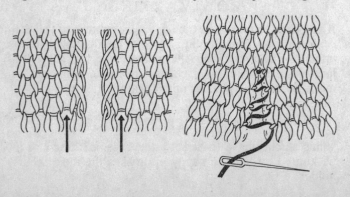

by sewing over the edge. Somewhere in the middle comes the invisible seam where you lay the two pieces edge to edge, right side up, and slip the needle through the bar of the stitch on one side and then through the bar on the other, to give a perfect row by row match.

SIZE ADJUSTING

As the sizes given on knitting patterns are geared to knitters with an average tension, it's essential to check if your tension is average before starting on the garment. Check the number of stitches and rows to the inch (or metric equivalent) that the pattern is based on and knit a sample which should turn out at least 4 in (10 cm) square by their calculations; measure carefully to see if it is exactly that size. If it isn't, you may need to go for a larger or smaller size in the pattern, or change to a larger or smaller size of needle.

It would be nice if there was a neat rule whereby a garment became smaller by a set amount if you chose a needle one size smaller. Unfortunately knitters and patterns vary so much that rules are impossible. If you do change the needle size, you must knit another square and check its size to see if it's any closer to that which the designers intended.

UNNECESSARY CASTING OFF

Quite often patterns tell you to cast off in places, such as the edge of a neck, where you will later have to pick up stitches and knit them. If you read ahead in the pattern and check if this is the case, you can often avoid the casting off, and the picking up of new stitches, by simply slipping the stitches on to a pin until you need to knit them. But before doing this, check that this isn't a place where casting off is needed to prevent the garment stretching, for in some places it is well used this way.

UNPICKING

When knitting needs to be unpicked, you can avoid the risk of dropped stitches, and make it much easier to start again, if you slip a needle through the first 'good' row, picking up every stitch, and then pull back the wool to there.

As it is usually easier to unpick from the end of a piece of work than from the beginning, children's sleeves will be easier to lengthen if they are knitted from the top down. But novice knitters should only attempt this if the top of the sleeve is really simple; reversing a pattern isn't always as easy as it sounds.

WOOL CARE

It would be good if balls of wool stayed on one's lap, but they don't. If you're working with a pale colour, be fatalistic and put the ball you're working with in a plastic bag, with the end sticking out, and a loose elastic band round the top. Then you won't find there are dusty stripes in the finished garment from when the wool rolled around a less than perfectly clean floor.

You And Yours

Hair and Beauty
Clothes and Shoes
Aches and Pains
This and That

HAIR AND BEAUTY

This chapter is a mixture of old and new tips on beauty and skin care. It includes some of the very latest ideas on how to make-up beautifully and some timeless hints which I've been using since my days as a model twenty-five years ago. There are tips on how to apply cosmetics and tips on how to make them last longer. And, unlike many of the beauty columns, there are tips for the not so young as well as for the young. Almost everyone can look really attractive if they know how; these pages are designed to provide at least part of the secret.

ARE YOU WHO YOU THINK?

It sounds odd but my first tip is that the biggest barrier to looking good is not knowing what you really look like. As an experiment, try closing your eyes and imagining your own face. Conjure every detail (without going to the mirror first), then go to a mirror and take a good look and, in all honesty, decide whether you really DO look the way you imagined yourself. If you think you look much less attractive than you imagined, you are probably wrong. Most people allow a quite mythical idea of beauty to blind them to their real assets; assets which are often a lot more interesting than the mythical ideal. So my next tip is to take another look at yourself and throw the mythical ideal, and modesty, to the winds and look for the good points – the things you'd compliment or admire if your head belonged to somebody else. Nobody can possibly make the best of themselves until they know what the best is. When you DO know, you can decide what you want to emphasize and start using some of the tricks in this chapter to achieve the look you want.

That isn't the end of the story. A face is like a river: it has the same elements and the same boundaries every day, but it never looks exactly the same two days running. Just as changes in wind and tide alter a river, so changes in our mood, our health and what we've been doing and eating subtly alter a face. The person who looks really good is the one who makes up, and dresses, for the face they have that day, not the one they had yesterday, still less the one they had last year.

That means looking critically at your face every day, watching for the changes, and accepting what you find there. Certain make-up shades and certain clothes which look wonderful one day can look very unflattering the next, and it's no good wearing them willy-nilly just because you planned to. From time to time I make a point of going clothes shopping when I'm looking my worst: tired, overweight and with my hair needing a wash. The tip is that if you find something you look good in when you're looking terrible, you always have it to fall back on for the other bad days. And the chances are that it will suit you on the good days as well.

ATTRACTIVE SMELLS

An old country tradition has it that if a man wants to win a woman at a dance, he should take a clean handkerchief and place it under his arm for a while, then put the handkerchief in his top pocket. The sexual attractants now discovered in sweat suggest that this tradition may have something to be said for it – though only FRESH sweat is potentially seductive. There is, alas, no equivalent gambit for women; however, it is no coincidence that most good perfumes contain a substance which is a sex attractant in animals.

BLUSHER

Applying
Powder blushers are made to go on top of other powder, not directly on to foundation. Put straight on top of foundation, they can look too heavy. One of the commonest mistakes is blusher which, instead of imperceptibly shaping the face, catches the eye and shouts at you. To apply a blusher subtly, use a large, very soft brush, take some blusher on it and then brush most of it off on the back of your hand. Apply the remainder carefully to the area of the cheek bones. Start at the point where you think you need the most colour and work away from it. It is much better to apply two or three tiny amounts than to slap it all on in one go.

If you find you've overdone the blusher, kill it by going over it with a neutral powder.

Shaping the Face
Anything red seems to be slightly more prominent than it really is, so blusher can alter the apparent shape of a face quite considerably. There are all kinds of rules for how to shape faces with it. For example, a long face will look more balanced if a touch of blusher is put at the hairline on the temples and a hint on the chin, but the rules can never be strictly applied. Any good make-up artist will take ALL the facial features into consideration and that's what one should do with one's own face. Sit down in front of a mirror and get to know your face. Look at it, feel the bone structure, and then apply a good foundation and powder and experiment with blusher in different places, on each side of your face, to see what works for your features.

BROKEN VEINS

As you'd expect from the rubicund beacons which stand
in for noses on some heavy drinkers, alcohol is extremely
bad for broken veins on the face. Surprisingly, it's almost
as bad to put it on your face as to drink it, but a lot of skin
toners contain alcohol. If you suffer from broken veins,
stick to skin toners which don't contain any. One of the
cheapest and best is a simple mixture of cosmetic rosewater
and witch hazel in equal parts, which you can mix yourself.

The other hazard to broken veins is extremes of temperature. So if you really must have a sauna, cover your
head with a towel and don't give your face a cold splash
afterwards.

Cover cream can be used to cover conspicuous broken
veins, but a carefully applied foundation usually provides
enough concealment. Go for a beige tone rather than a
pink one. Beige will neutralize the redness.

CLEANSING

The best way to apply cleanser is to put it on your fingertips,
massage it into the make-up, and wipe it off with clean
cotton wool – tissues are rough on the skin. Repeat the
process. If you normally cleanse your skin only once, you'll
be amazed how much comes off the second time.

COVER CREAM

A make-up artist I know was shocked to discover, during
a demonstration, that a lot of women didn't know about
cover cream. Most big cosmetic houses make one and it's
one item of make-up which everyone who wants to look
good, and ever has a late night or a spot, should possess.
A good cover cream, carefully blended in, will erase the
shadows under the eyes so subtly that even a man can wear
it without anyone knowing he's wearing make-up. And it's
a boon, on nights out, for teenage boys at the pimply stage.
Blend it carefully over the area you want to conceal before

you apply a foundation. Experts also use it on a fine brush over the foundation, but this takes a little more practice.

CRACKED LIPS

Lips usually crack because of a combination of lip-licking, harsh wind and a lack of oil. You can't stop the wind, but try to avoid licking, still worse chewing, your lips. Smear them with cocoa butter or lanolin night and morning to heal and protect them.

DANDRUFF

In addition to anti-dandruff shampoos, there are traditional ways to treat the problem which may be worth remembering if none of the shampoos seem to suit you. A method which some trichologists recommend is to rub witch hazel into the scalp after washing, and it does seem to be effective. Other traditional treatments include rubbing salt into the scalp before washing the hair or, pouring infusions of nasturtium leaves over the hair after washing.

DRY SHAMPOO

Today's aerosol dry shampoos are so effective there's no need ever to have lanky greasy hair. But I do find the makers overestimate the power of their products. They need more time to work than the instructions suggest – at least a couple of hours. And they produce their best results if applied the night before.

EYEBROWS

A face is so dominant that it's easy to forget that it's a very small place in which tiny details make a big difference. A lovely teenage ballet dancer in New York recently came to me for advice; she'd been turned down for a lucrative television advertisement because her eyes were too small. She wanted to know how to make them look larger and

expected to learn all kinds of complicated techniques using
eye-shadow. In fact all she needed to do was comb her
eyebrows. Unplucked bushy eyebrows may be in fashion,
but if they hang down they leave no space for the eyes and
make them look small. Eyes can look bigger and a face
look far better kept if the hairs are all combed upwards
and a comb run at right-angles along the top edge to shape
the upper hairs to the desired curve.

The surest way to darken eyebrows without getting a
hard line is to use block mascara. Moisten the brush that
comes with the mascara, rub it in the mascara and then
very lightly brush the mascara on to the eyebrow hairs, so
none of it gets on the skin. The eyebrows will look far
more natural than they would with a pencil. Comb the
brows to shape when the mascara is dry.

EYE SHAPING

Eye fashions change faster than almost any other aspect
of make-up, so any rules are out of date as soon as written;
and dated eye make-up is very ageing. Happily this is one
area in which fashion can be followed fairly safely by
women of almost any age, provided the older ones avoid
using the brighter or more sparkly colours – unless of
course they are in the mood to look garish and gaudy.
However, there is one useful rule of thumb. The easiest
shadows to wear successfully are those which are closest
to the natural colours of eyes (not necessarily your eyes)
– that is, soft browns, greys and sludgy greens. The hardest
colours to wear are those least like eye colours – yellows,
pinks, bright blues and, worst of all, turquoise.

Whatever the shape of the shadow and whatever the
colour, apply a pale eye-shadow base from the eyelashes
to the eyebrow before you start; this will stop the shadow
being absorbed by the skin and losing its effect. It will
also stop it creasing. Then, when you put on the shadow,
blend and blend and blend it, to combine the different
shades you are using, until you have a really subtle effect.
A single shade tends to look flat and dull, and most eyes

need a lighter shade close to the nose to give them
space.

If you apply a cream shadow, powder lightly over it
afterwards to stop it creasing.

There are days when, even with the best shading in the
world, the eyes look tired and dead. A minute dot of a
highlight (gold on a brown shadow, or light blue on a grey,
for example) put in the centre of the eyelid just above the
lashes – and shaded to nothing at the edges – will often
give the eyes a lift. It's a technique which was fashionable
a few years ago and, though it's now 'out', it's very useful
for the bad days on certain shapes of eye.

If the eyes seem to lack definition, during times when a
visible eye-liner is unfashionable, take a block eye-liner
(to match your mascara) and a *very* fine brush and apply
minute dots along the base of the eyelashes. When you
have finished, the eyes should look stronger but the colour
you have applied should be invisible among the roots of
the lashes.

FOUNDATION

Foundation is exactly that: the foundation on which we
base the rest of our make-up. So it's essential to choose the
right one. The big divide is between pink toned foundations
and beige toned ones: the wrong one for your colouring
will result in a hard and unnatural look however carefully
you apply your make-up. And remember that skin colour
changes with age, so you should always try a new foundation *on your face* before you buy it. If you can't endure
going bare-faced to a shop, to try it, get the sales girl to
put a little from a tester into an empty colour-film canister,
and try it at home.

The best foundation is the lightest one which will give
you the coverage you need. When buying one for the
summer months, go for the darkest shade which will suit
your summer skin tone. Don't be afraid to treat make-up
like paint and blend different shades. Mixing your summer
and winter foundation together on the back of your hand

will give you all the shades you need for the in-between months, if you choose the same brand.

If you start by applying foundation to the central parts of the face and work outwards it won't be thick at the hairline. Also, you can smooth it away under the jaw without getting a hard line. Make the last strokes downwards, so that they smooth the facial hairs flat against the skin – we are all downier than we suppose.

FRESHER TONING

In hot weather keep skin tonic in the fridge. Nothing is quite as refreshing as the feeling of the chilly liquid on the face. But don't do this if you suffer from broken veins.

HAIR ROLLER CLIPS

I was being made up in the make-up department of Harlech Television when I saw that one of the girls there had the perfect solution to the problem of clips for heated hair rollers linking together so you can't get hold of the size and colour you want – or at least not with the one hand that's free while you hold the roller in place. She simply hung them all round the rim of a small glass. Like that they never tangle and you can spot the right colour at a glance.

INSTANT SKIN SOFTENING

If you suddenly need to wear a sleeveless dress or go without stockings and find your skin is looking dry and neglected, the fastest remedy is to apply a mixture of rosewater and glycerine in equal parts. The skin should loose its parched appearance overnight. After that keep up the treatment.

LIPSTICK

The right lipstick shade and the right lip line can make a huge difference to a face. Yet the application of lipstick is often given the least attention of all.

Avoiding Runs up the Top Lip

There comes a time in everybody's life when lipstick yearns to travel into every microscopic line – and very unflattering this is. The way to avoid it is to shape the lips with a lip liner, blot it, apply a VERY light coat of lipstick, then powder over it, pressing the powder in. Then recoat the lips, making sure you don't go beyond the area you powdered.

Buying the Right Shade

Most women try out lipsticks on the backs of their hands, but, as one of the doyennes of the beauty business pointed out to me, the back of your hand bears no resemblance to the colour of your lips. So, predictably, the colours are distorted. Instead, turn your hand over and try out lipsticks on the tips of your fingers – they are always slightly pink and you'll get a far better idea of how the lipstick will actually look on your lips, and you can hold the finger tip in front of your lips to check the colour.

Colour Flattery

Whatever the magazines say, fashion isn't the only thing which should dictate the shade of lipstick you wear. Your colouring dictates the range of cosmetic colours which suit you and lipsticks need to be varied to suit different eye-shadows. A lipstick which looks marvellous when you wear grey eye-shadow will probably look terrible with brown eye-shadow, and vice versa. Anyone who tries to wear the same shade regardless isn't giving their looks a chance. You also need to think about the shape of your mouth: pale colours enlarge the lips; dark ones shrink them.

Finally, age is the biggest factor of all – the young can wear anything within reason, but an older woman needs to know a few tricks if she's not to look ridiculous in very pale shades or be aged by very dark ones. When very dark shades are being worn, apply a lighter, more flattering tone first and then lightly brush on the most attractive of the new dark shades over the top. Having the lighter lipstick underneath will take away the heaviness of the top coat. And use a glosser, so the darkness has some highlights on it. When very light shades are in fashion, do the reverse: put the mid-tone underneath and highlight it with the lighter lipstick to make it fashionable.

Shaping the Mouth

People tend to recoil with horror when I say that you don't have to go around with the shape of lips which nature gave you. I'm not suggesting that anyone should go in for great cupid's-bow curves half way up to their nose, as some film stars did in the thirties, but even tiny alterations can make a dramatic difference. Very few of the perfect lips you see on models are quite as perfect as they appear – yet even in a close-up photograph you can't see the alterations.

The shape of lips you choose should be a balance of three things – the natural shape of your lips, the lip shape which is in fashion, and the shape which would most flatter your other features. Start by looking at lots of top-fashion photographs, so you know what shape is in fashion. Unless you have a wonderful eye for line, you will need to try out various versions of it to discover how it can be adapted to suit your face.

Begin by taking the foundation and powder over your lip line; you then have a neutral base to use as your canvas. Now treat your face as a picture. Hold the mirror far enough away for you to see your whole face – NOT close up as you might have it to do your eyes – and with a fine lip pencil try to draw a version of the fashionable shape which suits both your face and your natural lip shape. To see that you have balanced the top lip perfectly, pull your chin in hard and look up into the mirror. To check the bottom lip, do the reverse: stick your chin out and look down into the mirror. When you have the line right, fill in the shape with a lipstick brush. Don't expect to get it right first time. I've been doing it for years and I often get it wrong even now – but it is worth the trouble.

LONG HAIR

To untangle long hair quite painlessly, comb it under water.

MAKE-UP PENCIL SHARPENING

When make-up pencils are due to be sharpened, put them in the fridge for a few hours. They are less likely to break when sharpened and you'll be able to get a really fine point if you want it.

MAKE-UP STORAGE

If, like me, you have an illogical conviction that even the most dated shades of make-up will come back into fashion, and are loath to throw away yesterday's colours, storage becomes a problem. A cutlery tray which will fit into your bedroom drawer is a good answer. It allows you to put each type of cosmetic into a different section and gives you a sporting chance of finding anything you want in a hurry. If you choose a cutlery tray with vertical sides, you can store your lipsticks on their ends, labels uppermost, so you can find the one you want at a glance.

If your dressing-table drawer is deep enough, store make-up pencils on end in something like a stumpy jam jar. You can find them faster if you can see the coloured ends.

MASCARA

A lot of people buy waterproof mascara to avoid smudges, but, unless you cry a lot, most of the smudging will be due to the grease in your make-up dissolving the mascara; therefore, unless you are weeping or swimming regularly, go for one which resists grease rather than water.

'The mascara on her eyelashes was so thick they looked like miniature iron railings,' comments Raymond Chandler in one of his classic thumbnail sketches. To avoid this effect, aim for lots of light coats, to build up the length and thickness; let the mascara dry well between each coat. Heavy coats just clump the eyelashes together and produce the iron railing effect; they are also more likely to flake off. If, despite this care, a few lashes stick together, you can brush them apart with an old, dry, mascara brush – so don't throw your old one away.

One good and inexpensive mascara remover is vaseline – though it doesn't suit everyone's eyes.

MOISTURIZING CREAM

Where moisturizers and night creams are concerned, enough is as good as a feast. Young skins only need a very light moisturizer and anyone should be able to tell, by the feel of their skin, whether they have used the right amount or not. Too much and the skin feels bloated; too little and it feels dry. Going for too heavy a cream too soon can age the skin just as much as not caring for the skin enough.

One of the cheapest and most effective moisturizing creams for dry skin is made by Crookes and goes under the name of E45. It costs least when bought in bulk, is unperfumed and can be used all over the body. It is, however, rather too heavy for use on the face.

NAIL VARNISH REMOVING

Rubbing away at nail varnish with remover on cotton wool tends to smear varnish on to the skin round the nail. Instead press the cotton wool on to the varnish for a few seconds, then wipe down the nail in a single sweep. Giving the remover time to penetrate should allow you to clean a whole nail in one go.

Wash the hands to soften the cuticles before you mani-cure them, then give the nails a final wipe with nail varnish remover. This final wipe removes the film of soap which prevents varnish adhering properly to the nails. Only the most expert can varnish ten nails without smudging a single one, so its worth training yourself to hold the cotton wool between the upper joints of your first two fingers; this way you can put the cotton wool aside and pick it up to wipe any smudges without endangering the unsmudged nails.

NECK MAKE-UP

To avoid a hard division between the face and the neck, take your foundation just under the jaw line, mix a little foundation with some moisturizer and use a fine sponge to shade the foundation away down the upper part of the neck. Then powder it very lightly.

The old saying that a woman is as old as her hands and her neck is very true. The neck needs as much skin care as the face if it's to keep the clock at bay.

ONION SMELLS

In *Supertips to Make Life Easy* I mentioned that vinegar or lemon juice removed smells from the hands. Between them they remove a whole spectrum of smells, but where onion is concerned the best cure is probably rubbing dry mustard well into the skin, then rinsing it off.

PERFUME AND AFTER SHAVE

Buying
The smell of perfume isn't simply what comes out of the bottle; it's a matter of interaction between the perfume itself and your body chemicals. The body's chemistry changes according to all sorts of factors. Most you can't allow for, but you can expect considerable changes during menstruation, so this isn't the time to try out perfumes.

The full reaction between the body and the perfume takes about an hour and a half. So, when choosing a perfume, it's important to take this reaction time into account. Smell various perfumes in the bottle until you find a couple which are close to the type you like. Then put one on the inside of each wrist and leave the shop. Smell each wrist an hour or two later; only then decide which you like. If you don't like either, try some others another day – don't put any more over those two.

Keeping

I always knew that perfume kept longest in the dark and cool, but what I have only just discovered is that it keeps best of all in the refrigerator. Make sure you keep it in its box and put the box in a tightly closed plastic bag to keep in the smell – perfume-flavoured milk is decidedly nasty.

Wearing

Many people find that their neck is sensitive to perfume and comes up in a rash. An easy way to avoid the rash is to put perfume on your hair instead – the area to each side of the temples is warm enough to bring out the scent.

It's wise to avoid putting perfume on the skin in sunlight. It can cause pigmentation changes in the skin and dark blotches may appear.

PIERCED EARS

If you haven't worn earrings for a while and the holes in your ears have closed up, making it difficult to insert an earring, put a smear of vaseline on the shaft as well as on the ear; the earring should go in far more easily.

POWDER

Powder is now back in fashion, but it has to be applied very carefully on top of a moisturizer and foundation. Choose a translucent powder with a beige tone if you are too pink and a pink tone if you're too pale. Shake the puff slightly before applying it, so it won't be too heavy, then press it lightly into the foundation. Don't necessarily apply it all over. Anyone with lines should avoid powdering the more lined areas – under the eyes, for example – where it will home in on the creases and emphasize them. They should just apply it to the more prominent parts of the face. Brush off any surplus with a soft brush.

RED CHEEKS

Tradition has it that a handful of parsley infused in a cup of boiling water produces a toning water which will reduce the redness of cheeks if they are bathed in it every day; I'm assured by one of my readers that it works, though I have no proof of it myself. If you want to try it, be sure to keep the spare liquid in the refrigerator or it will go off.

STAINED NAILS

Nails which are stained by vegetables can usually be cleaned by a good scrub with lemon juice. Nicotine-stained nails are harder to clean, but scrubbing with a smokers' toothpaste can improve them.

SECRETS OF THE EAST

One evening I and my co-author of *Pasta for Pleasure* decided to eat at my local Indian restaurant. As we sat down they brought us steaming flannels to wipe our hands with – and we were amazed to find how incredibly soft and smooth they left our hands. Clearly some ancient Eastern secret was responsible and I immediately decided that I must have it for this book. We asked the waiter to tell us what they put on the flannels. With exquisite Indian evasiveness he declined to tell us – clearly it was a very *special* Indian secret.

Even more intrigued, I brought my powers of persuasion to bear on the manager. He too tried to avoid answering, but after infinite wheedling and cajoling we won him round. 'Well, you see it is like this. We do not wash the flannels in soap, we wash them in Comfort. Then we rinse them, and then we are adding more Comfort, and some rosewater to make them smell good.' Such are the secrets of the mystic east.

I find that only a touch of Comfort and good dash of rosewater is the best balance, as rosewater is also a skin softener. And those who need to take a damp flannel when travelling but prefer not to put Comfort on their skin can wring a flannel out in water containing some glycerine and rosewater. The flannels will then leave the skin far softer.

TIRED EYES

When people are tired, the inner rims of the eyes often look redder than usual. Covering this up by very lightly running a soft white eyeliner along them can suddenly transform a tired face into a normal one. But be careful to choose a white pencil which is designed not to irritate the eye.

TIRED FACE

There are days when the face can feel tired and slack even though it doesn't need a real face mask. On such days a wonderfully easy way to give it the feeling of an instant tightness and freshness is to beat the white of an egg with a teaspoon of water, for just long enough to stop it being an unmanageable goo. Spread this on your face – avoiding the eye area – and allow it to dry. If you can spare the time, lie down until it has done so. Then rinse it off with cool water. It is extraordinarily effective.

CLOTHES AND SHOES

Since I wrote *Supertips to Make Life Easy*, people have contacted me, in letters and through radio phone-ins, about all kinds of problems to do with clothes and shoes. Sometimes they gave me their solutions to problems; sometimes they wanted my help over one I'd not managed to squeeze into the book, or hadn't even thought of. This is a compilation of the solutions I have found to such problems and also the tips they have given me which I have found successful.

ANTI-STATIC

It wasn't until I wore a man-made fibre on the BBC's 'Money Programme', and had it cling embarrassingly in rehearsal, that I discovered the existence of an anti-static spray called Croxtine, which the wardrobe mistress produced for me. You spray it on the inside of the fabric and it eliminates static, but leaves the material dry and unharmed.

If you can't get such a spray, another way to deal with static electricity is to rinse the garment in fabric softener. Wearing a natural fibre under the fabric is another solution;

even the most ham-fisted needlewoman can run up a waist slip from a couple of yards of Japanese silk. But make sure it's real silk. Some shops try to pass off the man-made version instead and it simply won't do the trick.

BEETROOT STAINS

This tip comes from a three-year-old – though his mother had to write to me on his behalf. First he got beetroot on himself and then he rubbed in a little pear. As a result he and his mother discovered that pear rubbed into beetroot stains makes them wash out remarkably easily. Improbable as it may sound, it most definitely works.

BELTS

In a drawer belts are about as manageable as a basketful of snakes. If you have cupboard doors which swing open, the best place to store belts is on hooks on the inside of the doors. The easy way to arrange this is to screw up one of those plastic-coated cup racks which have a whole row of hooks on a single strip of metal. A cheaper version, though more of an effort, is simply to screw in a set of cup hooks. If you use individual hooks, take advantage of the fact that you can space them as you like – give yourself room for big buckles by making two staggered rows instead of one.

BLOUSE CLOSER

Occasionally a crucial, but not visible, button comes off just as one is leaving the house; at other times one wants to wear a blouse done up to the neck and fastened with a brooch, but finds the buttons only go half way up. I came across the way to hold a blouse together in such circumstances when the sound men at the BBC were fixing my microphone cable out of sight. They used those little double-sided sticky pads which are sold to hold mirror tiles in place. They stick to the fabric just firmly enough to hold two layers together, but not so firmly that you can't peel them off afterwards. However, I wouldn't recommend them for any really treasured garment or for velvet, corduroy, or leather of any kind, as they might remove some of the pile or fail to come off altogether.

BRUSH SUBSTITUTES

If you need a clothes brush but don't have one, wet your hands, shake the water off, and wipe your damp hands firmly over the garment. The dampness will pick up most of the debris.

Another method is to wind a piece of broad adhesive tape, or adhesive bandage, around your hand – sticky side out – and wipe this over the garment.

When nap has become flattened and needs to be brought up and disentangled, a teazle head is much better than a clothes brush – teazles have been used for this purpose in the weaving industry for centuries. The little hooks on the teazle head enable it to tease out the individual thread, but it needs to be used carefully, and in the right direction, or cloth can become shaggy.

CHEWING GUM REMOVAL

Since writing *Supertips to Make Life Easy*, in which I gave a couple of homely methods of removing chewing gum, I have discovered that there is an aerosol for doing this job. You spray it on and it 'freezes' the gum to a point where it is brittle enough to break off in little pieces. The spray is made by a number of manufacturers but the one I have given at the back of this book proved the most effective in a series of tests by an organization which researches the efficacy of cleaning materials.

CLOTHES DRYING

Clothes keep their colour better if turned inside out before being hung on a washing line, so the sun doesn't bleach them.

Indoors

An ingenious way to dry smalls indoors, without putting
up a washing line, is to get hold of an old umbrella and
strip off the fabric. All you need then is a hook in a ceiling
and you can hang up the opened umbrella to provide a set
of drying arms which will fold away neatly into a cupboard
the next morning.

In the Wind

A splendid suggestion for how to hang washing on a hanger
on the washing line without the hanger blowing off was
sent to me by a 'Woman's Hour' listener. She said all you
need do is put two hangers in the garment with their hooks
hooked across the line in opposite directions. That way
the wind can blow the garment as much as it likes and the
hanger will never blow off the line. Just make sure the
buttons of the garment are securely done up – it's no good
if the hangers stay in place and the garment falls off.

CREASED CLOTHES

Happily, more and more hotels are providing each room
with a kettle, which is a godsend when clothes get creased
in packing. While doing a nationwide tour, with interviews
in every city, I managed to appear uncrumpled only by
holding my clothes over a steaming kettle in each hotel to
let the creases drop out. It works better than you'd believe
possible, though some fabrics are definitely more respon-
sive than others. Next time I shall give all my clothes the
kettle test before I go away and only pack those which
respond the best.

DYE RUNNING

I have received some agonized letters from readers who
want to know how to get dye out of garments which have
been stained by others which have run in the washing
machine, or by coloured paper they left in their pockets
before washing. It's a difficult problem to solve. If a gar-

ment is white and made of pure cotton, a soak in bleach at the strength suggested on the bleach bottle may kill the colour, but the chances of restoring a sparkling whiteness are very slim indeed. With other fabrics the best bet is to try Dygon. It's a product made by Dylon, the dye makers, and is specially designed to take dye out of clothes prior to dying them another colour. Failing that, the best solution may be to dye the garment a deeper shade of the colour which has run into it. Dylon has a consumer advice service which will advise you on the use of Dygon. They will also tell you how to get the best results if you end up dying the garment.

DYEING SHOES

My local shoe-mender doesn't bother to use the proprietory conditioner before applying paint-on-dyes to leather shoes. He conditions them with acetone or white spirit. He claims it does the job just as well. I haven't had reports from his other customers, but it has worked well for me and acetone is well known in the leather trade for its ability to strip the finish off leather. Though, of course, there may be some types of dye and some types of leather with which it won't work so well.

Bear in mind the power of acetone when using it to remove nail varnish; getting it on leather garments or shoes can be very bad news indeed. And never forget that it has an extremely low flashpoint – smokers beware.

GAP PREVENTION

I was about to demonstrate some 'Supertips' on 'Pebble Mill at One' when I discovered the ideal way to stop a belt riding up above one's trousers at the back and leaving an unsightly gap. I was searching through a haberdashery department for a solution when I came across sticky-backed Velcro. I bought six inches, and stuck the side with the soft loops to the inside of the belt at the centre back – I chose the soft loop side so any surplus wouldn't hook into the trousers. Then I stuck a piece of ribbon to the back of the other half of the Velcro – to stop it sticking to anything – and slipped it through the belt loop at the back of the trousers, with the rough side facing away from the trousers and towards the belt. When I put the trousers on all I had to do was press the two halves of the Velcro together at the back and the belt was firmly fixed in place. Even on the soft suede belt I'd chosen to wear there was no sign of the hidden fastening.

With some shapes of belt you may need to do a side or a front Velcro as well. Also, before attaching the Velcro, it's a good idea to put the belt on and check the position of the centre back when you wear it – this may not be the centre of the belt itself. And, of course, if the trousers haven't got a loop at the centre back, and you are sure you will always wear a belt with them, you could simply stick the other half of the Velcro straight on to the trousers. This method works just as well with skirts.

GLOVE CLEANING

For years the mother of a friend of mine has cleaned her gloves by putting them on and 'washing her hands' in petrol. She then removes the gloves and hangs them in the fresh air. It's a technique which the experts say will certainly remove a fair amount of grime, but it does create rather inflammable gloves and is not too good for the hands. So it's not a method of cleaning I'd use regularly, but if I was going to Buckingham Palace and my only suitable gloves were dirty I think I might try it.

GREASE STAIN

A grease stain on a leather or fabric shoe can sometimes be removed or reduced with potato flour. Stand the shoe on a large piece of kitchen foil, warm the flour in a pan until it's hand hot, then place it on the stain before wrapping the shoe in the foil, to hold the flour on the stain. Leave it overnight. How well it responds varies with the structure of the shoe and the nature of the stain. If potato flour fails, try the same method using Fullers' Earth.

GYM SHOES

If white gym or tennis shoes have become so filthy they are unwearable, they may come clean with a good scrub with detergent. If you haven't the energy for that it's worth seeing what the washing machine can do for them. Having brushed off any grit and earth, give them a wash in the machine with detergent. They may come up well or, if the glue is water soluble, they may fall apart – but at least you stand a CHANCE of being able to use them for a bit longer.

HAT CARE

If you lack a hat box, a precious hat can be somewhat protected by putting it in a large plastic bag, blowing the bag up like a balloon and closing it firmly.

JUMPER CARE

If you find you've run out of both glycerine and fabric softener, and need to give a softening rinse to a wool jumper, a little hair conditioner will do the job instead.

LEATHER

Leather for clothes, like the leather for furniture, comes in three main finishes – suede, aniline and pigmented. Both the suede and the aniline finishes lack a protective top coat and are prone to absorb anything which is dropped on them. It is always worth asking the shop to obtain a scrap of matching suede or soft leather for you when you buy a garment, as it is a great help when you need to deal with stains. The silicone sprays which are sold to keep the wet and stains off suede shoes can be used on some suede garments and on some aniline finishes. But check with the manufacturers before using them. If that's impossible test the spray on that scrap of leather or on the inside where it won't show.

Biro Marks

Methylated spirits is the chemical most likely to remove biro marks, but it could harm the leather. So test its effects on a part which doesn't show before trying it on the stain itself. And when you do the test, wait for it to dry completely before deciding whether it is safe to use. On really shiny leather, there is quite a good chance of it working safely, but the odds are not in favour of success on absorbent skins.

Dry Cleaning

When a leather garment needs dry cleaning, check that the cleaner you take it to has a leather dry-cleaning specialist. Many cleaners don't – they just take your garment in and clean it by guess and by God.

Grease Marks

When either suede or aniline leather gets a grease mark, the best treatment is to cover the mark with a little heap of Fuller's Earth and leave the garment in a warm place for a day. By the end of that time, the Fuller's Earth should have become darkened by the grease and slightly caked. Brush it away carefully, so you don't rub it into the skin, and then take a piece of the same leather and rub the place with it to remove the last traces of the powder. If any grease remains, repeat the treatment. When all the grease has gone, use the scrap of suede to rub up the nap on the garment.

Make-up Marks

If leather (other than suede) gets make-up on it, you should be able to remove it by dabbing it with the sticky side of adhesive tape such as sellotape. But don't press the tape on hard or it may pull off the surface of the leather when you lift it off.

Pigmented Leather

To test whether leather is pigmented or not, press a damp tissue against a part which doesn't show. If it doesn't darken with the moisture, it's pigmented.

Pigmented leather needs very little attention, but if a handbag, for example, becomes grubby, you can clean it carefully with a cloth well wrung out in warm water in which you have dissolved pure soap flakes. When it loses its shine, a rub with a colourless shoe polish will do no harm.

Stretched Knees

When the knees of leather trousers become stretched, you can get them back into shape with a little steam. The important word is LITTLE: if suede gets too damp it will be ruined. Bring a kettle or saucepan of water to the boil and hold the knees of the trousers, inside out, so they AREN'T in the strong jet of steam from the spout but simply in the larger clouds above. Don't leave them there for too long (and before you attempt this method, do check with the manufacturer that the steam won't harm the leather of your particular garment). Then lie them down and let them cool and shrink back into shape. Some leather manufacturers go one further and iron the inside of the leather, but this is a method that only experts can be certain to succeed with. Anyone less professional risks ruining the skin.

There is an old wives' tale going around that another way to shrink stretched knees is to put the trousers in a plastic bag and place them in the freezer overnight. Anyone who considers doing this should be aware that below a certain temperature some of the finishes on leather undergo permanent changes, which can make them become brittle and crack even at room temperature.

Water Marks

Water marks on leather are some of the most troublesome stains to deal with, because water actually undoes the treatment which was used to make the leather soft after it was cured, and the fibres themselves can become shrunken and hard. Rubbing the leather very gently against itself will sometimes improve its condition. Suede can be scratched VERY, VERY gently with a fine needle, in the direction of the nap, to bring up the surface again. The risk in doing this is that if you scratch too hard you may over-roughen the surface and produce feathering, which looks just as you would imagine from its name.

White Leather
To keep white leather clean, an Italian woman I know always uses milk. It's most effective, but it should only be used on leather which has a really shiny surface and won't absorb the liquid.

OSTRICH FEATHERS

I was taking part in a phone-in on BBC Radio Cambridge when a pearly queen rang, asking how to clean her ostrich feathers. It wasn't something that I'd researched, but I have now. The answer is that big ostrich plumes need to be cleaned very carefully or they may look tatty. Remove any surface dust by blowing on them and then clean them very carefully, working from the quill out to the edges, by brushing them with a clean soft brush dipped in white spirit. Allow them to dry in plenty of air.

Small pieces of ostrich feather, such as you get on a feather boa, can be dipped in and out of water in which you have dissolved pure soap flakes. Don't make the water too soapy and rinse them well afterwards. Carefully blow them dry with a hair dryer to fluff them up again.

PATENT LEATHER

If patent leather needs to be brought up to a shine quickly, and you have no milk to hand, use hand cream or hand lotion.

PEARLS

Pearls are curious. They react to the skin and can go dull
and lifeless if they are worn regularly by someone with an
acid skin, so they should be carefully wiped with a soft
cloth after use. They also lose their lustre if they are left
in a drawer for too long. Because of this, women with lots
of jewels used to have their maids wear their pearls at
night to keep the life in them. And one dashing – and virile
– old Etonian I know of, who lacks both a wife and a maid
to wear them for him, goes to bed regularly in nothing but
the family pearls.

Pearls can also be harmed by the chemicals in hair spray
and perfume, so these should be applied before any pearls
are put on.

PLEATS

Knife
In *Supertips to Make Life Easy* I suggested putting a big
tacking stitch in the bottom of each knife pleat, before
packing it, so it would hold in place. A reader wrote to
suggest using a kirby grip instead, which is a very good
idea – though it can't be used on fabrics like fine silk, or
velvet or wool with a delicate nap, for the grip would leave
an imprint which would be hard to remove.

Sun-ray
Every ten years or so sun-ray pleats come into fashion.
When they do, the way to pack this sort of skirt is to cut
the foot off an old stocking and pull the skirt down inside
the stocking, so all the pleats are held together in a tube.

PRINTING INK

To remove printing ink, you need to use a solvent such as
that in Dab-it-off, but the secret is in applying it so that it
doesn't leave the circular sweal which I explain in *Supertips
to Make Life Easy*. It has to be applied with light feathering

strokes to avoid a sweal; this is a tricky job with such a heavy stain.

SHOE STORAGE

Shoes must be one of the trickiest items to store tidily, and in *Supertips to Make Life Easy* I pointed out that boxes shoes are sold in are ideal containers for keeping the dust off them. So far as organising one's clothing is concerned they are ideal in other ways too. If you have plenty of space at the bottom of your clothes cupboard you can cut one end off each box and stack them, with the ends facing you. They then act as a neat set of pigeon holes and the shoes can be slid in and out as you need them.

If you lack space in the bottom of the cupboard the boxes can just as well be kept on end, in a small ottoman or chest, with the open ends uppermost. Of course, by cutting the ends off the boxes you do expose the shoes to dust which is bad for the leather, but those which are worn less often can always be protected by a polythene bag.

STARCHING

There is simply no comparison between the results one obtains with old-fashioned starch and with modern spray-on starch – the old way is much the best, and very easy. For most starching you need only follow the instructions on the packet. But if there are areas, like the fronts of men's dress shirts, which need to be extra stiff, here's one way to do it. Starch the whole garment with the starch at its normal strength. Then make up a small batch of starch in a jug at double or treble the strength and use a spotlessly clean pastry brush to brush this thoroughly on to the inside and outside of the shirt front and cuffs. When you iron it, you will then have part of the shirt very stiff and part of it just nicely crisp. Iron it while it is still rather damp; if it dries, the creases will be rock solid.

TIGHTS

Life

Tights last longer and look better if the part that gets rubbed by one's heels always stays at the heel. With today's anyway-goes tights, there's only a very slim chance of putting them on the same way every time, unless you mark the back. A quick X with a marker pen before you first put them on does the trick – but keep the pen in your bedroom or you'll never bother to do it.

The thrifty keep used tights in separate bags – mine read, 'Unladdered Tights', 'Ladders Above the Knee', and 'Ladders Below the Knee'. The first category can be worn for best, the second with skirts every day, and the third with trousers or long skirts. And, of course, tights of different denier go in different bags.

The ingenious and super-thrifty go even further and cut off the leg with the ladder in at the panty level and wear two legs from two different pairs of tights. The legs don't even have to match. A zany friend of mine who was once a top model has a penchant for going round like a court jester with one red leg and one blue one – and very good she looks, though not everyone could carry it off.

If you are taking off a pair of tights which have a hole or ladder, put a loose knot in the offending leg. Then, when it's washed, you can instantly spot that it isn't perfect and know which leg to look at to sort it correctly.

Washing

It is possible to wash tights in a washing machine if they are put into a large net bag. It protects them from snagging on the inside of the machine, but allows them enough room to move about.

TROUSER CREASES

If really sharp creases are needed in heavy wool trousers, rub a candle down the crease line on the wrong side before pressing in the crease.

TURMERIC

Turmeric is one of the trickiest stains to get out. On pure cotton it should come out with a soak in bleach at the strength recommended on the bottle. On other fabrics, the best way to get it out is to tamp it (as explained in *Supertips to Make Life Easy*) with pure soap and with neat cloudy household ammonia. On some fabrics this could cause the colour to bleed, so do a test patch where it won't show.

VELVET

As velvet can't be pressed in the usual way, a good way to get the creases out of a velvet dress is to put boiling hot water in a large bowl, hang the dress above it in the steam, and smooth it gently with your hands – but make sure it won't fall off the hanger into the water.

WOOD STAINS

If products sold for staining wood get on fabrics, treat the stains as for turmeric. It may also be worth trying ammonia if such stains get on Formica and similar surfaces.

ACHES AND PAINS

Despite the vast amounts which are spent by the National Health Service and the queues which form in every surgery, it has been calculated that nine out of ten symptoms are treated at home, and the British spend 400 million pounds a year on remedies such as cough mixtures which can be bought over the counter. The aim of this chapter isn't to increase that mounting expenditure, but to bring together some of the simple and inexpensive remedies which may be as effective as some of the proprietory medicines. Some of them are new and some are old, but it is always advisable to check any remedy with your doctor before using it. Only someone who knows your medical history can say what is safe for you.

ACNE

One of the functions of zinc in the body is to promote tissue formation. Maybe that is why some people find it remarkably effective as a treatment for acne. One of the herbal medicine companies which sells zinc tablets says that a shortage of this mineral may be indicated by the kind of aches which have long been described as growing pains. But they recommend that zinc should be used in combination with other tablets to keep a proper balance.

Before using the tablets, write to their manufacturer and find out what else they recommend; then discuss the combination with your doctor – zinc can be hazardous.

Another product which seems to reduce acne considerably in some people is a soap-free cleansing bar called Meadowblend, which is made by Shaklee, the American company that specializes in herbal remedies.

Some doctors recommend the Acne Aid Bar, which contains a vitamin A derivative, as a skin cleaner, but it doesn't work for everyone.

ARTHRITIS

There is some evidence that a medicament based on aspirin injected into arthritic areas may be able not only to relieve the pain of arthritis, but also to alleviate the condition itself. The work is still experimental, but it's interesting that two products – Balsona Ointment and Bengues Balsam – which have long been used for rubbing on arthritic joints, contain oil of wintergreen, which is, chemically, a close relative of aspirin.

Arthritis seems to be one of those complaints which respond to a whole range of remedies. I have had reports of people getting relief from taking garlic pills and others who say alfalfa tablets have cured the pain entirely.

BEDSORES

Increasingly the medical profession seems to be discreetly returning to some of the old-fashioned remedies. I interviewed one of the foremost authorities on the care of the bed-ridden and physically handicapped, for the BBC, and was interested to discover that she rated sugar as the best dressing for bedsores. It seems to kill bacteria and promote healing more effectively than more 'modern' dressings. But it is wise to consult a doctor before using it – it may not suit certain patients, such as diabetics.

Honey and sugar are also excellent treatments for cuts and grazes of any sort where a dressing is required.

CHOLESTEROL

Those who are worried about the build-up of cholesterol should use sunflower oil for cooking. It seems to be beneficial to people with this problem.

DENTAL RELAXATION

In a dentist's chair it can be difficult to relax the jaw to order, but there seems to be a natural interaction between the hands and jaw. Deliberately relax your hands and your jaw should relax too.

FAINTING

If there is a possibility that you may faint in the bath, tie a wooden cotton reel to a long piece of string and tie the other end to the ring on the plug. Have the cotton reel floating near your hand as you bathe, then you can pull the plug out without bending over if you feel bad. Of course, the other vital precaution is to leave the door ajar and make sure someone else is around to help you if you need it.

JET LAG PREVENTION

I've already named drinking alcohol and not drinking enough water as prime causes of jet lag. They both aid and abet dehydration – which is one of the hazards of flying – and that can make you feel pretty ghastly even if you haven't flown very far. Now there's another culprit – caffeine. It turns out that caffeine, in both tea, coffee and some soft drinks, makes it harder for your body to adapt to changes of time zone. On the other hand, eating a high carbohydrate meal, such as pasta, the night before, and changing your watch to the new time zone as you take off, will both make adjustments easier and reduce jet lag.

MOTION SICKNESS

In some parts of the world ginger has long been used as a

remedy for period pains and for nausea during morning
sickness, but until quite recently doctors dismissed it as an
old wives' remedy of no real value. Now research in
America has proved ginger does have real medicinal value.
Tests have shown that in preventing travel sickness ginger
is more effective than existing travel sickness pills – though
quite why is still to be discovered. To use it against travel
sickness, either eat a few pieces of crystallized root ginger
before you set off or drink a mug of boiling water, with a
teaspoon of powdered ginger, sweetened to taste. So far
there doesn't seem to be evidence either way as to its
effectiveness for dealing with morning sickness or period
pains, but it could be worth a try.

Car sickness can be caused by the motion and also by a
build-up of static electricity. If children suffer from car
sickness, it is a good idea thoroughly to spray the inside
of the car with an anti-static spray before a long journey.

If both these precautions have been forgotten and
queasiness ensues, actual sickness can sometimes be prevented if you can avoid swallowing your own spit – goodness knows why this helps, but it seems to.

PERIOD PAINS

A friend of mine had such excruciating period pains that
her doctor eventually booked her in for a hysterectomy.
While waiting to go into hospital, she met someone who
suggested she should try vitamin B6 first. She did. She still
has her womb and she no longer has pain. For some
women, the effect of B6 can be dramatic. Although it can
be bought across the counter, it is one of the vitamins
which can be harmful in excess, so its use should be
discussed with a doctor. The curious thing is that doctors
often leave it to patients to suggest it, even when they are
very happy to endorse the idea.

SINUS

Marjoram tea is used in Austria as a treatment for sinus

trouble and I have an Austrian friend who says it works extremely well. Simply make an infusion with a teaspoon of fresh or dried marjoram and a cupful of boiling water and drink this several times a day. My friend also recommends the stoic measure of sniffing the marjoram tea into the nose. If you can bear to, it may help – but make sure the infusion has cooled. But bear in mind that herbal remedies don't always act quickly, and this one needs to be persisted with.

SPLITTING SKIN

When skin becomes dry and liable to split, lanolin is the best general treatment for those not allergic to it. To heal an existing crack I know nothing better than a product called Lotil which is sold at most chemists.

STICKING PLASTER REMOVAL

If a lot of sticking plaster has to be removed, especially from anywhere hairy, it is well worth getting some surgical spirit. If you lift a corner of the plaster and rub the under-surface with the spirit, you can dissolve the glue little by little and remove the plaster without pain.

STIES

In Belgium some people swear by garlic as a cure for sties. They simply rub it on the sty several times a day. As garlic is antiseptic it may well help, but it does sting.

SUN DAMAGE

There's growing evidence that, however good a suntan looks, too much sunlight is bad for skin. But if you choose to lie out and age, two good treatments for sunburn are vitamin E and glycerine and rosewater. Apply glycerine and rosewater, mixed in equal amounts, to sooth the burning, cool it and take away the dryness. Use vitamin E, preferably out of an edible capsule, to help the burn to heal.

Scientists have recently discovered that very bright light cumulatively damages the eyes and causes them to age faster. Each time we go out in brilliant sunlight without sunglasses we are inviting the eye problems of old age to visit us that little bit sooner. The same goes for working in excessively bright light, or looking at flashes such as those from a photo-copier.

THORN FINDING

A drop of iodine on a place where you can feel, but not find, a splinter or thorn will often colour the wood and reveal its position.

THRUSH

Thrush seems to be increasingly common and should be taken to a doctor. But it isn't the kind of thing for which one calls a doctor out on a Sunday, so anyone who wants safe temporary relief until they can get to surgery may like to know that applying plain yoghurt will soothe the condition – but it should only be applied externally.

UPSET STOMACH

A traditional remedy for an upset stomach is, for adults, a teaspoonful of grated nutmeg.* Take it any way you can get it down – in a little hot water or even in a sandwich.

* Children should be given a smaller dose and at any age be careful not to take too much as nutmeg can be harmful.

WIND

In *Supertips to Make Life Easy* I mentioned port as the sovereign remedy for diarrhoea, but I forgot to say that it is almost magical in its effect on wind. A small glass full and the pain will begin to disappear almost immediately.

Teetotallers can use an infusion of camomile; it contains two compounds which affect the small gut and ease wind.

THIS AND THAT

In any book like this there has to be a place for the assorted bits of information which are too useful to throw out and too random to fit easily into any of the categories. Here is a collection of tips which covers everything from finding a contact lens to straightening out a warped record.

BEAN BAG PHOTOGRAPHY

One of the best photographers I know has thrown away his expensive tripod in favour of a bean bag. He finds that a bag the size of a large sock, filled with dried beans, can be pushed into any shape so it will support a camera at exactly the angle he requires. It is easy enough to make and anyone with a 'bean bag' chair can try it – though it isn't a technique for the wide open spaces.

CAR

Door Protection
If you have a narrow garage, it is far easier to glue a thin sheet of foam rubber to each wall, at the points where the door might hit it, than to warn each passenger to open the door carefully.

Electric Shocks

Now that man-made fibres are used both for car seats and for clothes, people can sometimes get a nasty shock from the build-up of static electricity in the car. Attaching earth straps to the back of the car solves this problem, or you can use an anti-static spray (see page 304).

Frozen Windscreens

One of the best, and cheapest, windscreen scrapers is a strong kitchen spatula. Moreover, it takes less space in the glove locker than other scrapers.

On very cold mornings, when frost covers the car windscreen, it often freezes back again almost as soon as you've scraped it off. The answer is some methylated spirits. Having scraped off all the frost and snow, moisten a rag well with meths and wipe it all over the windscreen. Since it has a lower freezing point than water, the windscreen shouldn't ice up again unless it is incredibly cold. As it evaporates, you need to do this just before you drive off; then by the time the meths evaporates the inside of the car will have warmed up enough to keep the ice off. If you have no methylated spirits, any spirit that's high in alcohol but low in sugar can be used instead – but at a higher cost. Incidentally, meths shouldn't damage modern car paint if your cloth happens to drip, but the paint on vintage cars could be harmed by it.

Misted-up Windscreens

Wiping the inside of a windscreen with neat washing-up liquid or glycerine will help to prevent it from misting up. After you apply it, the screen may look a little smeary, but, as it dries, the screen looks better and the benefits remain for some time.

Oil Pouring

If you have to pour oil into the engine from a can without a spout, don't forget that paper will funnel oil perfectly well. Either make a cone of several layers of newspaper, or cut the corner off an envelope and open it up to make a funnel.

Snow Clearing
If snow has to be cleared from under car wheels, a hubcap makes a natural scoop – not as good as a shovel perhaps, but better than your fingers. And if you aren't shovelling with them and want to keep hubcaps rust-free in winter, smear them with vaseline all over. It will hold the dirt, but they'll look better in the summer.

Traffic Film
By far the best cleaner for removing traffic film from a windscreen is a tablespoon of household ammonia in a pint of water.

Trailer
It's not a bad idea to put an old, slit tennis ball over the ball of a trailer hitch. It protects it from the weather and saves damage if you or another driver use the bounce-off-the-bumper style of parking.

Vinyl Cleaning
The vinyl used for car interiors and soft tops usually has a slightly rough, simulated-leather finish. The most effective way to get right into the dips is to use a soft scrubbing brush and washing-up liquid. Used regularly, however, the alkali in the washing-up liquid could attack the plasticizer which keeps the vinyl soft and prevents it from cracking. Counteract this by rinsing the plastic afterwards with clean water containing a dash of vinegar.

If the plastic interior still smells of cigarette smoke, even after washing, rinsing it with water containing bicarbonate of soda should reduce the smell considerably – a tablespoon to a pint of water (500 ml) is about right. Remember, the smell will also be in the carpets and any soft upholstery, so cleaning the vinyl isn't the whole answer. Once the bicarbonate has been given time to work, rinse the vinyl with vinegar and water as in the previous paragraph.

Vinyl Reviving

Dark vinyl, especially black, can still look old and dusty even when it's perfectly clean. To revive it, simply find a shade of shoe polish which matches it, rub it on and buff it off with a soft shoe brush. This works particularly well with black vinyl – one of my sons made his ten-year-old car look half its age that way.

CLIPPINGS

Most glues will make the printing ink from newspaper show through to the other side and spoil the look of any cuttings you may want to keep. One that doesn't do that, and is really easy to use, is the spray-on glue sold for mounting photographs. Don't get it on any furniture – it is harder to remove than you'd suppose.

CLOCK CHANGING

I could never remember whether the clocks went forward for summer and back for winter or vice versa until a friend gave me this simple rule: 'Spring forward, fall back.'

CONTACT LENS FINDING

If a contact lens is dropped on the carpet, the easiest way to find it is to use a vacuum cleaner extension covered with a nylon stocking. Take your shoes off, so you won't tread the lens to dust, and put the vacuum cleaner well outside the area where the lens was dropped. Then put the nylon TIGHTLY over the brush end of the extension so that it COMPLETELY COVERS IT AND THERE IS NO WAY THE LENS COULD BE SUCKED IN. Fix it firmly in place with a strong elastic band. (I'd use two elastic bands in case one breaks.) Switch the cleaner on and very systematically run the nozzle up and down the carpet, checking the bottom of it after each row. If it's there, so long as you don't switch off before checking, the lens should be sucked up and held in place against the stocking. Remember there's less suction when the cleaner bag is full; this could prevent the lens being picked up.

DENTURE CLEANING

If water is always put in the basin before any dentures are removed for washing, there's less chance of them breaking if you drop them.

MEDICINE

Preventing Drips
Most medicines tend to run down the side of the bottle and create a sticky ring where you put them down. If medicine comes in a box, remove the top flaps and keep the bottle in it, so it catches the drips.

PICTURE HANGING

Having fixed a nail or hook in the wall, it can be difficult to make the picture-wire hook over it. An excellent solution, sent me by a *Family Circle* reader, is to push the prongs of a fork over the nail so that the fork-handle sticks up and out. Then you just slide the wire down the fork-handle onto the nail, and remove the fork.

SPILL AVOIDANCE

When travelling with cosmetics in soft plastic bottles and tubes it's a good idea to squeeze some air out of them before putting on the cap. The tendency to suck air in, and go back to shape, will make them far less likely to leak.

WARPED RECORDS

When gramophone records become warped, the safest way to straighten them out, according to one of the technical experts in the record industry, is to put them in a warm airing cupboard between two clean sheets of glass.

One tip which I have been sent, which is NOT to be recommended, is applying direct heat by ironing the records: it would almost certainly distort the sound.

Your Children

There have been times when, faced with the demands of my own three children, I have felt that where children are concerned the only way to save time, money and energy is never to have any. Such moments of cynicism are short-lived. In fact there are quite a few ways to make life with children easier – the trouble is one usually learns them the hard way, after one has got it wrong with at least one child. So the purpose of this chapter is to pass on some of the ways which other mothers have found to smooth the path of child-rearing, as well as those I myself found useful as both a mother and a teacher.

It's a rather different approach from the one found in books on how to bring up children. There the emphasis is on the child. Children are very important, but I also believe they can only be happy in a home where the adults are happy, and an adult worn to a shred by the demands of the children is not a happy adult. In industry there would be a personnel officer to balance the demands of the employer (child) against the needs of the employee (parent), but the home is a cottage industry where the employee has to fight a single-handed battle. And recently the deck has been stacked rather too heavily in favour of the child. So this chapter tries to do a little to redress the balance and cut down on overtime. Though, paradoxically, the best way to do that is sometimes to look at things from the child's point of view.

ABSENCE

Life is much easier for parents if they handle time away from young children – for holidays, illness, or the birth of another child – rather carefully. Until they are about five, children have very little sense of time, so a parent who goes away has, in the child's view, gone away for ever. And, like an adult whose husband, wife or lover has suddenly walked out on them, they get most upset. On the parent's return they can react by being sulky and aloof, weepy and clinging, or downright aggressive and dis-obedient, according to temperament. Which makes for a bad homecoming, and some children take weeks to get over these reactions. Meanwhile, almost nothing is as exhausting as a miserable child.

In an ideal world – from the child's point of view – no parent would ever be parted from a child under five for more than a few hours. But when parents *have* to go away, one way to lessen such reactions is to make the child aware that he or she hasn't been forgotten. Anything that does this will help.

Hearing someone's voice brings them a lot closer, so a series of bedtime stories can be taped ready for playing each night; and telephone calls are a help, however brief or meaningless the conversation. Small presents can also be wrapped and left ready. They can be as tiny as you like, as they are just symbols of love, not compensation for absence. Then, each day, one can be given to the child with the information that it's from Mummy, or Daddy, who loves them.

To go smoothly the return also needs to be carefully handled. A child needs time alone with someone he or she loves, just as much as an adult does. This is particularly difficult, and particularly necessary, when a mother returns with a new baby – but with a bit of sensitivity from the rest of the family it can be arranged.

ABSENT MILK

Any breast-feeding mother who has a busy life may find it worth taking a tip from a friend of mine who always expresses any surplus milk into the tiny sterile plastic bags used to line certain types of baby's bottles. She then keeps all the bags in a sterilized box in the freezer to be used on days when she is too tired to have enough, is kept late at the office, or is out for the evening and unable to give the usual feed. Even a mother who isn't out at work may find this useful. Some family crisis may call her away, and not all babies accept other milk if it's suddenly given to them.

ALPHABET

It's always nice when there's something you DON'T have to do, and one thing you don't have to do is teach toddlers the alphabet. The alphabet – which is the NAMES of the letters in a particular order – is no help at all in learning to read: reading is about the SOUNDS of the letters, not their names. The alphabet is really only useful for looking things up in encyclopedias and telephone directories – and it takes a very precocious toddler to use those.

If you want to teach a child about words – and lots of children are eager to know about them – don't believe those who say this should be left to teachers. It won't do any harm, so long as you treat it as a game, not as a competition to have a more advanced child than some rival. Go at the child's pace, and stick to whole words rather than breaking them down. Start by writing the child's name in nice big letters (ordinary book-style print, not capitals) and teach him or her to recognize the whole word, plus any other basic words which are important to the child, such as Mummy, Daddy, Granny. Then the first steps to reading have really been made and you can just expand the vocabulary. Even better, have plastic letters and arrange them into the name (and later into other words); when it is easily recognized, let the child arrange the letters to make the name. The very latest research shows that children learn to read faster if they handle the letters of the alphabet and learn to arrange words with them – and there's nothing quite as restful as a child reading quietly to itself!

If you've already taught your child the names of the letters of the alphabet, don't worry. Children are used to adults doing confusing and contradictory things and simply make allowances.

BEDTIME

Babies
It used to be thought that babies needed silence in order

to sleep. Then it was realized that what with heart-beats and stomach rumbles the womb was a pretty noisy place, so babies probably feel more at home with a little soothing sound. You can now buy tapes which copy the body sounds a baby hears in the womb. Apparently they work very well. But you don't need to go to that expense: long before that discovery I'd found that a transistor radio in a baby's room, playing very gentle classical or popular music, sent my children to sleep far better than the sounds of silence. But make sure the radio is out of the child's reach, or he or she may learn to move the controls and accidentally wake you in the middle of the night with the guns of Tchaikowsky's '1812 Overture' blaring from some radio station.

Toddlers and Upwards

Some toddlers insist on rushing round the house like a whirlwind, evading every attempt to get them to bed whatever you do. The mother of one such child discovered that if she turned off all the lights except the one in the child's bedroom, and waited there quietly for him, he soon made his way towards the light and could then be got into bed.

Another useful ruse is to get the child to play parent and take a favourite teddy, or other toy, and put it to bed. Children who won't, as a matter of principle, admit to being tired themselves may happily admit that teddy is tired and then lie down and join him.

It's hard for older children to enjoy bedtime if it's the time when all the enjoyable things stop – television, playing in the garden and so on. If these stop so they can tidy up (and they don't have the fun today unless they tidied up yesterday), and bedtime is story-time, it is easier to get them to bed.

BROKEN NIGHTS

When my first baby was born, the GP who had looked after me since childhood gave me a tip that saved a lot of lost sleep. She explained that babies love milky feeds in the middle of the night, and find them well worth waking up for, although a bouncing full-term baby doesn't really NEED them much after the first six weeks. So, at about six weeks, she advised me to give the baby very slightly sweetened water if she woke in the night, instead of milk. As she said, 'It will take it a few times, dear, but she will soon get bored and sleep through till the morning.' Her advice worked like a charm with every child, and I blessed her for it. Check the timing of this with your GP.

BURPS

The acid smell from a baby's milky burps can be removed by rinsing the stain with water containing a little bicarbonate of soda. Bicarbonate of soda is also effective on the smell which sometimes remains even after vomit has been cleaned up. But before using this solution on a carpet or any coloured fabric, test the solution of bicarbonate on a scrap of the same carpet or a corner of the garment which won't show – some dyes may fade with this treatment. If you find your carpet is one of those, you may be able to improve the smell by cleaning up and shampooing the carpet in the normal way, letting it dry completely and then sprinkling on DRY bicarbonate of soda and leaving it for a few days before vacuuming it up.

CARROT AND STICK

A friend of mine has the rather good catch-phrase that 'love is attention', and certainly the greatest reward any child can get is the attention of his or her parents, and the worst punishment is being ignored by them. Sometimes children do dreadful things in the spirit of innocent curiosity, sometimes out of a natural desire to know where the limits come; both (harassing as they are for adults) are just part of growing up and can't really be prevented. But I've often seen children being naughty or demanding because it was the only way they could guarantee the attention of adults. That sort of naughtiness can be kept to a minimum by giving lots of attention to the good things they do, and giving tantrums and bad behaviour a cold shoulder. This policy won't make them good, but it will steer them in the right direction.

By the same token, seeming to reward a child for bad behaviour is just asking for trouble. A child who cries for sweets in a shop, and gets them, knows just what to do next time. A child who cries for them and is swiftly removed from the shop without any, but given a treat next time he or she behaves well, has learnt a lesson which will make shopping far easier in the long term – even if it ruined that first shopping trip. Being a parent is a bit like being a politician – short-term solutions bring long-term problems. Yet we all fall into the trap some time or other.

CHRISTMAS

There is no God-given rule that children must receive *all* their presents on Christmas Day. In fact I have found it an excellent idea to spread present-opening over as many of the following days as possible. There's less risk of toys being broken in the welter of wrapping-paper, and instead of being satiated with gifts, the children can enjoy those they have opened. Also the days to come are less of an anti-climax – and if Christmas Day itself leaves them over-excited, over-tired and reluctant to go to bed, you have the useful sanction of no presents tomorrow unless they stop yelling and go to bed today.

CO-OPERATION

For reasons which psychologists still don't understand, children seem programmed to enjoy rhymes and word games of all kinds. This can be a marvellous tool in getting them to do what you want. For example, a child who doesn't like having his or her fingers wiped will usually be delighted to sit having them 'counted' with a wet flannel – and learn to count at the same time. In the same way children will giggle delightedly at the most feeble spur-of-the-moment rhymes, and get the message without umbrage. It doesn't even matter if they don't understand all the words; it's the sound which pleases them. The only catch is that children have remarkable memories, especially for things you don't want them to remember, so you could well find a rhyme like, 'Oh, you are a silly moo/ you shouldn't have taken off your shoe', being used on Grandma. Who might be less than amused.

CUTS AND GRAZES, BUMPS AND BRUISES

As cuts and grazes are unavoidable in childhood, it makes things a lot easier if children learn to handle them calmly. That means the adults mustn't seem upset either. The first weapon is humour. One man I know still recalls with pleasure the way, when he fell down or bumped himself as a toddler, his mother would exclaim, 'Oh, poor pavement,' or 'Poor chair.' He says that even as a toddler the idiocy of an adult sympathizing with the pavement made him giggle and forget his hurt.

That doesn't mean hurts should be totally ignored. Loving attention is also reassuring and a parent 'kissing it better' is one of the best pain-killers. Most childhood knocks need little more. Run-of-the-mill shallow cuts and grazes do no great harm, provided a child has been innoculated against tetanus. All anyone need do is rinse the injury well with a clean cloth and pure cold water. Encourage the child to help – children are reassured by being able to DO something about their hurts. There is usually no need to cause pain and tears by washing the graze with stinging antiseptic – in fact it has now been found that some strong antiseptics make things worse by killing the bacteria which aid healing. Antibiotic creams should never be applied unless a doctor recommends it. Wrongly used they can delay healing and breed resistant organisms.

In some families there is a tradition of covering even the slightest graze with a piece of sticking plaster. Plasters can be useful to staunch dripping blood, and to keep dirt out of wounds on vulnerable places like feet, but they tend to be over-used. Most cuts and grazes heal faster if the air can get to them. It is also worth remembering that children tend to ritualize the care of cuts and, if having a plaster becomes an essential part of the ritual, it will be a great nuisance when an accident occurs and no plaster is to hand. The lack of plaster alone may cause quite unnecessary tears.

CUTTING THE SHEET WASH

When toddlers grow out of their cots and move into normal beds, they are only half the size of an adult, but they seem to have twice the ability to get the bedclothes dirty – my daughter's favourite method was smuggling bananas into bed. At this time a good way to halve the washing and bed-making is to make the bed with only one sheet, like an apple-pie bed. Tuck the sheet in at the top, taking it halfway down the bed. Then fold it back on itself, so the foot of the sheet comes up to the top of the bed. Put the blankets on and fold down the top of the bed in the normal way. When the toddler gets the bedding dirty, you only have one sheet to wash, and the clean sheet can be put on without having to untuck the foot of the blankets. This halves both lots of work.

Mind you, you do have to be careful that no elder sibling enters too much into the spirit of an apple-pie bed and puts nasty things at the bottom of it.

DIARY KEEPING

It doesn't make things one wit easier at the time, but the piece of advice I most wish someone had given to me when my children were young was to keep a diary about them. Not a boring baby book of how much they weighed and what they ate, but a book of the charming and peculiar things they said and did. The early years seem so consuming and interminable it's almost impossible to imagine the day when those same toddlers will tower over you; and it seems equally unlikely that you will forget the events which occupied so much of your time. But you do, and when the children are big the haziness of the memories is a real loss. The brief diary I did keep is a delight not only to me, but to the children themselves. I would have kept it for longer had I realized how much I would forget.

DISCIPLINE

When I was newly married, a near neighbour had an almost miraculous way of getting his children to do what he wanted. He would ask the child to do something and, if he or she refused, would simply say in a mock threatening voice, 'I'll give you until I count five.' Then he started counting very slowly and loudly with his voice becoming more and more ominous and giant-like. Invariably they had done what he wanted before he got to five. I found the method just as invaluable with my children.

Young children vary the amount of time they spend pretending not to respond, and delay the moment of obedience according to their age and temperament. But, if you start this method when they are young enough, there are very few children who will push you to the limit – though you may have to resort to 'four and a quarter, four and a half, four and three-quarters', in a voice ever more laden with foreboding.

As the object is to get them to do what you want WITHOUT tears or punishment, giving them the leeway to disobey a little is in your interests as well as theirs, so long as they comply in the end. When, eventually, they challenge you all the way to five, you know they are too old for the game. Chase them to the desired obedience, roaring like a lion, and don't try counting with that child again.

Whatever system you use, always do what you say you are going to do – children are very quick to learn if they can get away with things.

DIVIDE AND RULE

Children have a great feeling for precision and fairness when it comes to someone else not getting a bigger share of a treat. If there are two children, let one child cut the cake (or other treat) in half and let the other have first choice of the two halves. It is a powerful incentive to fair cutting, a great lesson in fractions, and whatever happens you can't be accused of favouring anyone.

Incidentally, when it comes to dividing Mars bars and similar chocolate, a bread knife is the best choice.

DRESSING UP

Dressing up is one of the cheapest and easiest games, and keeps children happy for hours. Silly hats, high heels and flowing colourful garments of any kind are top favourites. A small white-wood chest which will store such things and double as a seat in a bedroom is a godsend.

Even if there isn't room for dressing-up clothes, masks take very little space, are wonderfully easy to make, and just the occupation for a wet afternoon. Just blow up a balloon, cover it well with vaseline and then use wallpaper paste to stick on layer upon layer of newspaper torn in little pieces. Let it dry out overnight every few layers, then add more until you have a rock hard covering. Finally saw it in half down the length. With elastic to hold them on, and holes for eyes, you have the basis of two masks which the children can paint into any characters they like. And older children can build up elaborate noses and cheek-bones by sticking shaped sections of crumpled chicken wire on to the basic mask with strong glue, and covering these with yet more paper. Such masks are marvellous for Halloween.

EARLY WAKING

It's one thing for young children to wake early and quite another for them to wake everyone else. A young child (though not a hungry baby) should be able to play quite happily until a civilized hour if the parents want him or her to; it's just a matter of getting the circumstances right. Think twice before taking a child into bed in the night or the small hours of the morning. What seems like an easy solution at the time can make things far tougher later. Most children are companionable creatures and would rather be in their parents' bed than alone in a cot – so if they think there's even a sporting chance that yelling will get them there, they will yell.

They will also, quite reasonably, kick up a rumpus if they are bored or hungry. So the formula is to wait until they've gone to sleep and then put plenty of safe toys in the cot with them (on elastic if they are prone to chucking them out). And, if they are old enough to eat without choking, put something to eat within reach of the cot. If a child then yells to come into bed at the crack of dawn, he or she can be told that it's not going to happen, and firmly ignored until morning has thoroughly broken. Children stop yelling when they realize you aren't going to give in.

Of course, some children are so active that a cot is a kind of imprisonment. An easy way to give them a bit more space is to abandon the convention of a cot altogether. Beds were originally put on legs to get away from draughts and vermin, but if a home is rat-free and reasonably warm there's nothing wrong with a mattress on the floor. The cot mattress can be put into a play pen, where there's room for more activity when the child wakes and a shorter fall for those who try to climb out, as the very active child surely will.

FINISHING FOOD

Children refuse food for all kinds of reasons – because they genuinely dislike it, or because they are being over-fed, for example. But one of the commonest reasons is that eating is one of the few areas in which children can exercise power and decide something for themselves – and children don't like feeling impotent any more than we do. So the more concerned grown-ups seem about their eating, the more powerful they feel; and the more incentive they have for playing them up.

The easy solution is simply to give very much smaller helpings, and casually offer seconds. Children, like animals, will eat when they are hungry, and it's no bad thing to turn the tables and have them ask for food. That way they can exercise their power not by REJECTING what you offer, but ASKING for what they want. If they say no to a second helping and come crying for more between meals, it's just a matter of sensing the situation. We all get peckish between meals occasionally – but equally if they have proved they can turn down a healthy piece of fruit at lunch and get an ice cream half an hour later, they'd be daft not to try it on a regular basis.

Another useful dodge with the very young is to use an incentive scheme which focuses attention away from the food itself. Put the food on a clear pyrex plate. Then sit the plate on an old Christmas card or a picture from a magazine and make a game of finding the picture through the food as it is eaten. Some children like to keep finding the same familiar picture, others like variety. Watch their reaction and ring the changes accordingly. But when the child realizes that he or she can find the picture by lifting up the plate or scooping the food off on to the floor, it is time to stop this particular game.

GLOVE KEEPING

Gloves hanging at the bottom of coat sleeves on the ends of elastic have become the stuff of comedy. Nannyish they may look, but they make a lot more sense than searching for the lost gloves in the snow while a toddler bawls his frozen fingers off. What's more, the gloves are always with the coat, so there's no need to scour the house for them. Let the comedians laugh, say I – provided they dress and take the toddlers out too. (Make sure you loop the elastic through the coat loop before you sew on the gloves. It's safer than pinning it up with a safety pin.)

HAIR WASHING

Washing hair with the child's head bent forward is almost bound to make water run into the eyes, and bring tears. Washing hair in the bath with the head tilted back won't.

HELPING

It's tempting to wait until children are old enough to be genuinely helpful before asking for their assistance. Unfortunately, by the time their help is much use, they may be at the stroppy stage and be less than enthusiastic about giving it. So, if you want to make life easy for yourself as they get older, get them into the way of helping while they are still young enough to think it's a big game at which they can be very clever. Children under five love to imitate adults and it's surprising how well they can do a simple job like dusting if you show them how. Then you just add on a little bit of responsibility as they get older.

In practice there is far less fuss if each child has his or her own particular job or jobs than if each bit of assistance is argued out on a one-off basis. For example, there is no reason why a six-year-old shouldn't routinely take his or her dirty clothes to the laundry basket; any eight-year-old can easily make a bed; and by the age of ten a child is perfectly capable of cleaning his or her own room thoroughly at least once a week. If the increases in responsibility are linked to birthdays on which pocket money is routinely increased, and failures to do the jobs are linked to a deduction of the increase, the trade-off between privilege and responsibility is quickly grasped by even the very young. Of course they won't always do these things well, and in adolescence they may be rather less thorough than they were at five, but that is par for the course and no reason for not holding them to at least token gestures.

ICE LOLLIES AND ICE CREAM

The drips which can smother young children when they eat these ever popular products can be largely prevented by cupping the bases in a large circle of foil so it makes a rim to catch the drips as they form. Some people also put a marshmallow in the bottom of an ice cream cone to stop drips coming out at the bottom. Unfortunately, if children KNOW there's a marshmallow in there, they are inclined to make things worse by biting off the bottom of the cone to get at it.

ILLNESS

When young children are ill in bed, boredom is the big bugbear. Having something to bash and bang and make a mess with is a good outlet for their frustration at being cooped up; but clay and plasticine can play havoc with the sheets. Instead, make the old nursery-school dough of 1 teacup of salt to 2 teacups of plain flour and just enough water to make a very firm dough. This gives as much satisfaction as messier mixtures, but, once dry, it can be brushed off the bedding with no trouble.

Ill children often revert to behaviour from an earlier stage, so it's worth bearing in mind that their current toys and books may be less appealing than those they have officially 'grown out of '.

JIGSAW TIDYING

Jigsaws are great for teaching children to observe details, but hell to put away. The solution is to count the number of pieces in a new jigsaw the moment it comes into the house and then assign it a letter of the alphabet. Then on the back of every single piece write its letter of the alphabet and the number of pieces in the set. Then, when the children tidy up, they can just gather together those with the same letter and count them into the container. That way you know at once if any pieces are missing.

As the boxes of jigsaws always seem to break in no time, collect the nylon net bags which supermarkets sell fruit in. With a drawstring threaded round the top, each will hold a puzzle nicely and the bags can hang on hooks inside cupboards and take much less space than a stack of boxes.

KEEPING PROMISES

If you tell a child you'll do something – return at a certain time, for example – KEEP YOUR WORD. A child who has been let down won't trust you next time, and may well yell the house down. Worse still, as a teenager he or she may follow your example and keep you up half the night wondering why they haven't come home. If you are always reliable there is a sporting chance that some of the reliability may rub off on them.

MILK REJECTION

It's all very well for doctors to say that it doesn't matter a bit if a toddler won't drink milk, but milk is a very convenient way for a busy mother to give a child nourishment either by itself or in dishes of various kinds. Luckily children are usually beguiled by novelty and a glass of milk dyed lurid green with a safe food dye may disappear in no time when its white twin is rejected. In fact children usually love food to be curious colours and are far less likely to become bored with any basic food if you ring the changes by colouring it. Just be careful visitors aren't coming – it's not every adult that can stomach pink mashed potato.

Of course you have to be careful not to use this to persuade a child to eat something which really doesn't suit him or her.

NEW BABY

Helping children adjust to a new brother or sister is a delicate business, and nothing is more calculated to put children's noses out of joint than a new baby usurping all the attention and all the presents while they wait on the sidelines. But it's amazing how often visitors, who come to coo over the baby, will totally ignore the other children. So it's useful to have a bag of tiny presents hidden away, so that when a visitor arrives bearing gifts for the baby the other children can be given something to unwrap too. It isn't so much the gift that matters, as not being left out.

Children are fairly good at cupboard love, so a baby may get a better reception if he or she arrives bearing gifts for the other children – unless, of course, they are too old to be taken in by the deception, or have the wisdom to know that, like ancient Greeks, babies 'are to be feared even when they come bearing gifts'.

NOISY CHAIRS

It is far easier to stick a little pad of white felt (coloured felts run) to the bottom of each chair leg than to teach your children to push chairs back quietly on a hard floor.

PARTY GIVING

Finding You
Parties get off to a very bad start if half the guests arrive late because they can't find you. So it's worth making it easy for newcomers. A few balloons tied to the gate or door should do the trick.

Food
Only the greatest optimist would suppose that young children will pass food to one another at a party. The best children's party I ever gave was when I decided to stop rushing round the table like a clockwork mouse, offering plates of food to one child after another, and abandoned plates altogether. You can do it like this.

Cover the table with slightly overlapping sheets of aluminium foil, tucked firmly under the edge of the table. Then regard the whole table as a plate and dot the different types of food all over it, so that everyone can reach something of everything. (Soft foods like jelly are, of course, OUT.) Then fill in any gaps with scatterings of tiny brightly coloured sweets such as Smarties. The table looks splendid, the children have the treat of a seemingly limitless feast to be eaten in any order they choose – which they love – and you don't have to pass a thing.

But give very small helpings of drinks, so there isn't too much to spill, or it could ruin a lot of food. And, if the table itself is precious, put a sheet of polythene under the foil.

Games

The best games to start a party with are the ones which tire the children most – then they won't bounce around too much at tea. The best games to end with are the gentle ones – then they won't be sick if they've over-eaten. And at intervals (for the sake of your sanity) build in some games which ensure total silence – picking up small beans from the floor and depositing them in a jar by sucking at a straw is one; Kim's Game (listing all the objects on a tray after seeing it only for a brief time) is another. While forming two teams which each have to pass a match box, by nose, from one end of the team to the other ensures that at least two children in each team are silent at any one time. Though it's not a game for the season of colds and mellow fruitfulness.

Help

What one needs most at a children's party is another pair of hands. There's no way you can keep even ONE child amused while taking another one to the lavatory, or welcoming someone at the door – and there's no telling what children will do in a strange house. The best way is often to beg, borrow or hire a teenager who is good with younger children and old enough to keep them amused and in order. Other adults tend to make a take-over bid for control. Parties go distinctively better if other parents are banned: children behave best when they know exactly who is in charge – with two adults around they play the parent off against the hostess.

Prizes

Young children like mystery rather more than they like big prizes. An easy way to achieve this is a lucky dip out of which they can pull their prize. Instead of wrapping umpteen tiny parcels, put things like large chocolates or funny rubbers or balloons in the cylindrical boxes colour film is sold in – most photographic shops are happy to give you any number – and put these in a tub of sand or sawdust. What looks like a dreary old film box to us has a grown-up air to the very young.

PILLOW FIXING

If you want to make sure a pillow stays in place – to stop it being pulled down into a wet bed for example – get hold of some old-fashioned bolster covers which were designed for a double bed. Being unfashionable, they sometimes go very cheaply in auctions. Then slip the pillow into the centre of the case and tuck the ends of the case firmly in place underneath the mattress on each side. Alternatively, use long strips of sheeting, say, from an old sheet, wide enough to wrap round the pillow and long enough to tuck into either side of the bed. If you put some tapes on the edges in the area where the pillow will go, you can just tie the pillow in place.

ROUTINE

The golden rule of old-style nannies used to be that children needed routine, and meals and rests had to be at fixed times. It was a wonderfully wise bit of double-think because, of course, children have little need of routine. It's the ADULTS who need the children to learn a routine. Put a child to rest after lunch EVERY DAY and, once it's established, you can count on a blissful hour to yourself.

Try and get a child to rest every so often and you're likely to have trouble.

In the maelstrom of child-rearing it's easy to be carried along, simply surviving from minute to minute. But it's worth grabbing a short time while the child is very young to sit down and work out a pattern which allows you to draw breath. Only when you've planned what you would like can you begin to organize the family in that direction. No plan works out perfectly where children are concerned, but if you know what you're aiming for, you stand a better chance of achieving it than if you just let the children take the lead. After all, you have rights too, and a right to a rest every so often is one of them.

SHOE LACE TYING

Shoe laces on small feet seem to have a life of their own. I tried all kinds of ways to keep my children's laces done up, but the best plan of all is one I have only just discovered from a friend who used it for all her children. Make the bow in the usual way, but just before you pull the bow tight take one of the loops over the top of the central 'knot' and back through the hole a second time. Then pull both loops to tighten the bow as usual. This way the bow is much firmer, but it pulls undone in the normal way.

STAIR NEGOTIATING

When children have legs which are too short to allow them to walk down the stairs, they can negotiate the descent quite safely if they are taught to slide down, feet first, on their tummies (preferably in dungarees), or to work their way down, step by step, sitting down.

STARTING SCHOOL

Doing Up Clothes

A five-year-old faced with trouser flies for the first time, with nobody to come to the rescue if he can't manage, is liable to have an accident. Try to stick to garments with familiar elastic tops for the first term or so. Or, if the uniform prevents this, let him wear the garments around the house for a few weeks before school starts, so he can get used to coping with flies while he is at home.

Even familiar fastenings, like buttonholes, can be a problem on stiff, brand-new garments, and a child who can't do up a coat to go outside may get cold and miserable. So it's wise to buy the uniform for starting school some weeks ahead and let it become worn-in at home until it's familiar and easy to handle. If putting on the uniform is used as a treat, and much is made of how nice and how grown-up the child looks in it, the child will associate school with pleasant things and approach the first day far more happily.

Familiarity Breeds Content
New schools will seem less big and frightening if they have already been visited on a happy occasion. Most schools have fun events, like fêtes, during the summer term and any good head teacher should be delighted for parents to bring along a future pupil to share the fun and get to know the building.

Name Tapes
All name tapes look alike to a child who can't read. To help the child find his or her own garment in a sea of identical clothes, add something distinctive to the name tape – a button, or a tag of ribbon for example.

STROPPY ADOLESCENTS

There are very few adolescents who don't go through a stage when they are exasperating beyond measure. Psychologists say it's an important part of their finding their own identity – but it can leave parents wishing they'd go and find their identity somewhere else. However, there is a compensation: nature has devised things so that, just when parents might be feeling sad at the prospect of their little darlings leaving the nest, the little darlings are so impossible that they can wave them goodbye with nothing more painful than a sigh of relief.

TELEPHONE-MAD TODDLERS

Some toddlers can't leave phones alone. At the very least, a child who is constantly picking them up blocks incoming calls, and there are dreadful stories of those who have accidentally dialled long-distance and brought a mammoth bill on their parents' heads. The way to prevent both hazards is to put a wide elastic band round the phone so it holds down the rests when the receiver is picked up. Then the child can pick up the phone to his (it usually is a he) heart's content with no repercussions, and any adult who wants to use the phone only has to snap the band aside.

TIGHT SUSPENSION

To stop little girls' tights sagging and wrinkling down their legs, put small buttons on the vest seam at either side, fairly near the armhole, and attach a piece of buttonholed elastic (the sort with ready made buttonholes all down the length) to each side of the tights. Then the tights can be buttoned on to the vest. Of course this only works while they are young enough to need help in the lavatory and when they are old enough to manage the buttons: there is an in-between stage when it would only cause problems.

TOILET TRAINING

Toilet training is a vast subject and one which is full of pitfalls, so this isn't the place to go into it in detail. But there are a couple of points to bear in mind. The first is the oft repeated (and almost as oft forgotten) rule that no child can be toilet trained until he or she has enough physical development to control the activity, and children vary as to when that is.

The second point is that there are no prizes for speed, and the best time to toilet train a child isn't necessarily the instant he or she is old enough to respond. The best time is when it suits the whole family. If you're moving house, or staying with other people, a few nappies may be no real problem, but a child who may wet the carpet at any minute can be a real harassment. And the worst time of all can be just when a new baby is due. Well-meaning friends talked me into getting my first child out of nappies before the new baby came 'to save me two lots of nappies'. It took her about a day to realize that the only infallible way to get me to put down the baby and attend only to her was to ask to go to the lavatory. After that, scarcely a feed went undisturbed. Nappies would have been half the trouble.

TOYS

There comes a stage when children really mind whether they have the same patent toy as the child next door, but in the early years improvised toys can be some of the best. A small child gets a lot of pleasure from 'painting' an outside wall with a big brush and a bucket of water and watching the bricks turn redder from the water. A wooden spoon and a saucepan lid make an excellent drum (if you can stand the din); a bowl of water, a funnel and a plastic mug or two will keep a small child busy for a surprisingly long time and teach him far more than more expensive toys ever could. Even a sheet of plain white tissue paper (the dye comes off coloured paper) will intrigue a toddler with its crisp rustle. It's just a matter of looking around and seeing objects from a child's point of view – then rejecting any which are small enough to be swallowed or have other dangerous features.

Sometimes improvised toys have other advantages. If a young child wants to thread beads for necklaces, but an even younger one might try to eat the beads, tiny beads of pasta dipped in food colouring and dried are much safer. And simply by having improvised toys the child learns that all fun doesn't come ready-made and pre-packed.

TOY TIDYING

Choosing the best containers for toys depends very much on the space available. Small objects like crayons and Lego can be stored in the large plastic sweet jars which sweet shops will gladly give you for nothing. And when floor space is short, all you need do is drill a hole in each lid and bolt them to the underside of a low shelf, so the jars hang below the shelf with their contents nice and easy to see.

Heavy toys need tougher housing. Specialist shops now sell large plastic boxes for toys, but, before you buy them, it is worth pricing a few ordinary washing-up bowls and laundry baskets: they do exactly the same job and are sometimes much cheaper. What is more, you can use them for something else when the toy stage is over.

TRAVEL

Even on a short outing with a baby it's wise to plan for delays and changes of plan. Nothing puts a damper on fun more than having to drag oneself away from friends because of the baby; and nothing makes a bad situation worse more quickly than the yells of a hungry child. Even if you plan to be back for the next meal, the train could be late or the car could break down, so take spare nappies and spare food, or milk. If a baby is on powdered milk, the right amount can be measured into a bottle and the water carried separately in a suitably clean thermos flask.

Children's ears will be less affected by the pressure changes when flying if they suck a sweet on take-off and landing. A pocketful can save tears.

There is a stage when, given half a chance, children will take every toy they possess away with them on holiday. A friend solved this rather neatly by making a child-sized rucksack for each of her four children and saying they could take anything they could get into their own rucksack. It proved a powerful incentive to restrict the load. The added advantage was that they each had a container in which to carry a towel and bathing costume, and their hands were free to carry their buckets and spades on the way to the beach. So that was another job their parents didn't have to do.

TROUSER AND JUMPER REPAIRS

It is the wildest optimism to imagine that any young boy can wear trousers for very long without going through the knees. The easy solution is to fortify them when they are new, rather than wait for a difficult-to-mend hole. A patch stuck or sewn on the inside of each knee, or in the seat of the trousers, will almost double their decent life, and save a lot of work.

Prevention is also better than cure when it comes to the elbows of jumpers which will be rubbed daily on the tops of school desks. It is far easier to sew on the leather patches, sold by most good haberdashers, when the sleeves are new and unstretched than when they are baggy with holes.

WALKS

Somewhere in the grand mythology of childhood the idea got around that babies need to be taken out in their prams for walks, and some mothers still believe this. It is, happily, a fiction. Babies need fresh air, they also need lots of new things to see and do, but a walk is by no means the only way to achieve either. Mothers who loathe walking can rest their consciences.

WASH SHYNESS

A *Family Circle* reader wrote to tell me that she'd found the solution to a teenager who wouldn't wash before going to school – she took away all his school uniform until he did, and that saved any argument, even though he was late for school the first time. This is a practical method with those children who WANT to go to school. Indeed, unless the children are liable to ransack the house, almost any garments can be hidden until the required standard has been reached.

WEANING

Children have a penchant for the familiar and will sometimes learn to drink quite happily from the rim of their old familiar bottle, when they would kick up a fuss if asked to drink from a cup.

WELLINGTONS

To make sure one child's wellingtons don't get muddled up with the next ones, clip each pair together with a clothes peg. If the clothes peg hangs from the right length of string, and the string is attached to a coat hook, the boots will also keep upright.

To dry wellingtons quickly, invert them over the grilles of underfloor heating (having first tipped out any water), or give them a blow with a hairdryer.

To prevent wellingtons from smelling, put charcoal in the feet of a pair of laddered tights and put one foot of the tights into each wellington.

Your Food And Drink

When I first learnt to cook, I used to wonder why more experienced cooks seemed to get better results, but put in far less time and effort than I did. Gradually I realized that they had all sorts of little 'tricks of the trade' which made it easy for them to prepare dishes successfully with a minimum of effort. Of course, these little tricks never make a bad recipe into a good one, but they do make a big difference. Yet, surprisingly, very few recipe books bother to give them. Maybe it's because the recipe writers are so experienced that they just take their little tricks for granted and don't even realize they are using them. This chapter is designed to make good that omission. It includes a lot of tips which people have sent me since I wrote a similar chapter in *Supertips to Make Life Easy*, as well as a whole lot I have recently picked up or devised myself. The lovely thing about cooking is that there is always something new to be discovered and always a better way to do almost everything.

APRICOTS

A friend in France taught me that the flavour of fresh apricots is tremendously improved if you take out a few stones, crack them and cook the kernels with the apricots. Adding a few kernels also makes a great difference to apricot jam. Damson jam is also far more delicious with damson kernels – though cracking the minute damson stones is a real labour of love.

ASPIC

Improving the Flavour
For the best-flavoured aspic of all, substitute dry white wine for some of the liquid – the better the wine, the better the flavour.

Keeping It in Place
Aspic has a nasty habit of running off a sloping surface before it has time to set. The way to prevent this is to

thoroughly chill whatever you want to coat and to cool the
aspic until it is close to its setting point, but not yet
beginning to set. Then when you put the aspic on to the
cold surface, it sets very rapidly and stays put.

AVOCADOS

A ripe avocado is SLIGHTLY soft if you press it. However,
if your greengrocer slips you a hard one, it will ripen well
in a paper bag in any warm place, such as a high kitchen
shelf. Ripe avocados keep best in the refrigerator.

BANANAS

If your family, like mine, disappears for meals the instant
you do a really big shop, console yourself that you can
stop most fruit over-ripening, for a few days, by keeping
it in the fridge. Bananas will look black and deeply unappe-
tizing, but the fruit itself will be fine.

If bananas over-ripen, and nobody in the family will eat
them, they still make excellent banana bread. And if you
have a freezer you can freeze them until you're in the
mood for baking. Banana bread also freezes well, so you
can save time by doing a bulk bake, slicing it and freezing
it for picnics, packed lunches and so on.

BEANS

Cooking Dried
The length of time which dried beans, such as butter beans,
red kidney beans and so on take to cook depends very
much on their age – the older they are, the longer they take.
The cooking time also depends on the other ingredients in
the dish. Bean skins become tougher when they encounter
salt or acid; this means they take longer to cook. Therefore
it's best to add salt near the end of cooking and pre-cook
them, separately, if they are to go in a dish which contains
lemon juice, tomatoes, or other naturally acid foods.

Being an alkali, a pinch of bicarbonate of soda has the

opposite effect and speeds up cooking. But it does this at the price of destroying important vitamins and sometimes affecting the flavour – though in strongly flavoured dishes the difference is unlikely to be noticed.

Whatever method you use, the larger dried beans can take a good while to cook. As it's as easy to cook 4 lb (2 kg) as to cook 2 lb (1 kg), anyone with a freezer can save time and fuel by cooking twice as much as they need and freezing half. And, as explained in *Supertips to Make Life Easy*, red kidney beans *must* be boiled rapidly for at least 10 minutes to be safe.

De-stringing
If fresh beans need de-stringing, a potato peeler does the job fastest.

BEAN SPROUT KEEPING

Normally vegetables rot if they have too much water around them. Bean sprouts are an exception. If you try to keep them in a nice dry bag they'll rot to a stinking sludge in a day or two. To keep them beautifully fresh, use the Chinese method recommended by Kenneth Lo and put them under water in a tightly closed jar in a refrigerator. Like this, they last well for almost a week – if they were fresh to start with, that is – but you need to use a really large jar so they won't be crushed and be sure to change the water every couple of days. Water chestnuts like the same treatment.

BEATING

Short Beaters
If you are short and find that beating and mixing by hand normally forces your shoulders up to your ears, try working with the bowl in the sink. You should be much more comfortable.

Without a Beater
If you have to beat food without a beater, it isn't as hard with a pair of forks as you might suppose.

BEEF WELLINGTON

Have you ever wondered how Beef Wellington can be cooked so the pastry is perfect outside but the meat is very rare inside? Well, opinions differ, but one New York chef insists that the answer is quite simple. All you need to do is to seal the outside of the meat in the usual way, wrap it in foil, then put it in a refrigerator to chill thoroughly until it is given its coating of mushrooms and pastry and cooked. He says the colder it is when you cook it, the rarer the beef will be.

BEETROOT

Keeping It Fresh
If you want to keep a cooked beetroot from going mouldy, but don't want the acid taste from keeping it in vinegar, try grating it into a bowl and covering it with cider. You can then drain it and use it in any way you like, or you can heat it in the cider and, with the addition of seasoning, a touch of vinegar and some brown sugar, create delicious sweet and sour beetroot which, if the sweet and sour flavour is balanced nicely, is perfect with pork. Bear in mind, though, that beetroot loses its texture and becomes pappy after a while however you store it.

Skinning
Immediately after boiling the beetroot, drop it in cold water and the skins will peel off far more easily.

BISCUITS

To keep biscuits crisp for longer, all you need do is put a few lumps of sugar in the box with them. If you have already let them go slightly soggy, they can be revived by baking them in a low oven until they are crisp again. Breakfast cereals, crisps and salted nuts can be revived in the same way. However, baking won't improve the dreary musty taste which marks the old age of such food.

BRAZIL AND COCONUT SHELLING

It's not often that one finds a food tip in the pages of *New Scientist*, but I was browsing through it when I discovered an article on how to get Brazil nuts out of their shells without breaking them. The author had established that if Brazil nuts were put in a freezer for several hours before being cracked, they came out intact almost every time. Since I rate broken Brazil nuts, which invariably cling to their fragmented shells, as one of the great frustrations of Christmas, I quickly tested his method. As one would expect from *New Scientist*, it worked – the nuts came out perfectly almost every time. Presumably the freezing makes the shell more brittle and also causes the kernel to contract and pull away from the shell – but, happily, the taste and texture are unaffected. The same can't be said for the method of cracking coconuts (which some cook books recommend), whereby they are baked in a low oven for a while. For though the heat makes them easy to crack, it spoils the texture of the flesh quite markedly.

BREAD MAKING

Adding Fat
Some bread makers find that in recipes where a little fat is added to the bread, the best way to add it is to put it on their hands at the kneading stage and knead it in. Like that, it stops the dough sticking to their hands. Moreover they say the texture is better that way.

Crust Making
Bread recipes often forget to tell you that you can alter the character of a crust by painting it with different things when the loaf is nearly cooked. For example, if you paint

it with melted butter, you get a soft crust, but if you paint it with water, you get a crisp one. And those aren't the only effects: egg yolks with a little top of the milk will give a dark top; apricot jam will give a shiny one. So you can choose the effect which best suits the bread you are making.

BREAD SAUCE

Bread sauce may be indispensable to Christmas, but it can also take up time, a saucepan and a burner just when you have none of these to spare. Happily the secret of a good bread sauce is to cook the flavourings with the milk before combining it with the breadcrumbs. This means the main cooking can be done the day before – or you can even prepare the milk weeks in advance and freeze it if you wish; and the bread can be crumbed and frozen too.

For ½ pint (250 ml) of milk, you need a large peeled and halved onion, 4–6 cloves, 12 peppercorns and a good pinch of nutmeg. Let these stew very gently in the milk, in the top of a double saucepan, until the milk is well flavoured. Adjust the seasoning, strain, cool, cover, and put it in the refrigerator or freezer until you need it. When the time comes, all you need to do is heat the milk and breadcrumbs together in the oven or on top of the stove.

BROTH

It's a shame to throw away the left-over carcass of a chicken when its broth could make all the difference to another dish. A good basic broth, which can be used in soups and sauces, is easily made by boiling up the carcass of a chicken – or any other bird one cooks – with an onion, a carrot, a bay leaf and a little thyme, parsley, pepper and salt, and perhaps a finger-length of celery. If you don't want to use the broth straight away, it can be a bulky item to store in a freezer. An excellent cook I know gets round this by cooking the broth until most of the liquid cooks away and it becomes highly concentrated. He then puts the concentrated stock in an ice-cube tray and, when it's frozen, stores the home made 'stock cubes' in a bag. Being small, they take no time to melt when needed and can be diluted with water to give whatever strength the dish requires.

BURNT FOOD

Cakes

The trouble with burnt cake is that it is usually dry right through, as well as burnt. With fruit cake all you can do is cut off the black bits and follow the directions for dry cakes (p. 234). With sponge cake, you can treat it like one of the cakes designed to be biscuity: having cut off the black bits, cut it across into as many thin layers as possible and sandwich the layers with plenty of rich butter icing.

Alternatively, abandon the idea of having cake and use it up in a trifle, well doused in alcohol; or, if your family likes the combination, put it in a bowl, pour a jelly over it and leave it to set.

Casseroles

The trouble with burnt food is that the taste of burning often gets into the whole dish. But if a pan of food has caught at the bottom, start by tipping all the loose food out into a clean pan – and don't be tempted to pull away burnt pieces which are stuck to the bottom unless the pieces are so big you can cut the good unburnt top from the burnt part. Taste the rescued food. It may taste fine, but if there's a suspicion of charcoal about the flavour you may be able to mask it by frying some spices separately in a little oil and stirring them in – curry powder, cumin, coriander or cinnamon for example – provided the dish will blend well with such flavours.

Meat

If grilled or roast meat is burnt, you will find it easier to scrape off the burnt part if you cover it for a minute or two with a piece of damp cloth or kitchen roll.

Tarts

If the burnt filling from tarts clamps them firmly to the tin, just hold the bottom of the tin over a gas or candle flame until the stickiness bubbles and melts. Then whip the tarts out instantly. A curved grapefruit knife is one of the best tools for getting them out.

Toast

When toast burns, it is usually only on one side. So proceed as for 'Melba Toast' (p. 253), but throw away the burnt half.

CAKES

Dry

If a cake is SLIGHTLY overcooked and rather dry, pop it in a plastic bag with a piece of fruit cut in quarters (but not touching it), close the bag tightly and leave it overnight. It won't be as good as it would have been when perfectly cooked, but it should absorb enough moisture from the fruit to be quite pleasant to eat. Almost any not too juicy fruit will do – an apple, pear, peach or nectarine for example – but you don't want the juice to get ON the cake, so don't risk anything runny like a slice of pineapple or melon.

If a large fruit cake, such as Christmas cake, is over-cooked, you can put fruit with it as above, but you can also add moisture more directly. With a skewer make holes almost all the way down into it, and all over it. Then spoon on any alcohol which will suit the recipe – brandy, sherry, or a liqueur, for example. Teetotallers can use a touch of fruit juice instead. Put it in a tightly closed box or a plastic bag for a day or two, so the moisture has a chance to work its way right through the cake.

Fruit-Stretching

If you are making a rich fruit cake and find yourself short of dried fruit, or simply want to economize, you can make a beautifully moist fruit cake by using 12 oz (350 g) finely grated carrot as part of 2 lbs (1 kg) of dried fruit.

Lemon Flavouring
A little lemon zest in a quite ordinary sponge can make it delicious, but if you lack lemons and have a herb garden, try putting a few leaves of lemon balm in the bottom of the baking tin instead.

Tin Shortage
If you run short of cake tins, you'll find cakes bake perfectly well in the aluminium containers used by Indian take-aways.

Transferring to the Tin
If you don't want to savour the delights of licking the cake mixture from a spoon or spatula, and would prefer to have the mixture slip neatly off them, grease them with a butter paper before using them to spoon it out.

CAULIFLOWER

Cleaning
On a recent radio phone-in, someone rang to tell me that if a cauliflower was soaked in salted water, it killed the creepy-crawlies but left them in the cauliflower; if, however, you soaked it in vinegared water, it drew them OUT of the cauliflower. This is an impossible tip to test, for one would need to count the insects in the cauliflower to start with to know how many stayed in and how many came out by each method. But she may be right and you may like to try it for yourself. Either way, a limp cauliflower will revive more rapidly if you remove all its leaves and cut a deep X in the base of its stem.

Cooking
When I was compiling *Supertips to Make Life Easy*, I was told that if you put a slice of bread in the water when boiling cauliflower, cabbage or Brussels sprouts, it prevented them

from smelling. I tried it and didn't find it nearly as effective as leaving the lid off the pan. So I didn't recommend bread in the book. Since then I've talked to people who insist on keeping the lid on and DO find that bread helps. So maybe I'd better give the facts behind all this.

The reason these vegetables smell when cooked with the lid on is that they release natural acids into the water. In small amounts thē acids don't smell; but if the lid is on, the acids rise in the steam, hit the lid, condense and fall back into the water. So the longer the vegetables are cooked, the stronger the acids in the water become and the more they smell. When the lid is off, most of the acids just drift away in the steam and only become strong enough to smell if the vegetables are very overcooked. If the vegetables are cooked with the lid on, a piece of bread could possibly absorb some of the acids and so reduce the smell – but it is bound to be less effective than stopping them building up in the first place.

Cooking Whole
Occasionally one may want to serve a small cauliflower whole, as the centre-piece for a dish of mixed vegetables. The way to guarantee that it comes out perfectly, without any of the florets getting crushed as you turn it into a colander, is to place it on a square of muslin and tie the corners over the top of the cauliflower, as you might tie up a Christmas pudding. You can then lower it into the water by the knots, and lift it out the same way.

Make sure you cut a deep X in the bottom of the stem, so it will be cooked by the time the florets are tender.

CENTRIFUGAL SAUCE

Whenever a small amount of sauce or ketchup gets stuck in the bottom of a bottle, call science to your aid. Grab the bottom of the bottle and hold it so the top (with the lid screwed tight!) points towards the ground. Then whirl your arm round and round in circles (as if trying to improve your chest muscles – which, if you have enough ketchup bottles, could be a bonus). The centrifugal force you create will shunt all the sauce from the bottom of the bottle to the top, where you can get it out.

CHAMPAGNE OVERFLOW

An old trick, which waiters sometimes use surreptitiously, will quickly stop a bottle of champagne overflowing. As soon as it starts to overflow, simply wipe a finger across your forehead and hold it over the opened neck of the bottle. You literally stop the fizz with the sweat of your brow, for it is the perspiration which does the trick. Not hygienic, but it works.

CHEESE THRIFT

The cheapest way to buy cheese is usually in family packs, or when it's on special offer – but it may not be needed in that quantity or at that time. You can still take advantage of this saving if you remember that, for cooking and even for sandwiches, most hard cheeses are none the worse for a spell in the freezer. Grate them first, then you can use them straight from the freezer and just shake out what you need – so saving cooking time as well as money. This applies to the British style cheese, from Cheddar to Stilton – wherever they come from – and to most hard Italian cheeses. This way you can have good quality cheeses always to hand to cook with, without the waste of them going mouldy.

CHESTNUTS

A woman in Cheshire has written to tell me that if chestnuts are put in a pail of earth they keep well; they don't dry out or go mouldy. As chestnuts haven't been in season since I heard this, I haven't been able to try it myself, but as squirrels bury nuts to keep them – and presumably don't like dry or mouldy ones any better than we do – I think she may well be right. It is certainly worth a try, especially when you consider how the prices rise in Christmas week.

CHOCOLATE

Melting

If you've ever had problems with chocolate not melting to the consistency you expect, take heart. Chocolate is naturally unpredictable and not even the manufacturers know why it behaves well one day and badly the next. Their best guess is that it's affected by the storage temperature – a hot summer or a spell in the fridge may be equally bad for it.

When you melt it, there are also a few dos and don'ts which can increase your chances of success. Never use milk chocolate: being fattier, it is far more difficult to melt successfully. Melt plain chocolate over hot, NOT boiling, water and use it as soon as it melts, which takes about 4 minutes – overheating makes it lose its shine and become slightly granular. And don't be tempted to stir it until it is completely melted – and no more than necessary even then. The usual method is to put it in a bowl over a saucepan of water which has been taken off the stove; in fact it melts faster on a pyrex plate over the pan, as more of the chocolate touches the plate.

Once chocolate has melted, it can be spread on grease-proof paper, left to set and cut into squares or triangles as a decoration for cakes, as well as being used in all the normal ways.

Skinless Drinking Chocolate

Drinking chocolate is much less likely to develop that much-disliked skin if you beat it to a froth in the pan just before you pour it out.

CITRUS FRUIT

If you are taking the juice from citrus fruit, it is worth removing the zest first and putting it in the freezer to use in other dishes when you need it. If you have zest always to hand, you never need to spoil another piece of fruit which you aren't juicing by taking the zest from it.

COFFEE

I've already explained in *Supertips to Make Life Easy* that making coffee is one of the things I'm bad at. But I have to admit some improvement since a friend returned from South America with the news that in that home of coffee they never put absolutely boiling water on it; they bring the water to the boil, turn it off and let it stand a few moments before pouring it on to the coffee. Using water which is just off the boil seems to make both instant and fresh coffee taste far less bitter.

COLOURINGS AND FLAVOURINGS

If you don't want to end up with a carmine cake when you planned a pink one, or have your Victoria sponge reeking of vanilla, put colourings and flavourings first on to a spoon – away from the mixture – and not straight into the food itself. And, of course, the same goes for salt and gravy browning.

CRAB CRACKING

If you have smart crackers for crab and lobster claws read no further. If you don't, and have to use a hammer, remember to put the claws in a plastic bag first, then the fragments won't fly everywhere.

CREAM DISPENSERS

The pressurized cans which dispense rosettes of whipped long-lasting cream are useful but wasteful, as a lot can remain in the bottom. To get the dregs out, when the canister seems empty, run it under a hot tap for a moment or two just before you use it. The resulting cream will be thinner and less attractive than the rest, but at least you'll have it all.

CREAMING

The business of beating butter and sugar to a cream is a matter of moments with a mixer or a food processor. If, however, you have to make a cake without one, try grating the fat into the bowl on a coarse grater and then standing the bowl in the sink, in warm water, for the creaming. Most working surfaces are too high for such a job and the warm water makes the creaming much easier. Alternatively, you may like to heed the words of a woman who was making cakes long before food processors had been invented.

The renowned nineteenth-century cook, Eliza Acton, says in her delightful book *Modern Cookery*: 'For all large and very rich cakes the directions are to beat the butter to a cream: but we find that they are quite as light when it is cut small and gently melted with just so much heat as will dissolve it.' She adds, 'It must on no account be HOT when added to the other ingredients.'

She is right: a lot of cookery writers instruct you to cream the butter when they haven't bothered to think whether it is really necessary or not. But you need to be careful where you apply Eliza Acton's advice. Good cakes CAN be made without the creaming normally suggested; but it is not the size or the richness which determines whether a cake needs to be creamed or not. The determining factors are the other ingredients, and the kind of texture you want the cake to have.

Creaming the butter puts air into the cake; when the air heats in cooking it expands, pushing the cake up and making it lighter. But not all cakes need very much lightness, and some contain a raising agent such as baking powder, or bicarbonate of soda, which may give the cake enough lightness without any air being beaten in. Fruit cakes, for example, are not usually designed to be light, so if you fail to cream the butter it may be no great loss, and the same goes for most tea breads. Chocolate cakes often contain raising agents, and anyway a slightly heavy chocolate cake will still taste good.

But a plain sponge which is heavy is not worth eating.

If you do omit the creaming, add a bit of extra air by sifting in the flour, even if it isn't lumpy, and if the recipe uses both a raising agent and a little milk, use sour milk – when the acid of the milk reacts with the alkaline raising agent, the gas which is given off helps to lift the cake. Equally you can use a touch of lemon juice or vinegar to create this effect, providing it won't make the cake too runny.

CUCUMBER – PICKLED

Anyone who has a taste for Central-European-style cucumbers pickled in vinegar may like to try slicing some fresh cucumber into the liquid when all the whole pickled cucumbers are finished. In two or three days the cucumber has a deliciously close resemblance to the fresh pickled cucumbers sold in Jewish restaurants. Of course the flavour will vary with the brand of cucumber you choose. I find the Krakus brand works very well indeed.

DATE CHOPPING

It is almost impossible to chop a block of stoned dates finely, because they stick together again as soon as you cut them. If the dates can be added just after the flour, there is an easier way. Slice them, drop them into the flour and just pull the slices into fragments, under the flour, with your fingers.

DESSERT AVOIDANCE

Among the ultra-luxurious shops of New York's Trump Tower there's an exclusive chocolate shop where, for a truly astronomical price, you can buy enormous fresh strawberries dipped in chocolate. They are sold singly, each in its own paper case. You can use this idea to avoid making a dessert for a special meal. If you are in a hurry, or have more than enough cooking to do already, it only takes a moment to melt plain chocolate (see 'Chocolate', p. 238) and dip the ends of a punnet or two of strawberries in it. Fresh strawberries with chocolate are infinitely nicer than chocolates with a strawberry filling and they look enchanting. Have the cheese course after the main one, as they do in France, and eat the strawberries with the coffee, as a sweet punctuation mark to the end of the meal.

Strawberries aren't the only fruit to be delicious dipped in chocolate. I have successfully tried small white grapes, very small ripe greengages and apricots. Put them to set in a cool place, on a biscuit tray lined with greaseproof paper. It is best to avoid the refrigerator if you can, as condensation can spoil the surface of the chocolate.

DIPS FOR EASE

Most dips and soft creamy pâtés, whether of meat, fish, vegetables or cheese, freeze very well. It saves a lot of money and hassle if you keep a few handy in the freezer, against the arrival of unexpected guests. Pack them in the smallest possible containers so they will thaw quickly.

They can keep the wolf from the door while a guest overstays his or her welcome, or they can be used as a first course, and there's no real reason why this has to be taken sitting at table. If the main course is the sort that needs last-minute attention, giving it that attention can leave an embarrassingly long gap in the meal. A far easier way is to serve a dip or other finger food with the drinks which is substantial enough to act as a first course. Tell your guests that is what it is, so that they tuck in. Then, if any guest is late arriving, the rest of the party aren't starving and the sit-down meal can start when the main course is ready. Moreover, you don't have to rush from the room to put the finishing touches to so many courses.

EGGS

Mashing

The easiest and quickest way to mash hard-boiled eggs for sandwiches is not to mash them at all, but just grate them on a coarse grater. Start at the round end: the distribution of the yolk makes it work better that way.

White Whipping

When I wrote *Supertips to Make Life Easy* there was no evidence that the traditional chef's copper bowl made egg whites beat any better. Since then a series of extraordinarily complex experiments in an American university have shown that a copper bowl IS better. It seems that minute traces of the copper combine with the egg whites to increase their elasticity and help them to foam.

Whatever you beat them in, egg whites are like the rubber of a balloon – enough air is a good thing, too much and they will collapse on you. As soon as the whites are stiff enough to stand in peaks, and you can JUST turn the bowl upside down without its contents falling out, they have reached their best. If you go on whipping after that – which it is all too easy to do with an electric beater – the whites will be overstretched and tend to collapse. Overbeaten egg whites are a common cause of meringues which fall and weep miserably over the tray.

ELDERFLOWERS

In *Supertips to Make Life Easy* I mentioned that if elderflowers are stewed with gooseberries, they give the gooseberries a wonderful flavour. Elderflowers are just as good with tinned gooseberries as with fresh ones, and in some years the elderflowers and the gooseberries aren't both ready at the same time. So, if you are planning an outing at elderflower time, take a few large plastic bags with you. If you put the flowers in these as you pick them, and close the bags to keep in the moisture, they should keep fresh for about 24 hours in a cool place. To have the elderflower flavour available at all times, simply put the flower heads to cook in a little water with enough sugar to sweeten it pleasantly; let them cook until the water has absorbed their delicious aroma. Strain the flowers off and cook the syrup until it's fairly concentrated. Then freeze it in an ice-cube tray, and store the cubes in a bag, ready to pop into any gooseberry dish you make. You can also use the syrup as the basis for an elderflower sorbet which tastes delightfully fresh and unusual, but costs only pence. Equally the cubes can be watered down to make a wonderfully refreshing elderflower cordial at any time of the year, although bottled elderflower cordial does not keep well.

A word of warning. It would be highly dangerous to cook with elderflowers which had been sprayed with insecticides or herbicides. Therefore they should only be picked if you can be sure they are totally free of such chemicals. Moreover, some people are allergic to elderflowers in large quantities.

FAT SPITTING

Fat is most likely to spit when damp food is put into it. As the water in the fat dries up, it will stop spitting; but if you want to speed up the process, sprinkle a little flour on the fat – it will absorb the moisture and quell the reaction.

FIZZY DRINKS – MAINTAINING FIZZ

In *Supertips to Make Life Easy* I said that, if you dropped the handle of a teaspoon down the neck of a newly opened bottle of champagne, it would keep reasonably fizzy until the next morning. An ex-chalet girl from a ski resort wrote to say that I was right about champagne, but that it also worked for most other fizzy drinks. In her ski resort they only sold tonic in crown-top bottles; she used a teaspoon to keep the lunchtime leftovers fizzing for the pre-après-ski top-up.

FRAGILE FOOD

Now that few homes have fish kettles with perforated bases, on which to cook and lift out fragile food, other methods have to be employed. One of the best is simply a sling of butter muslin. If a large square of butter muslin is put in the base of a big pan, a fish can be poached in it and lifted out on the fabric every bit as easily as it could in an old fish kettle. The same goes for any other fragile food.

FRENCH DRESSING

Instructions on making French dressing always tell you to stir the ingredients together; but it's very much easier to put them all in a screw-top jar and shake well. It mixes better and it's in a jar ready to store.

FROSTING FRUIT

Frosting fruit perhaps ought to go in the children's chapter, as it's a lovely job to give children if you are preparing for a party or Christmas dinner and they aren't quite old enough to join in the major cooking. Grapes, cherries and strawberries look especially pretty, but the frosting needn't be limited to fruit: you can also frost flowers and leaves. Wash and dry any fruit well. Beat up an egg white with 2 tablespoons of water and brush it on to whatever you're frosting with a fine paint brush; then sprinkle or dip the surface in castor sugar and leave your handiwork to dry on a tray of greaseproof paper.

You can use this method to make decorations, or serve frosted fruit with coffee – see 'Dessert Avoidance', p. 242.

If you prefer to have glazed fruit, just heat 1 lb (500 g) of sugar and ¼ pint (125 ml) of water together very gently in a large pan, until the sugar has completely dissolved. Then bring it to a rolling boil and cook it until a little dropped in cold water forms a crisp droplet. Let it cool very slightly, dip in your fruit, and leave it to cool on greaseproof paper.

FROZEN FOOD

Closing Packets
Some people, especially the elderly, find it hard to twist those little wire ties to get a good grip on a plastic bag. The solution is simply to close the bag with a plastic clothes peg instead.

Cutting
The only easy way to cut through frozen food is with a heavy cleaver. Failing that, or if you want to cut off smallish pieces, use a saw-bladed knife – such as a bread knife – and, if it is really tough-going, heat the blade in boiling water from time to time.

Drying
When blanching and freezing fresh vegetables, there shouldn't be much water left on or they clump together, making it difficult to get out small quantities. A good way to dry them is to give them a whirl in a salad spinner.

Layering
It's useful to freeze chops, hamburgers and so on separately, so you never have to defrost more than you need. All you need do is place greaseproof paper, or the paper from inside cereal packets, between the slices of meat. Simple cakes, like tea breads, can be sliced in advance and layered in the same way for easy access.

FRUIT

Cooking
The acid from some fruit can help to clean blackened aluminium saucepans. This may improve the saucepan, but it doesn't do a lot for the flavour of the fruit. Acid foods should really be cooked in enamel or stainless steel saucepans, for there are indications that traces of aluminium drawn into food by acidity could be harmful.

Grape Pipping
The pips can be taken out of grapes with a quick twist of
the curved end of a well-scalded hair pin.

Ripening
Ripe fruit gives off a gas which has the effect of speeding
up the ripening of other fruit around it. So if you have one
ripe piece of fruit and want to ripen up a whole bag full,
put the ripe fruit in the paper bag and close it to trap the
gas. Conversely, if you want to avoid over-ripening fruit,
keep the less ripe fruit well away.

It has also been claimed that the ethylene gas given
off by apples will act on potatoes and keep them from
sprouting. There is some truth in this. Under certain conditions it will: the snag is that if the conditions are wrong,
it can have the opposite effect and speed up sprouting. So
it isn't a technique you can employ at home. Instead you
may have to make the best of a bad job and, if you have
a garden, just plant your sprouting potatoes instead.

GLACÉ FRUIT

It saves time to use a wet knife when chopping glacé fruit.
It sticks far less to a wet knife than to a dry one.

GRAVY

If you put at least a couple of unpeeled onions, with their
roots removed, in the roasting tin with meat, the sugary
juices which ooze from them and brown will add a delicious
flavour to the gravy and provide gravy browning. You can
then take the onions from their skins and eat them with
the meat.

HERB STORING

Basil, more than any other herb, carries in its aromatic
leaves the taste of summer; a flavour doubly welcome in
the dark days of winter when its delicately pervasive flavour

recalls holidays in Italy and meals in the sun. The best way to keep it for winter is to place freshly picked, clean dry leaves on a biscuit tray in the freezer; when the leaves are frozen, pack them in a plastic bag. The texture of the leaves is lost in freezing, but the flavour remains and is infinitely better in dishes than dried basil. Two other special flavours of summer can also be frozen like this – dill and coriander. And root ginger, which is always useful to have to hand, can be peeled and frozen too.

Dill is a perfect partner for potatoes; another way to keep it for the winter is to chop it up and beat it into butter. The butter can then be shaped into rolls, wrapped in greaseproof paper and frozen, ready for slicing on to winter potatoes. Alternatively, dill can be beaten into sour cream for using on jacket potatoes. Parsley can also be kept like this.

If you lack a freezer, basil can be kept for winter by chopping it finely and covering it with fine cooking oil. This preserves the flavour perfectly, but you do have to keep it in a refrigerator and make sure that the basil stays under the oil. If it comes to the surface, it goes mouldy easily.

ICINGS

Butter Icing

A way to make rich chocolate, or coffee, butter icing even richer and more luscious is to beat an egg yolk into it. One egg yolk will enrich enough icing to fill and cover a cake from a 7 in (17 cm) tin. Add two yolks and the icing is luxury itself. Beat in the yolk(s) as soon as the sugar and butter are thoroughly creamed together.

The egg makes the icing set slightly less firmly, so it's a good idea to keep the cake in a cool place until just before it is served.

Chocolate Caraque

The classic way to produce those wafer-thin curls of chocolate which professionals use to decorate cakes is to melt the chocolate (see 'Chocolate', p. 238), pour it on to a flat surface (the underside of an upside-down cake tin will do) and let it set. Then you cut diagonally into the chocolate to make the thinnest possible slices, which will curl automatically as you cut them. A far easier method is to use one of those Scandinavian cheese slicers, rather like a fish slice with a blade in the centre. If you draw one of those across the surface of the chocolate you produce immaculate curls in a fraction of the time it takes to cut them with a knife.

If you want little crumbles of chocolate to put round the side of a cake rather than real caraque, all you have to do is run a potato peeler down the side of an ordinary block of chocolate. The easiest way to coat the sides of a cake with these is to cover the sides in butter icing and roll the cake over the chocolate crumbs BEFORE you ice the top.

Dusting with Sugar
The simple way to dust small cakes with icing sugar is to put the icing sugar in one of those little perforated double-sided teaspoons used for infusing tea.

Piping
If you have to hold an icing bag with one hand while you try to spoon icing into it with the other, the chances are that most of the icing will end up near the top of the bag – where you want it to be clean to hold – rather than by the nozzle where it should be. An excellent method, which was sent to me by a listener to 'Woman's Hour', avoids this. Instead of holding the bag, put it, nozzle down, into a tall jar and fold the bag back over the edge of the jar so that the lower section of the bag is fully open and ready for you to spoon in the icing. If the weight of the icing pushes the bag down, you can clip it to the edge of the jar with a couple of clean plastic clothes pegs.

To dry the icing bag after washing it, just slip it upside down over a milk bottle and leave it to dry in the air.

Royal Icing
One of the less thoughtful British traditions is that of topping cakes with rock-like royal icing on all those occasions to which elderly relatives are invited – weddings, christenings and Christmas – thus serving them with a veritable obstacle course for false teeth (or indeed teeth of the standard variety). A kinder royal icing is made by adding ½–1 teaspoon of glycerine for every 1 lb (500 g) of icing sugar. The glycerine is perfectly edible (it's used in sweets) and holds just enough moisture in the icing to make it reasonably easy to eat, without spoiling its other qualities.

Smoothing Royal Icing
Some people are less then adept at getting a completely smooth surface on royal icing (myself among them) and, if you find it hard, it is worth remembering that what is really needed is a CONSISTENT surface. One 'Woman's Hour' listener achieved this ingeniously by sprinkling icing sugar on a clean tea towel which was woven in a waffle pattern, laying it on the moist surface of the icing, and running a rolling pin over it so the waffle design was pressed into the surface of the cake.

JELLY

To turn out a jelly easily, dip the mould VERY BRIEFLY in hot water. Rinse a plate in water, put it over the mould and, holding the two firmly together, turn them upside down. If the jelly doesn't land smack in the middle of the damp plate, the thin film of water should allow you to slide it to the correct position.

LETTUCE

My statement in *Supertips to Make Life Easy* that a peeled potato in the water helped a lettuce to crisp up fastest brought protesting letters from readers saying, 'What about coal?' So I experimented to see whether coal was

better than a potato. Having exercised stringent fairness –
even to the point of comparing the effects of each on
different sections of the same lettuce leaf – I find there is
little to choose between them. A lump of coal in the water
or a peeled and chopped potato will each crisp a lettuce
much faster than plain water. So will a drop of vinegar. So
why not use whichever you have to hand.

If you don't have a salad spinner, there are two other
ways to get the worst of the water off the leaves. Put a
small quantity of lettuce in a clean tea-towel, hold the
towel by the corners with one hand and swing it round and
round in rapid circles. The water will fly everywhere, but
the lettuce will be drier.

If you have a large quantity of lettuce, you can go one
further and put it in a clean pillow slip and give it a quick
spin in the spin-drying programme of the washing machine.
This method should only be used in emergencies and at
the last minute, for, though it dries the lettuce rather well,
the vigour of the washing machine can bruise the leaves
and they would go brown if left about too long.

MANGOES

Ripening
Mangoes are often on sale when they are under-ripe, but
like many other fruit they will ripen quite well at home.
Just wrap them up in several layers of paper – newspaper
will do – and keep them in a reasonably warm place. As
the heat from cooking rises, a fairly high kitchen shelf is
ideal. Look at them every day to see if they are ripe. The
delicious perfume of ripe mango should greet you as you
open the paper and they will be slightly soft to touch.

Eating
The considered opinion of my family is that the best
possible place to eat a mango is in the bath – an exotic
combination of steam and lusciously dripping juice – but
not all families are so decadent.

For the less sybaritic, there are two ways to handle this

perfect fruit. If a mango is very ripe you can treat it rather like an avocado pear. You cut it all the way round as you would an avocado, then hold it between your two hands and smoothly twist the two halves in opposite directions. If it is ripe enough, both halves will come loose from the stone; if it isn't, then the riper half will part from the stone and the other half retain it. The flesh can then be scooped out and eaten with a teaspoon.

The other way is to stand the mango on end and, with a very sharp knife, slice off each of the flatter sides. If each cut is positioned about ¼ in (5 mm) away from the centre of the fruit, the knife will slide neatly down the outside of the stone and cut off two perfect 'boats' of mango. The section of flesh which is left surrounding the stone can be carefully cut free, skinned, diced and heaped on each of the 'boats'.

MARINADES

The quantity of liquid given for most marinades simply doesn't cover the amount of meat in the dish. To get round this put both the marinade and the meat straight into a strong plastic bag. The meat should then be completely covered by the marinade, but even if it isn't, it's far easier to turn the bag and marinade the other side than to turn individual pieces of meat in a dish.

MEAT CARE

Modern methods of cattle and poultry rearing, and abattoir practices, mean that more and more meat and poultry is contaminated with the salmonella bacteria which causes food poisoning. Cooking kills the bacteria, but cooked meat can easily be reinfected by contact with uncooked meat, or with knives, boards or hands which have touched it. Yet it's not unusual to see a butcher gut a chicken and then turn and slice ham, giving his hands the merest wipe in between. We may need to eat a peck of dirt before we die, but the saying could have more sinister meaning if the dirt contained this bacteria. It is safer not to buy cooked meat from butchers who serve it from the same counter as raw meat. In the kitchen it's worth taking care that the two are kept well apart and that anything which touches raw meat is well washed before being used on cooked meat.

MELBA TOAST

Delicate, curling slices of melba toast are a wonderfully easy addition to a meal when you're serving soup or pâté. They take almost no time to make, yet give the impression that you have taken a lot of trouble. You simply toast a slice of bread in the normal way, cut off the crusts, and hold it firmly in place with the flat of your hand while you slice through between the two toasted sides – to make two much thinner slices. This much can be done in advance. Then, when you need it, you just toast the uncooked sides of the split slices. The only tricky part is keeping an eagle eye that you don't burn these extra-thin slices.

MERINGUES

For most purposes there is no difference between cane sugar and beet sugar. Chemically they differ only in minute quantities of trace elements, but these slight differences do seem to make a difference when it comes to meringues. Many people find that those made with cane sugar are better; and, for reasons which even the major sugar refiners can't explain, the same applies to jam.

MINCERS

Mincers have a nasty tendency to spill the food in unwanted directions. The way to stop this is to attach a plastic bag firmly over the outlet with a rubber band – then the food can be minced straight into it without a crumb spilling.

MINT SAUCE

I heard that some acquaintances kept mint through the winter for sauces by chopping it finely and covering it with golden syrup. When I tried it, I found that with a little seasoning and a touch of vinegar it did indeed make a good mint sauce. It seems a splendidly trouble-free way to keep the mint, and my test pot has kept perfectly for over a year in a warm kitchen.

MOUSSES

At their best, mousses should look frothily excessive, standing above the bowl like cold soufflés; there is something inhospitable about a mousse lurking in a bowl, unable to raise its head above the edge. To get the right effect, choose a soufflé dish which is slightly too small for the mousse and tie a band of greaseproof paper very tightly round it, so a collar stands a couple of inches above the rim. Then pour in the mousse so it rises above the bowl and is held in by the paper. Just before you serve it, you can peel off the paper and leave the mousse standing proudly above the rim.

OIL STORING

In Italy they say that oils, like herbs, keep longer in the dark. Those who have their own olive groves put the oil into dark bottles – an argument in favour of buying large quantities of olive oil in tins rather than in bottles.

ONION HIDING

Some families suffer from having one member who turns his or her nose up at food the moment a piece of onion is detected, but will eat it with gusto provided they don't *see* any onion. An ingenious solution given to me by one housewife is secretly to peel and liquidize a number of onions when everyone is out of the house and then freeze the onion purée in very small quantities in an old ice-cube container. She can then pop an innocent-looking block of onion into her soups and stews without her family being any the wiser. It seems that her 'onion-hating' husband has been eating onions for years, quite unawares, and congratulating her on her cooking. Of course, it isn't only onions which can be treated this way, but one does have to be careful to distinguish between dislikes and allergies.

ORANGE SKINNING

The quick way to skin an orange for a fruit salad is to cut a slice from one end, so that you cut off both the pith and the skin enclosing the segments. Then cut round and round the orange in a spiral, so that the pith and inner skin come off in a continuous piece. You will then have an orange with only the segment divisions left. It can either be sliced as it is or, with a small, very sharp knife, you can cut each segment from the skin to either side of it to produce absolutely skin-free sections of orange. Which method is the better depends on how you wish to use it afterwards.

There is usually a little flesh on the spiral of peel and the juice from this can be squeezed out with your thumbs and added to the pieces of orange.

PASTRY

Baking
To get a glossy top to a pie, all you need do is brush it with egg beaten with a pinch of salt before it goes in the oven.

Flaky pastry rises best if cooked at a high temperature in a steamy atmosphere. The steam can be created by damping the baking sheet or by putting a dish of water in the bottom of the oven.

Choux pastry also seems to like steam. This is usually provided by a wet baking sheet, but in her invaluable book, *Talking About Cakes*, Margaret Bates describes her discovery that putting éclairs and 'snowballs' to cook under a cover, such as an inverted baking tin, improves them enormously. It appears to trap the steam and make them even larger and lighter, though they do take about twice as long to cook. As soon as any choux pastry emerges from the oven, poke a skewer into the centre to let the steam out, otherwise it may go soggy in the middle.

It's worth remembering that the crispness of any pastry depends on the heat that gets to it. Metal conducts heat well, but china and pottery don't – so don't expect good pastry if you bake a flan in one of those elegant china flan dishes. They may look lovely in colour supplements, but the proof of real cooking is in the eating, not just in the looking.

Rolling

Rolling out pastry needs a clean surface and is a messy business, even if you do take my tip and use cold water to clear up afterwards. If you want to avoid the mess, or are short of clean space, or simply have rather crumbly pastry, try rolling it out between two large sheets of plastic. A friend of mine swears by this and says the crackly type of plastic is best. She has a circle the size of her baking tin drawn on the plastic, so she can easily see when the pastry is the right size; she claims the great advantage is that you can use the plastic to hold crumbly pastry in a neat sheet when you move it to the tin, and then just peel the paper off when it's in place.

I find that though this certainly works, and saves a lot of mess, it makes the actual rolling slightly harder as the plastic tends to slide about. The only way round this is to use a really large sheet which will drape off the edge of the work surface; you then have to lean firmly against this end as you work, to stop it moving – the only situation I can think of where a touch of paunch would be an advantage.

PEACHES

At the end of their season peaches are often a touch flavourless and woolly. But you can transform them into something delicious by peeling them and marinading them for a day in red wine and a little sugar.

PEARS

Ripe pears need to be kept in a refrigerator – at room temperature they rapidly turn woolly and inedible. If you have too many for the refrigerator, you can peel, core and liquidize them. The pulp makes a most delicious sorbet.

PEPPER

Ground pepper, like any other spice, tends to lose its aroma with keeping. To help it keep its aroma longer, put a few whole peppercorns in the container with it.

PINEAPPLE EYES

If you look at a pineapple, you'll find the eyes grow round in a spiral. So, if you want to get the most from a pineapple, remove the eyes by cutting diagonal channels round the fruit. Then cut off the remaining skin and slice it.

If thrift isn't a consideration, it is even easier just to cut the skin off in thick slices, taking the eyes with it.

POTATOES

Cooking

The vitamins and minerals in potatoes are drawn out by water. So the longer potatoes are soaked in water after peeling, and the more water you cook them in, the more goodness you lose. Luckily there's a limit to how much the water can absorb; so if you use a small amount of water, most of the goodness stays in the potatoes. This means it's best to put the potatoes in the pan and just add enough

water to cover them, instead of throwing them into a
boiling sea of liquid.

Steaming potatoes is the best way of all to keep in the
goodness; this is also a solution when the weather or soil
conditions have made them impossibly floury and prone
to breaking up.

Peeling

It's much less work to leave the skins on potatoes, and
they are far better for you. Even chips can be made without
removing the skin; the dark ends look really rather nice.

If you prefer to peel old potatoes, the peelings can have
a life of their own. Scrub the potatoes well before you peel
them, and deep fry the peel to make crunchy potato crisps.
You can eat them hot or cold sprinkled with salt, and
maybe a touch of curry powder.

Storing Packet Crisps

It sounds crazy to suggest putting something in the freezer
to keep it crisp, but it's perfectly logical. The process of
freezing extracts moisture from food – that's why ice builds
up inside a freezer – so if you want to keep potato crisps
crisp, put them in a freezer. Just make sure nothing else
sits on them, or they'll end up as potato crumbs instead,
and you won't enjoy them however crisp they are.

Beware of thinking that what is good for a crisp is good
for a raw potato. Cold changes the texture of potatoes and
rapidly causes them to produce sugars. So if you make
the mistake of storing your potatoes in the fridge, both
their texture and their flavour will be spoilt.

QUICKER BUTTER BLENDING

There are some recipes, such as those for pastry or short-
bread, in which the butter has to be rubbed into the flour
until it resembles breadcrumbs. This is done instantly in a
food processor, but is a tedious job if you haven't got one.
The quick way is to chill the butter thoroughly in a freezer
– or the refrigerator ice-box – and grate it into the flour.

Stir the flour occasionally as you grate it in, so it won't clump together; it will then rub in remarkably easily. There is also the bonus that, as the butter stays colder this way, you get even crisper pastry.

RADISHES

The best way to deal with the ridiculously large bunches of radishes which shops insist on selling is to cut them all from the bunch, leaving about an inch of stalk on each – they keep a better flavour with a bit of stalk. Then put them in a polythene bag in the bottom of a refrigerator. That way they will keep their texture and flavour for some time and you can eat them at leisure.

RICE

Every rice-eating country has its own sovereign solution to the problem of cooking rice so that it is tender but separate. I personally put my faith in a method given by an elderly nanny from Ceylon. You can weigh the cupful of rice and adjust the quantity to suit your dish.

Wash a cup of long-grain or basmati rice very thoroughly in plenty of cold water, stirring it constantly with your hands so the loose starch is released into the water. Keep changing the water until you can stir the rice without the water clouding with starch. Then drain the rice and put it in a small casserole with 1 ½ cups of water, a tablespoon of cooking oil and a little salt, and cover it well. Put the casserole in the oven at 400°F (200°C), Gas Mark 6, for about 20 minutes, by which time the rice should be perfectly cooked and the liquid absorbed.

The great thing about that method is that it's so easy to make rice more interesting. Try frying a sliced onion and a chopped clove of garlic until just golden in a little butter and oil, then stirring in the uncooked rice. When the rice looks transparent add not only the water, but also a bouillon cube, a bay leaf, a couple of inches of cinnamon stick and two or three cloves and cardamoms. Then cook it as before.

If you have ordinary boiled rice which has been drained and has then clumped together, pour boiling water over it, stir it quickly to separate it, drain and serve immediately. If you want to reheat cold rice, use the same method, but let it stay a little longer in the water. Exactly the same method can be used for separating or re-heating pasta, but pasta is not at its best treated this way.

SALAD SERVING

The longer a green salad sits in its dressing, the mushier it will become. But the French have a neat way of getting round this problem which still allows them to prepare it in advance. They put the dressing in the bottom of the bowl, then place the crossed salad servers over it and rest the salad on the servers, well clear of the dressing. The salad can be tossed in the dressing just before serving.

SAUCE KEEPING

If you want to make a sauce or custard in advance and keep it hot for the meal, rinse a wide-necked thermos flask with hot water (this warms it up and the damp helps the sauce not to stick), then put in the sauce and cork it tightly. It shouldn't form a thick skin, such as you'd get if you left it in the saucepan, but if a slight skin forms, you can beat it in with a loop whisk before you tip out the sauce.

SAUSAGE COOKING

It was during a radio phone-in in Leicester that I discovered the easiest way to grill or fry sausages. A canny housewife rang me to say that she always pushes a skewer through her sausages, so it goes in one end and out the other. This does a number of things: it keeps the sausages straight, so you can turn and cook them evenly all round; it makes it easy to turn several sausages at a time; and, as the skewer heats up, the sausages are cooked from the inside as well as the outside, which saves fuel by slightly reducing the cooking time.

If sausages are put into cold water and brought to the boil before being fried, they are said to be far less likely to split. It's a difficult one to prove, as one never knows what the sausage would have done if one hadn't treated it that way – and in any batch of fried sausages there are always some which split and some which don't. But if splitting matters to you, it's worth a try.

SCONES

However good scones LOOK in country tea-shops, I am almost always disappointed and find they leave a dry after-taste in my mouth. The culprit is baking powder, which all too often has this effect in cakes as well. If you use self-raising flour (and no added raising agent) in scones, they never have this aftertaste; and if you mix them with sour milk or add a touch of lemon juice or vinegar to the mixture, they will rise beautifully. Another solution is to use plain flour, bicarbonate of soda and sour milk. On its own, bicarbonate of soda doesn't leave an aftertaste.

In cakes for which plain flour and baking powder are recommended, it is worth experimenting and seeing if they rise just as well with self-raising flour instead, for the taste will often be far better.

SERVING

When giving a party, it's easy to run out of containers. If you find yourself short of bowls, look for the cheapest ones the season has to offer. Pimentos with the tops cut off and the seeds removed make attractive holders for savoury dips. The same treatment given to a large pumpkin will convert it into a soup tureen, and scooped out melons make excellent bowls for fruit or salads.

If you have to use a vast bowl to serve a less than vast

amount of food, raise the food by putting an inverted plate in the bottom of the bowl.

Serving things prettily can make it seem as if you've taken far more time preparing a meal than you really have; in fact it's often just a matter of having a small touch of something the right colour and flavour to hand. Chopped parsley is an easy option on a whole range of meat and vegetables; a single THIN slice of lemon can make all the difference to fish or delicate meat; and a slice from a pimento-stuffed olive or a few thin rings of onion are equally effective with the right food. The most impressive decoration of all is piping. Yet it's very easy to beat chopped herbs into very soft butter, then pipe the butter into rosettes on greaseproof paper and freeze the rosettes until you need them. Top a plain grilled steak or chop with such a rosette and it instantly looks cordon bleu.

SPINACH

The way to prevent spinach becoming a repellent watery mess is to wash it well, removing all the coarse stalks and spoiled leaves, then cook it without water – it has enough of its own. Just put it in a closely covered saucepan with a hint of salt and cook it gently, turning it over from time to time, until it is JUST tender. Then drain it.

It is then nicest if tossed in a pan with some butter or cream to evaporate some of its moisture and give it extra flavour. But if you want to eat it plain, put an inverted saucer in the bottom of the bowl before you put the spinach in – that way any water it releases trickles down under the saucer and the spinach stays nicely dry on top. This trick is also worth using with marrow.

One of London's newest and smartest oriental restaurants thriftily serves spinach stalks as a separate vegetable. They are cooked in chicken broth with a touch of garlic; the broth is then thickened with cornflour. The result is delicious.

STEAMING

When buying a colander, it is economical to choose a metal one, as it can also sit on top of a saucepan and do duty as a steamer.

A little vinegar in the water reduces the discoloration of an aluminium pan when a pudding is being steamed in it.

STRAINING

When dishes call for liquid to be strained through muslin, you needn't worry about not having any muslin – one of those conical paper coffee filters will do very well instead. Just prop one up in a sieve and pretend it's muslin. The only limitation is that coffee filters can't handle large quantities.

STRAWBERRY JAM

Strawberry jam is often over-sweet and sets badly. To cure both these problems at once, a friend of mine adds the juice from rhubarb stewed without sugar.

SWISS ROLL

A Swiss roll will be far less likely to crack if you turn it out on to greaseproof paper while it's still quite hot and use the paper to help you roll it up. Let it cool as a roll, then unroll it carefully, spread on the filling and roll it up again.

TEA

Making
The simplest way to warm a teapot, if you have a kettle with a spout, is to hang the teapot on the spout while the water comes to the boil.

Special

If you have run out of decent coffee, or have guests who prefer tea after a meal anyway, you may like to try a tip from the Malabar restaurant in Notting Hill.

For a ½ pint (250 ml) jug, they put in a good-quality tea-bag, about 1 in (3 cm) of cinnamon bark, 4 cloves and 5 crushed cardamon pods. They then pour on boiling water and leave the mixture to infuse until the tea is a fine golden brown. With the right tea-bag, it is a subtle and delicious way to drink tea without milk and far more suited to the end of a meal than the sharp taste of tea with lemon. But you do need to stop the infusion at the right point. To do this they make the tea in one of those French glass coffee jugs called Le Cafetier, which has a filter plunger you press down when the tea (or coffee) is the right strength, trapping the tea-bag beneath it. An alternative would be to strain the tea off, when it's ready, into a hot jug. Though tea-bags are convenient in a restaurant, the mixture of spices can just as well be used with loose tea.

THERMOS CARE

The corks on wide-necked thermos flasks easily become contaminated by food and are difficult to clean thoroughly. So it's best to cover the cork with cling film each time the thermos is used, so it stays perfectly clean.

TOMATO SKINNING

When I was working on my book *Pasta for Pleasure*, I skinned and froze whole boxes of tomatoes so as to have fresh tomatoes to use in the sauces I tested during the winter. It was only after I'd done all the work that I discovered that tomatoes freeze perfectly with their skins on and – even better – need only be run under a hot tap to peel beautifully afterwards: the perfect solution for tomatoes for soups and sauces. But do peel them while they are still frozen solid; they are too mushy to handle easily once they thaw.

VEGETABLE PERFECTION

When I have people round for a meal I often bless a friend in the catering business who taught me how top restaurants produce perfectly cooked vegetables, with just a hint of crispness, with a minimum of effort. The trick is to prepare the vegetables and drop them into boiling salted water for JUST long enough to leave them slightly less cooked than you want them. Drain them rapidly and drop them into plenty of cold water to refresh them and get the heat out – if they stay hot they keep on cooking and lose their crispness. Then drain them again. All this can be done hours before they are needed, when you are feeling relaxed enough to time them perfectly. At serving time you just toss them in butter in a wide pan until they are heated through, which is a matter of moments. Rounds of courgettes or leeks, peas or mange tout, cabbage, carrots and French beans are all excellent by this method and you never have to wonder whether the vegetables are over-cooking while a talkative guest corners you.

WATER

Nowadays even water can be unpredictable. They add more chlorine in some areas than in others and water can also acquire peculiar flavours from contact with plastic pipes, certain types of tap washers, and even the insides of plastic kettles. The experts say that if water is in prolonged contact with any of these – say, sitting in the pipes over-night, or in a kettle between one boil-up and the next – it will draw out chemicals which, though perfectly harmless, may taste most unpleasant when they interact with the traces of chemicals like chlorine which have been used to purify the water. As the chemicals interact fastest when hot, you may only notice the flavour when water is boiled to make tea or coffee.

An obvious solution is to run the water for a while before drawing any for drinking and to put fresh water in the kettle each time. But if you want to be even more thorough, ask a chemist for some sodium thiosulphate, a harmless chemical which neutralizes chlorine. If you put 1 small crystal of it in a 2 pint (1l) jug of water, it should prevent any peculiar flavours. If you have to replace a tap washer, it may be worth making sure you use the kind which won't react with water. Unfortunately the only guarantee of this is to go to the people who manufacture taps; for though there are regulations controlling the type of washers which can be sold IN taps, there are none, as yet, controlling the standards of replacement washers sold in hardware stores.

Incidentally, if fish are using the water, rather than people, you can use sodium thiosulphate to neutralize the chlorine in an aquarium instead of a proprietory water conditioner. Use 3 crystals in a 5 gallon (22 l) tank.

WINE

Corking
The first time I made home-made wine I was alarmed to discover that none of the corks would fit in the bottles. In desperation I put them in a steamer to soften them – they then went in perfectly. Only later did I discover that steaming or boiling was the usual way to treat them.

Flies
The innocent-looking little fruit flies which make a beeline for wine have a curious property: they are sometimes called vinegar flies, for they will rapidly turn wine or beer into vinegar. This means that home-made wine which is waiting to be corked, or even wine left over from a meal and about to be kept for cooking, should be kept covered with cling film to prevent them flying in.

Left Over
If left-over wine goes sour, don't throw it away; it can be used instead of some of the vinegar in certain marinades and in cooking things like red cabbage.

YEAST

Fresh yeast (sometimes called compressed yeast) makes the best bread. For though dried yeast will rise perfectly well, it can have a slightly beery flavour. Many bakers will sell you fresh yeast if you ask for it, even though it isn't on display. If you have a freezer it's worth buying it in bulk (if you make bread regularly) and freezing it ready for use. The easiest way is to weigh out 1 oz (30 g) pieces and wrap and freeze each one separately; then put them together in a freezer box. This way you can find them easily and don't have to defrost more than you need.

YORKSHIRE PUDDING

The secret of perfect Yorkshire pudding is largely in the heat of the fat. Put the dripping in the pudding dish or pan and let it get smoking hot in the top of a hot oven before you pour in the batter.

ZEST

Normally I'm dead against one-job gadgets – they usually take up more space than they earn. I make an exception for a lemon zester. I had never heard of one until the deputy editor of 'Woman's Hour' asked me if I knew about them and assured me they were wonderful. As she's not the kind of woman to waste time on gimmicks, I found and bought one – and she has my blessing for suggesting it. At a stroke, its row of tiny sharp-edged holes will remove perfect strands of zest from the outer skin of any citrus fruit, without a trace of the bitter pith clinging to them. In a matter of moments you can garnish a fruit salad or ice cream with delicate strands of orange, or have slivers of lemon zest to add a piquancy to fish or veal.

You're Organized

I confess to writing this chapter with some hesitation, and very much at the request of others. The remark, 'Oh, you're so well organized,' from a friend or acquaintance, always leaves me wondering whether they know me less well than I suppose, or whether perhaps my efforts to stem the threatened disorder work better than I imagine.

Just as some people are born with the ability to eat anything and remain thin, while others wage a constant battle against their 'too too solid flesh', so I suspect some are born with a natural flair for tidiness and organization, while others must forever fight to keep at bay a rising tide of chaos. I am neither naturally tidy nor naturally slim, so I am an experienced fighter in the battle against both flab and disorder; anyone who has even the occasional skirmish with either has all my sympathy.

Half the battle is making things easy for yourself. Of course, that means deciding what you, and those around you, find difficult – even if it means admitting to the kind of laziness you may not be able to justify logically (but then who's logical?). For example, it's no good hanging a coat rack in the cupboard under the stairs, if you, or your family, will never take a coat further than a yard inside the front door, but a few hooks right beside the door might just stop everything ending up in a heap.

I am also convinced that most of us fail to become any tidier (or more houseproud, or thinner), not because we don't try hard enough, but because we try TOO hard. In one of those dreadful moments of clarity, we look at our surroundings, or our figure, with fresh eyes. And, seeing the truth, decide something has to be done and vow to take draconian measures. From that day on we will keep the place spotlessly clean and wonderfully tidy, or give up every fattening food we crave. Such large-scale resolutions may do great things for the soul – for a short while – but in practice they do very little for anything else. Human beings are simply not designed to acquire great bouquets of virtue all of a sudden. So within hours or days, the effort to be perfect becomes unbearable and we lapse into behaving just as we did before. Far easier, and far more effective, is the making of small resolutions. Decide that you will fold up and put away ONE garment when you take it off at night, or organize one area of your life, and it may become a habit which will spread to the rest of your days. So the tips in this chapter are all designed to help you iron out the little hassles which eat into your time. Once you've started using one time-saver, it should be easier to move on to the next.

BILLS

The very essence of any budget is cash flow – and a happy cash flow is when more money is flowing in than flowing out. You only have to organize the outflow a little to help this happy state along. The golden rule is that the later a bill can be paid, the better. The advantage of this is that if you are short of money it gives you time to find the cash, and if you have plenty it can be invested to earn you interest in the meantime. Though you should apply this rule only to large organizations which are geared to endure a proportion of late payments; small companies often have real cash-flow problems themselves and need prompt payment.

There are all kinds of ways of legitimately delaying payment: major bills like rates can usually be paid in instalments if you ask. If you buy a large item, like a refrigerator, some big stores will also let you pay in instalments, at no extra cost, especially at sale time – but beware of those who arrange loans; the rates are usually higher than those at your local bank.

Having an account at a shop delays payment for a month or so. And, though credit cards are often seen as an invitation to extravagance, they can be even greater money-savers. If you use a credit card to buy something on the first of the month, the bill won't come in until the month is over. You then have about a month in which to pay. So they have effectively lent you the money for two months without charging a penny of interest. That has to be good news. And if you had the money invested, in the meantime you were making money on the arrangement. The snag is that the interest is high if you accidentally go over the interest-free period without paying. The simplest way to avoid this is to write the cheque and send it off as soon as you get the account, but post-date the cheque for the 'pay by' date. That way you keep the money for as long as possible, but never incur any interest. I'm not saying the credit card companies LIKE you doing it that way, but it is well within the rules of the system – and, if they have the nerve to return your cheque for re-dating, you can tell them so, and ask them to file it till the given date.

BURGLARS

Burglar prevention is an expensive business, but there are a few relatively cheap measures which anyone can take. The majority of burglaries aren't done by experts, but by people who take an opportunity when they see it. If your house doesn't look like a good bet, they will pass it by.

A light or, better still, a couple of lights going on and off while you're out or away makes a casual burglar think twice. Inexpensive timer switches make this easy, but they are very under-used. Anyone who wants to be really thorough could tape-record a big dog barking and have the tape on the timer too. A friend of mine has a neatly printed notice by her door saying, 'Please face the camera when ringing the bell', which may well have deterred the odd burglar or two.

In addition to simple things, like actually remembering to cancel the papers and milk and lock up, you can have an arrangement with a neighbour that, if either goes away, the other will do a daily doorstep check and remove telltale free literature. If you are away for some time, arranging for a neighbour to park a spare car in front of your house at night is another easy precaution which costs nothing.

BUYING PLANTS

The trouble with plants is that one often orders them in one season and plants them in another. In the gap between the two some of the enthusiasm for the project may have waned. So, while the enthusiasm for ordering is still with you, make a plan of exactly where they will go. Then you can get them in with the minimum of time and thought when the time comes. And the bonus is that if you keep the plans, you have a record of what you put where. Then when the fruit trees produce a crop, you can jog your memory and discover which were eaters and which were cookers.

CAR

Life becomes a great deal easier if you plan for trouble where cars are concerned. Apart from obvious equipment like tissues, maps, restaurant, hotel and bed and breakfast guides, and an accident triangle, other items well worth carrying are a pair of transparent plastic gloves – invaluable if you need to fill up with petrol or do anything to the car when going somewhere smart – a spare coat and a dustbin liner. The dustbin liner can be used for unexpected rubbish from an impromptu picnic, as a disguise for something worth stealing if it has to be left in sight when the boot is full, or as an emergency rain cape. A penknife – for the picnic or for cutting the cape – is also useful, and so are a nail file, moist tissues such as Wet Ones, and a notebook for jotting down anything *en route* and for communicating with traffic wardens. Also I never go anywhere without a pair of jump leads in my car – it's too easy to forget to turn off one's headlights after going through a tunnel in the daytime.

CHILDREN

When nursing a feverish child or listening to his or her yells at an innoculation, it seems impossible that you will ever forget who was ill or who had the innoculation. But the awful truth is that, after several children and a number of feverish nights and innoculations, the whole lot can blend into one, so you are left with no idea who had chicken pox and who had measles, or whether any of them ever got tetanus boosters. So, even if you're certain you'll remember, it'll save time if you keep an index card for each child with his or her 'medical history' – then, when a school or doctor asks for one, you won't have a guilty feeling that you're getting it all wrong.

CLEANING

It's amazing the way people make life hard for themselves when it comes to cleaning. That dreadful old ethic which linked virtue with drudgery has meant that some families have two cars, but only one (often delapidated) washing-up cloth. But cleaning is like carpentry: to do it well you need the right tool for each job. To make life easy, I think every kitchen needs a sponge cloth for work surfaces, and ANOTHER for wiping up spills on the floor; a plastic washing-up brush of the type which has a straight edge at the end for scraping with (mops and cloths don't clean between the prongs of forks); a looped nylon scourer for scrambled egg and similar debris; soap-filled wire pads for metal saucepans; and a foam pad with a rough green scourer on one side for casseroles and for cleaning the sink itself. One of those foam/scourer pads should be next to every basin. They make far shorter work of cleaning it than a sponge cloth.

Of course people get used to working in a certain way and you may disagree with my list; but anyone's time is worth a great deal more than the cost of a few items to speed things up. And each one can have several lives. When the work-surface cloth is past its best, it can be pensioned off to wipe the floor; the looped nylon scourer cleans insects off the car in its old age; and the old foam scourer pads from the kitchen can be used on basins.

As dusting is one of those jobs which can be done in

odd moments – while waiting for the kettle to boil, or for toenail varnish to dry, for example – it also helps to have a duster hidden in every room.

For thorough cleaning, the secret is to have everything you need to hand. If you have to leave the room to get what you need for each new job, you'll get tired of walking to and fro and leave half the jobs not done. The best plan is to wear one of those gardening aprons which have a big pocket in the front. Then you can carry everything you need in the pocket – but put damp cloths into plastic bags. Failing that, there's the old-fashioned method of a box or basket which you carry from room to room. And if you are lucky enough to have someone doing the cleaning for you, it will save you money if they use the same system. If they don't have everything conveniently to hand, you could be paying more for walking time than for cleaning time.

Another way to cut down on the walking is to put a long extension lead on the end of the vacuum cleaners, so you can clean from room to room without a pause.

COOKING

Any experienced cook knows that it's almost as quick to cook for an army as for a couple. So anyone who has a freezer can save themselves a lot of work by cooking double and putting half in the freezer, whenever the food will freeze well.

CREDIT CARDS

Credit card companies always exhort you to keep a note of your card number. What they don't tell you is that the simplest way to do this is to photocopy them all on a single sheet. Then you have them all noted in one place if they are stolen – for if you lose one, you usually lose them all. If a handbag is stolen or a pocket is picked, credit cards aren't the only things which may go, so use the same method to note your passport number, social security number and numbers of any bank accounts, savings accounts, driving licences and so on.

Put the sheets where the rest of your household can find them if you have to phone up in an emergency – it's when you're out of the house that the cards will be stolen.

DO-IT-YOURSELF

If you don't know how much paint or paper it takes to decorate a particular room, you'll usually have to overestimate. But that extra cost need only happen once. If you make a note of just how much you used, you will be able to buy exactly what you need next time.

ENTERTAINING

Avoiding Repetition
After a memorable evening with one's friends, it's all too easy to imagine that you will remember who was there and what you gave them to eat. Three months later the memory may not be so vivid. So, if you don't want to risk repeating the same menu to a well-nigh identical group of guests, it saves a lot of memory cudgelling if you keep a notebook on whom you entertain and what you give them to eat.

Cutting the Work
Nobody needs me to tell them that the easiest way to cut the work is to pay somebody else to do it, but it's worth remembering that, provided the food is good, none of your guests will mind who made it. Nobody who's busy should be ashamed to use their local Indian, or other, take-away if it does a good job – and anyone who feels compelled to impress can always hide the containers and serve it as if it was all home-made.

Failing such a drastic short-cut, there are a number of other factors which make entertaining easier or harder. Organize yourself so as to include as many as possible of the former and as few as possible of the latter. This will mean spreading the work over days, or even weeks. And getting things done in advance means doing the little things, like making the French dressing, as well as doing the big dishes. Left to the last minute, little jobs eat into far more time than you'd expect. It's well worth making – and keeping – a list of all the things which have to be done everytime, such as laying the table and opening the wine. Then, if you're tired and a bit frantic, you'll be spared the worry of 'What have I forgotten?'.

The following dishes make a meal easier to organize:
 ones which can be prepared long in advance and frozen;
 ones which can be made at least twenty-four hours before they are needed;
 ones which combine meat and vegetables and rice, or beans or pasta – requiring only a salad to accompany them;
 ones which can be prepared a few hours in advance and served cold;
 ones which will keep without spoiling if guests are late;
 ones which are quick to prepare.

The following dishes make a meal harder to organize:
 those which require last-minute attention – especially tricky sauces;
 those which will spoil if they are not served at a particular time;
 those which can only be made just before they are eaten;
 those which must be served hot – especially if hot food is to be served at every course;
 those which take a long time to prepare;
 those which need a lot of vegetables or accompaniments.

That said, it's only fair to add that entertaining is not about being perfect, it's about having fun. Anyone who would *enjoy* cooking a hideously complicated meal which breaks all these rules should do so. If your guests find you unprepared and you have to shell the peas in the sitting-room, take comfort from the fact that, in addition to a marvellous meal, you are probably giving them a sneaking sense of superiority – which few human beings are averse to.

Fads and Fancies

Most people have at least one food they really detest (in case any of my friends are reading, mine is herrings) and some are genuinely allergic to certain foods. If you don't want to watch the dismal sight of a guest pushing to one side your choicest creation, or find yourself rushing to make an omelette for the vegetarian you unexpectedly discover in your midst, it's as well to ask every guest what foods he or she doesn't eat at the time when you invite them. Make a permanent note of it in the back of the book where you list who came to the house and what you cooked for them, then you will never have to ask them twice.

If you want to make people feel REALLY cherished, go one further and make a note of their other preferences: whether they drink coffee after a meal, or what they like instead, and whether or not they take sugar, and how much they put in. Note down their favourite drink before dinner, and make sure you are never out of it when they come. This way you could find yourself with a reputation as the hostess with the mostess even if your meals aren't always superb.

All that sounds horribly like advice from that notorious American book, *How to Make Friends and Influence People*, but the fact is that whether we like it or not, what people enjoy most isn't marvellous food or superb wine, but feeling that THEY matter. And if you are trying to give people pleasure when they come to your home, it's really rather reassuring to know that it's the little things, which take very little time, money or energy, which make all the difference.

A word of warning though: if someone claims something is their favourite food on earth, don't believe them unless it is something you HAVEN'T cooked for the meal – it could be an excessive compliment about a dish they secretly loathe. Even if they DO love it, don't give it to them every time they visit you – predictable food is never fun. And if they are under twenty, assume their taste may change at any time. Think how many grandmothers have caused anguish to their grandchildren by serving their 'favourite food' at every visit; when in truth it was only favourite for some fleeting period of toddlerdom.

Party Drink

It is always worth buying drink for a party from an off-licence which will supply free glasses. Many will also offer a discount on a bulk buy of drink – but only if you ask for it – and let you buy on a use or return basis, so you can get in a good stock without having to drink the left-overs for weeks. But, if you don't want to be left with a huge number of half-used bottles which you can't return, put the extra bottles (which you don't EXPECT to use) in a locked cupboard until they are needed. Some people can sense a closed bottle at a hundred paces and feel duty-bound to open it if it isn't locked away, however many others are in sight.

Parties are quite tiring enough without having to prise ice-cubes out of their trays. A few days ahead of time start stocking up plastic bags with ice-cubes, so you have more than enough to hand. The same, incidentally, applies if you have Americans coming to stay in anything but arctic weather: some can deplete an ice-tray faster than a cat drinks milk.

Quantities

If you are making a note of what you served people when they visited you, it's easy enough to make a note of the amount you cooked and whether it was the right quantity or too much or too little. That way you have an ever-growing reference book on how much your particular friends eat of your favourite dishes. For, if a dish tickles the tastebuds, people may eat far more of it than you could reasonably expect. I once made a double quantity of pilaf, plenty for sixteen normal helpings, so I wouldn't have to cook for the children next day – my plan went awry when my seven supper guests enjoyed it so much that they ate every last mouthful. Now I always assume people will eat double quantities of that dish, and I'm seldom wrong.

Keeping a record is particularly useful when it comes to

the quantities needed for large parties. The big problem when cooking in bulk is what I call the 'and a bit' rule. This is the one whereby five little new potatoes feed one person, but ten stretch to feed two and a bit people, and twenty feed five people not four – because the more people you have, the greater the chances of someone going easy on that particular food. So just multiplying up will always land you with more food than you need. (The opposite is true of drink: at a party some people always drink more than could reasonably be expected.) Parties get easier and easier to cater for if you make a note of exactly how much you cooked of each dish and how many people came. Then, after the meal, and before the family gannets have been at it, note how much was eaten and how much was left over.

FREEZER

Clearing

Even in the best-run homes, freezers can accumulate an assortment of unwanted or unidentified bags and packets, which, month after month, never quite suit the needs of the moment. Katherine Whitehorn has dubbed such packets UFOs – Unidentified Frozen Objects. One of the best solutions to this problem was long ago devised by a producer on 'Woman's Hour'. She suggested to her husband that if they ate their way through the contents of the freezer, instead of buying food in the normal way, the money they saved on the housekeeping over that time would buy them a short holiday in Paris. With the pleasures of French gastronomy ahead, they happily ate their way through the most extraordinary combinations, saved a great deal of waste, and had a fabulous weekend away.

Of course, it doesn't HAVE to be a stay in Paris. You can plan for a night at the opera or a week in Salcombe if it's more to your taste. But the treat must be enticing enough to persuade your family to eat what they would otherwise shun – even if it IS sardine sandwiches and ancient trifle.

(Assuming, of course, that whatever it is hasn't exceeded its safe storage life.)

Keeping Track of the Food

There are two good systems for knowing what you have in a freezer. The least demanding system is to write two identical labels and put one on the food and another on the outside of the freezer cabinet – grouping foods of the same type together. Then you can see at a glance what you've got; all you need do is strip off the duplicate label when you remove the food. Turn a corner of the label under as you stick it on, so it's easy to remove when the time comes. There's just one problem: the paint on your freezer may not like the constant sticking on and pulling off. But the other side of the coin is that if the freezer is out in a garage the labels will, in a way, protect it from rust.

Another way is to keep a freezer book in which you list everything you buy and delete it as you use it. It's useful to divide the book into sections, so that all the meat is listed in one place, fruit in another, vegetables in another and so on; then you don't have to wade through pages of frozen peas to discover whether you have anything for pudding. If you cut the tops of the pages in steps, like an address book, you can find each section quickly. The snag is that its usefulness depends on everyone in the household being organized enough to cross things out as they use them.

Labelling

The labels for sticking on frozen food are a silly price. If you don't mind the food looking rather less tidy, a strip from a reel of masking tape is cheaper and allows you to write larger and add any details you want. Make sure those details include the date. Masking tape is also far easier to remove from plastic boxes, or the top of your freezer cabinet, than a conventional label.

Power Cuts

If there is any chance of a power cut while you are out or away, put some ice-cubes in a plastic bag and put the bag in the top of your freezer. If you find they have changed shape, you'll know there was a cut long enough to thaw some of your food.

Space Saving

An enormous amount of space is wasted in freezers because the containers which are put into it are all shapes and sizes. You can get far more in if the containers are straight-sided; also, as they sit neatly cheek by jowl, warm air can't circulate between them when you open the freezer, so money is saved on the electricity bills. The neatest containers of all are the rectangular cartons from milk or fruit juice. They may look decidedly odd, but opened up, well washed and clearly labelled, they do a far better job than most plastic containers. Stick them firmly closed with masking tape, but make sure you store them upright until the contents are hard.

GETTING THERE

As I have almost no sense of direction, one of my most useful files is labelled, 'How to Get There'. In it I put all the directions friends have given me on how to find their off-the-beaten-track houses. To those, I add the simplified maps of towns and cities which good bookshops and local radio stations often give away. Then I never have to ask anyone for directions twice.

GUARANTEES AND INSTRUCTIONS

Any instructions about machinery which need to be referred to frequently are best kept in a plastic folder stuck to the side of the machine – or nearby. For the rest, it makes things simpler if all instructions and guarantees are filed together, in a place known to the whole family. And

it's worth noting the serial number of all appliances on the
guarantees in case of theft.

HOUSE SELLING

Every house with a garden, and any flat with window
boxes, is likely to look its best at a particular time of the
year. If there's any possibility that you might move within
twelve months, it's worth taking a set of really good photographs of the outside when it's looking its best. Then, if
you put it up for sale in an off season, you can use the
photographs to convince prospective buyers of its delights
in the months to come – far more persuasive than going
on about the daffodils like some would-be Wordsworth.

JUST REWARDS

One of the nicest tips I have ever been sent came from a
woman who said that chores get done much more easily if
one makes a list of them and has the satisfaction of crossing
them off as soon as they are done. She added that the list
should have the nastiest chores at the top – so you get them
over and done with early and don't have them looming over
you – and, best of all, it should have rewards included in
it. So, when you've done a certain number of jobs, you
come across some instruction like 'Have a cup of tea', or
'Ring a friend and have a chat', or whatever else you
enjoy.

This suggestion is as sensible as it's charming: all too
often the days when people achieve the most are the ones
when they feel least satisfied. All they can see are the
things they HAVEN'T done and, instead of enjoying the
breaks they took (and needed), they feel guilty about
them. But build them into your plan of action and you
can't possibly feel guilty – though it may take a bit of
self-control to get yourself back to work after the break.

I also suggest that anyone doing a mammoth task, which
will take more than a day to complete, should stop BEFORE
they've done as much as they feel like doing. If you drive

yourself until you are dropping and are sick to death of the job, you will be in no mood to start again the next day, and the rest may never, ever, get done. But if you stop while you still have at least a vestige of enthusiasm for the task, that/enthusiasm will be there to get you going again. And the tougher the job, the better the reward you should plan to give yourself when it's done. It isn't only OTHER people who should be dangling carrots in your path.

Lesser Evils
Another tip I like is that when you really can't face doing a dreaded task, you should think of an even nastier one which you ought to do instead – then you will get down to the lesser of two evils with a sense of relief.

LETTER POSTING

If there's a place by the front door where everyone in the house puts the letters they want to post, and the first person to go out acts as postman, letters tend to reach the postbox rather sooner than when there's no system at all.

MAGAZINE CLIPPING

If you or your family like to cut articles out of magazines before throwing them away, it's easy to end up with a heap of magazines which can't be thrown away because somebody just MIGHT want something from them. To avoid this, put one of those self-adhesive address labels (cheapest by the roll) on the front of each magazine as it comes into the house. Then anyone who spots an article they want can write the name and page on the label, and whoever is doing the throwing away can clip whatever is needed. If people don't note their cherished articles on the front, the thrower-away can't be blamed.

If you keep magazines or journals for reference, and they don't have an index on the front cover, listing articles of special interest on a label on the cover also saves a lot of leafing through to find them later.

MEDICINE

Repeat Prescriptions
If you take medicine regularly, and live the kind of life where you might have to go away suddenly at any time, it's worth taking a photocopy of each prescription and packing it when you travel. Then if your return is delayed and you need a repeat prescription before you return home, you can show the photocopy to the local doctor and he or she will know what to give you. But do remember that you need your most recent prescription: your doctor could have changed the dose without mentioning it to you.

Taking It Correctly
Taking a lot of different medicines can be a confusing business. With the elderly there is a risk that they will take a second dose, forgetting they took the first one. Psychologists are working on all kinds of systems to make it easier for patients. Meanwhile, a simple home-made system is to use one of the pages of rows of little plastic pockets which are designed to hold photographic slides or a coin collection. Each pocket can be labelled with the day and the time that a particular medicine, or group of medicines, has to be taken: 'Monday breakfast' on one, 'Monday lunch' on the next, or whatever is appropriate. Then the pills can be allocated to their proper places by the patient, or a relative or friend, and they can see at a glance what has been taken and what hasn't.

MENDING

The counsel of perfection is to mend each garment as you finish ironing it. If you keep some needles and cotton near the ironing board, putting in the odd stitch here and there is a matter of moments, because you always catch holes before they grow and buttons when they are beginning to get loose. Then everything is put away in perfect order ready to wear next time.

Failing that, put everything that needs mending in one

place -- then, when you have a spare half hour watching television, you can instantly lay your hands on whatever needs attention.

The best way to be sure you can instantly find a button when you get round to replacing it is to have a box clearly marked 'Buttons Off Clothes' into which everyone in the household puts any buttons which come off. If they are put in 'safe' places or tucked into a general button box, you may as well give them up for lost.

MESSAGES

Taking phone messages is one thing; making sure people get them is another. Any household with teenagers in it which fails to establish that all messages will be written down and put in a set place EVERY time may be at the mercy of teenage imagination as to what might be appropriate. In my house we use the pads made by 3M which have a slightly adhesive top to each page which will adhere to anything. That way notes can be stuck on walls and doors where nobody can miss them.

MOVING HOUSE

First Night Blues

The first night in a new home should be a night for celebration. It won't be unless you remember to pack everything you need for it in one box. Experienced movers say you shouldn't stick to necessities like soap and towels, but, as you're bound to be tired and need a fillip, should also make sure you include a few treats, like delicious snack food. Whether you also put in a teapot and kettle or a corkscrew and bottle is up to you.

A further precaution is to come to an agreement as to whether the previous owners will or won't take the light bulbs with them. A friend who thoughtfully left all her bulbs behind for the next owner moved into her new home one Sunday afternoon in winter to find that every single bulb had been taken. It was a black start.

Freezer Moving

It is tempting to stock up on food before a move, but it is wise to do just the opposite. The stock in a freezer should be run down as low as possible. Freezers can become fragile with age and may not take kindly to being moved. The shaking *en route* can bring them to an untimely end. With all the expense of moving, the last thing you want is a freezer full of rotting food.

House Warming

A house-warming party gets off to a better start if your friends can find you easily. Since most British house-numbers are positioned so that they are invisible at night, you can make things easier for them by putting a coloured bulb in the porch or front window and warning them to look out for a bulb of that colour.

Knowing What's What

Anyone who has lived in a house for a while knows its little ways: the cistern which won't flush unless you pull it twice; the correct position of the stopcock for the water system; the address of the only electrician in the area who understands the wiring, and so on. Very few people volunteer such information to the new owner, but (once you've signed the agreement) few people mind passing on their expertise if you ask them. Get the previous owners to label the stopcocks and leave you those addresses, then you won't have your arrival spoilt when the central heating won't work and all the lights fuse and you don't know where to begin to get either sorted out.

Placing Furniture

It can be difficult to envisage familiar furniture in new surroundings. One excellent solution, for those with exact minds, is to measure up the new rooms and make a scale drawing of each on graph paper. You can then cut out scale outlines of your furniture and move each piece effortlessly around the rooms until it fits nicely. This may seem fiddly, but it's far less tiring than moving the furniture itself when you change your mind about its position after the removal men have left.

Once you know where every piece will go, it will save a great deal of trouble if each one is labelled with a sticky label. Give each room a letter of the alphabet, and stick that letter on the door of the room. Then put the same letter on the sticky label of everything that should go into it. Then even the least competent removals firm should be able to put everything where it belongs. But do be careful that you don't put labels on any surface which could be damaged by them.

Sorting Out
Experienced movers often say that the secret of easy moving is to sort out what you don't need BEFORE you leave the old house, and throw it away, instead of waiting until you find it won't fit in the new one.

Who Pays What for Which
With stamp duty in mind, all sorts of curious arrangements are reached regarding payments for fixtures and fittings. So it's easy to get a false impression of what the previous owners actually are leaving behind. Discuss it in detail and ask them to give you a list. That way you can be sure you are both on the same wavelength. Don't forget to include the garden. There are stories of people arriving to find the rhododendrons they loved so much have vanished with the owners.

PHOTOGRAPHS

If photographs come back from the printers when you're too busy to put them in an album, at least put the details on the back of each photo and date it. It's amazing how alike different holidays look after a while. And if you're too busy to date the photos, at least date and name the packet you keep them in. If you have to rely on who was wearing what when, it can take hours to get a backlog of photos in chronological order.

POST PROBLEMS

There's no denying that things do get lost in the post. If you might need to prove that you put something in the post, you don't have to go to the expense of sending it by registered post or recorded delivery. Ask the post office to give you a certificate of posting. You just write the destination of the letter or parcel on a form and have it stamped by the post office. This service is free and it's well worth using if you are returning goods to a company and might be charged for them if they don't arrive.

If you need to send through the post a document which would be hard to replace, take a photocopy of it and – if possible – send the photocopy, not the original. If you have to send the original, file the photocopy safely.

PRESENT GIVING

In an ideal world, present giving is a delight: you think fondly of the recipient and put time and effort into choosing something to give them pleasure. In reality, presents often have to be given to people we do NOT think of with any marked fondness; and there can be moments in one's life when there may not be time even to think properly about presents for one's nearest and dearest. In these circumstances a bit of organization is essential.

Knowing When
The first problem is simply remembering the occasions. Only those with amazing memories, or very little else to think about, are likely to remember all the birthdays, anniversaries and other special days of all their friends and family. There are two solutions to this. One is to opt out entirely: you thereby at least offend everyone equally, but they get used to your omissions after a while. The alternative is to develop a system. The most labour-saving, but most impersonal, is a good secretary (male or female) who does all the remembering and present-buying for you. The next best is to have a calendar on which all such dates

are marked, and routinely scan it each month. One person suggested to me that it should go on the back of the lavatory door – on the grounds that this was the only place in the house where you had time to sit and stare. She has a point.

Listing

Present-giving is yet another of the areas where a list makes life a lot easier. It's a good idea to keep a list of who gives YOU what for Christmas and birthdays as well as what you give them. This means that, if anyone gives you something which suits them better than it suits you, it can go in the present cupboard with no risk that you will accidentally give it back to them the next time they are due for a gift – which is very easy to do if you aren't careful. It also helps you avoid the trap of always giving the same present to someone year after year.

Organizing Shopping

Even having a list of the dates fails if you have no time to buy the gifts. Ideally, you need to have one place where you can keep things until the day comes around, so that you can buy presents whenever it suits you and tuck them away until they are needed, with no worry that you'll forget where they are. This can also be a money-saver. Aunt Jemima's favourite scent for Christmas can be bought at leisure, and duty free, on the way to or from a summer holiday, and you can pick up the gardening book for Uncle George when you see it remaindered at half-price. January and July sales are equally grist to the mill and, though it may SOUND mean to buy in the sales, it actually means you can give nicer presents and give them on time – for the money goes further and they are never delayed because you are too busy to go shopping. So the recipient benefits as much as you do.

Few things are more embarrassing than finding that the supper you are going to is actually a birthday party and you have nothing to give, or having people arrive unexpectedly at Christmas with presents when you have nothing for

'
them. The solution is to have a selection of general-purpose
presents tucked in a cupboard. What goes into it depends
on your purse and the type of friends you have: it can
range from pencils with silly things on the end for young
children, to bottles or delicacies of various kinds, or the
odd mink or two (whoever refused a mink, even if it wasn't
her size?).

Planning A head
The most expensive occasions for present-givers – eight-
eenth birthdays, major wedding anniversaries and so on –
are happily predictable. And some of the nicest presents
only take a little planning. Collecting the birthday or
wedding-day issue of a particular newspaper for each year
after the event is easy and makes an interesting gift when
the birthday or anniversary comes round. Even better, a
bottle of port put down every year up to a coming of age
costs relatively little over the years, but makes a splendid
gift on the day.

Receipts
When buying clothing as a present, there's always a chance
that it will be the wrong colour, wrong style or wrong size.
If you don't want to condemn the recipient to wearing it
willy-nilly, you can explain to the shop that it's a gift and
ask them to let you have a receipt without the price on to
put with the gift. Then it can be changed without question
– and YOU won't have to be involved in the changing. The
paperwork of some shops may make it impossible for them
to do this, but with others it will be no problem.

RECORD KEEPING

With an expensive item which you might want to sell at
some time – be it a mink, a car or a house – it pays to keep
a record of any care and attention it receives. Simply keep
a file for each such object and put in all the receipts and
slips showing repairs, painting, cleaning or whatever. A
prospective buyer is far more likely to pay the price you

want if there is concrete proof that something has been well looked after. And, the very fact that you bothered to keep a record makes you look like a careful owner, quite regardless of what you had done. So if you're the buyer, examine those receipts and see what really was done.

SEED STORAGE

It's a nuisance to have to go through a drawer full of seeds and decide each month which ones need to be sown. The way to avoid this is to keep a cardboard concertina file, with a section for each month, and simply drop into each section the packets of seeds which need to be sown that month. Those which are sown in rotation can be used and then moved to the next month when they are due to be sown.

SELLOTAPE

Some people find that putting a button under the end of Sellotape is more effective than just trying to remember to turn the end in: if you don't put the button back you're left with it sitting there to remind you.

SEWING THINGS

One of the neatest ways to keep a small quantity of sewing things – such as hooks and eyes, packets of needles and so on – tidy, and to hand, is to lay them out on one of the adhesive pages used in photograph albums and simply smooth the film over them.

SHOE CLEANING

As shoe polishing is often a last-minute affair, it saves a lot of hand washing if a pair of rubber gloves is kept with the shoe polish.

SHOPPING

Cutting the Journeys

With a little care, a car and perhaps a freezer, household shopping – even for a large family – need only occupy a few hours a month. It's just as easy to buy two or three months' supply of basics like washing-up liquid as to buy a month's. The same applies to all the stand-bys like rice, pasta and dried fruit. Correctly stored basics like cereals, bacon and butter will keep for at least two weeks. So you only need a quick twice-weekly trip to buy fruit, vegetables and meat to have everything you need.

When my children were all very young, and I was too harassed to remember what I did and did not have in the house, I found it helpful to keep a typed checklist of everything I normally used under a sheet of clear plastic. I put a stroke to mark each packet, jar or toilet roll in store and crossed them off as I used them up. This way I could see at a glance if nappy pads or light bulbs or whatever were running low and buy more before I ran out. It saved a lot of crises.

Lists

Everyone makes shopping lists, but lists are better if you write things down at the time when you find you've run short – by the end of the week you may know you need SOMETHING, but have no idea what it is.

Some people like to keep a regular list of things they buy every week. This is fine for predictable families, but if your family is unpredictable you'll just end up overstocked.

A 'Woman's Hour' listener wrote to me suggesting that shopping lists should be written on cardboard and tied to your handbag. This means you don't have to give an open invitation to pickpockets and muggers by repeatedly opening your handbag to take out the list – a tip for the elderly and anyone shopping at Christmas, or in markets.

STORING

If you have items such as surplus glasses or china which are only used once in a while, the bother of covering them with cling film to keep out the dust pays off. It takes far less time to cover them than to wash them and you can cover them up in any odd minute; whereas if you are getting them out, the chances are it's for an occasion and you have more than enough other things to do.

If you're thinking that it's easier still simply to keep glasses upside down, beware: they may pick up the smell of the shelf and spoil the taste of whatever you drink from them.

TELEPHONE ANSWERING

Answering Machines
One of the snags about answering machines is that one can never tell whether the brand one is talking to has room for an unlimited length of message or will suddenly shut off after a few words. To save your callers being panicked by this dilemma, it's a good idea to say, on your recording, how long a message your machine will take.

During Messy Jobs
When doing a messy job, avoid making the telephone dirty by putting an open paper bag near the phone – if it rings you can put your hand in the bag and pick the phone up through the bag.

THANK-YOUS

If you find yourself going blank before an empty sheet of paper and feel quite unable to write a succinct thank-you after a party or a visit, the answer could be postcards. Really attractive postcards make a more interesting thank-you than a piece of paper – especially if you can suit the postcard to the interests of the person. Moreover, you only have a tiny space in which to write, so the problem of what to write, and the time you take to write it, diminishes considerably.

TRAVEL

Case Care

If you are going to check in luggage, bear in mind that airport theft is rife, but an efficient thief wants to get through as many inviting cases as possible. Using smart luggage invites theft – logically the more valuable the contents, the dowdier the case should look. And the case should present some obstacles to access. A hard case, locked and with a tough strap round it, is the safest bet. It won't stop a determined thief, but it will make him give it a miss if he's in a hurry.

If your suitcase is a popular brand, reduce the chances of someone accidentally walking off with it by putting an unusual strap round it or binding the handle with coloured tape.

In America they have found that most of the luggage lost at airports was checked in towards the end of the check-in period. So early birds are less likely to lose their bags.

Clothes

Unless you are a celebrity, and likely to be photographed as you emerge at your destination, there is very little point in travelling in smart clothes which you will hesitate to crumple by curling up and sleeping.

For packing, the ideal is to take so little it can all fit in a case small enough to count as hand baggage on a plane. With a fully co-ordinated set of clothes, this is easier than you might suppose, but it gets harder and harder the more colours you take. One much-travelled businessman I know buys only white shirts and black socks, and wears only clothes which go with both. For a woman, a good starting point can be to restrict the packing to two neutrals (say, black and white, or brown and cream) and one colour. If you bear this in mind when shopping for a journey, you may find far more clothes go together than you thought possible – and you won't need to take a whole assortment of shoes, accessories and make-up to go with them. Your wardrobe is also likely to date less quickly; neutrals like black and white never go out of fashion. Mind you, I am talking about a normal person's range of new clothes: I once saw an article on travelling light which advocated a similar idea and then showed more clothes than I had in my entire summer wardrobe.

Coming Back
Pack an extra, fold-up, bag in the bottom of your case. Then you can take advantage of the good buys wherever you go without returning laden with awkward carrier bags.

Customs
If there could be a customs query on any valuables you take away with you, it's worth packing photocopies of the receipts, or customs payments, when you pack the items. If you aren't carrying the documents to prove it, customs officers can't be blamed for not believing that you bought and paid duty on your Japanese camera on your previous visit. But their doubts can waste a lot of your time.

Home Lists
If you have children or other relatives you leave behind when you travel, or ever let others use your home while you are away, it is useful to have a ready-made list of names and addresses they might need – doctor, butcher, reliable plumber and so on; also, possibly, the numbers of a few people they can ring if anything goes wrong. If such a list is put somewhere conspicuous – on a board in the kitchen, for example – it can double as an emergency list for babysitters.

Make sure this list has the name of relatives you are likely to visit, and gives their relationship to you. Then, if you leave your house empty and the police have to come in because of a burglary, they can easily see who might know where to find you.

Loss Leader

Whatever you do, there is always a chance that your
luggage will be lost at an airport. If your appearance
matters to you it takes a lot of worry out of a journey if
you carry everything you need for one night and one *smart*
day in your hand baggage. There are always some garments
one loves more than others, so I always make sure that
the one I pick for my hand luggage is the one I would most
hate to lose. Then if the rest are lost I can at least comfort
myself with the thought that my favourite is still with me.

Make-up

Most cosmetic manufacturers seem to make a special point
of packaging their wares in containers which are (thanks
to extra cavities) either so large or so heavy that a decent
selection of make-up can virtually put you into excess
weight all on its own. One way to cut the weight down
is to buy some tiny trial-size bottles of skin cleanser,
moisturizer and so on when they are on special offer. Then
keep them packed in your sponge bag, ready for any
journey. Remember to top them up, from your main
bottles, at the end of each journey – it's the kind of fiddly
job which is annoying when rushing to leave, yet a quietly
satisfying reminder of good times when you are just
back.

Make-up Plus

Another solution to packing make-up is to save the little
plastic canisters which colour film comes in – or beg a few
for free from a photographic shop. They weigh next to
nothing, have lids which usually seal perfectly, and can be
labelled to show what they contain. They look too small
to take all one needs for a couple of weeks, but, in my
experience, they are quite big enough.

   These canisters can also be used for other things:
   for shampoo,
   for toothpaste (no more heavy tubes),
   for taking pills and tablets of all kinds;
   for containing a miniature sewing kit (thimble, needles,

safety pins, spare buttons and a few shades of cotton
wound round a piece of cardboard);
   and for holding salt, pepper and mustard (invaluable on
holiday picnics).

If you replenish your set of containers each time you
return, keeping them ready filled with all the things you
personally like to take with you (bar anything which will
deteriorate with keeping), and keep them ready in a plastic
bag, you can pack them all in seconds, without the horror
of rushing round the house only to discover that you've
run out of something essential and the shops are shut.

Money
If there's the slightest chance that you'll go to a country
again in the next few years, it is well worth hanging on to
all those little coins one finds in pockets after a trip. Put
each type of currency into a different small plastic bag and
label it clearly – sorting through hundreds of small coins
all heaped into a box when you are already busy packing
is hell. I know, I've done it.

PACKING – LISTS

In practice, though every journey has its own special
requirements, certain things are needed every time. It's a
great saving of time and energy if you keep a basic list of
essentials ready to use each time you go away. It may seem
a bit pernickety to stick the list to a piece of cardboard
and cover it with clear plastic, but it does mean you can
tick things off with a chinagraph pencil as you pack, and
wipe it clean afterwards for the next time.

In addition to a basic list – or even instead of it – journeys
can be divided into different types, each with their own
particular requirements and special lists. The things you
need for a two-day business trip will be much the same
wherever you go; all cold-weather camping holidays require one type of clothes; and all hot-weather beach holidays another; and so on. This saves you racking your brains
while you try to pack. It also allows you to delete items

which experience proves are unnecessary and insert others which you discover you need.

A friend who travelled frequently with four small children found she could keep track of what she was packing for whom by putting each child's list on a different coloured piece of paper.

If you always use the same case, the lists can be kept in it, so they are there to hand. Otherwise keep them in a slim plastic file in a drawer.

Such lists don't have to be restricted to clothes. For years I kept a camping list, which got better and better as I gained experience, and my camping went more smoothly every year because of it. For example, it wasn't until I experienced the amount of brushwood underfoot in some allotted spaces that I realized that secateurs are essential on a camping holiday.

Postcards

If you are obliged to send postcards while you are away to people whose addresses you don't know by heart, write out the addresses on a series of self-adhesive labels of the sort offices use to address letters and take these with you. Then you can just stick the label on the back of the postcard and you'll know by the remaining labels who still needs to get a card.

Sundries

You can save yourself a lot of searching if you keep all the odds and ends you need abroad, and nowhere else, together in one place. Things like an adaptor plug for foreign sockets, a small plastic bag of soap powder, a travelling radio, razor, iron, alarm clock and so on. And, though I wouldn't recommend it to those not experienced in matters electrical, I always carry a small screwdriver, so I can change the plugs on any of my equipment if the adaptor fails me.

TOOLS

Garden Tools

It's too easy to drop the tool one is using, rush inside to the phone, be distracted by a series of children, and find that by the time you get back to the garden you've forgotten where you put the tool down. To guard against this, spray the handles a bright colour so you can quickly spot them – yellow has the advantage of showing up well in moonlight if you get really delayed! Also, if your neighbours are tool borrowers, they will have a vivid reminder to return them.

To be sure that you find what you want in a shed – or to make it easy to see if it's missing – hang all the tools on a rack.

Nails and Screws

Any system which keeps each type of nail, screw, bolt and so on separate is worth using. Sifting through them for what one needs is a waste of time. A stack of tobacco tins used to be traditional, but a set of very small jars is better, because it allows you to see what you've got without opening them. The ultra-organized way is to make a small hole in the lid of each jar and to screw it to the underside of a shelf. Then the jars hang in a neat row with everything instantly visible.

Working Tools

Basic tools – pliers, screwdrivers and so on – are easiest to find if they are stored on a hanging board, held in position with clips. If you want to be sure to notice if anyone in the family fails to put them back, the solution is to mark each tool's place by drawing round its outline; then fill in the outline with paint. The sooner you know that someone has spirited a tool away to their room, the better the chance of getting it back before one of the culprit's friends borrows it – forever.

VALUABLES

When valuing furniture and effects, a good valuer should supply photographs, as well as a detailed description, of any special pieces. Even if your possessions don't merit that level of valuation, photographs are a worthwhile record of anything you treasure and can make it easier for the police to recover them if there is a burglary.

WASHING

Airing Cupboards

It's extraordinary the way a teenager looking for a shirt can almost instantly convert a tidy airing cupboard into something resembling the aftermath of a rummage sale. An excellent way to prevent this is to buy a set of small rectangular plastic baskets, of different colours, and allocate a basket to each member of the family. Then, as the clothes are ironed, they can be put straight into the correct baskets and go into the airing cupboard in these. The problem then solves itself. And, with a bit of luck, everyone will be so pleased at being able to find their clothes that they actually return the baskets to beside the ironing board.

Socks

Breakfasts can be ruined by debates over sock ownership. So in any household where there is more than one male – be they sons or lovers – some system of sock sorting is useful. One of the simplest methods is to allocate a particular colour code to each person and make a couple of firm stitches in the back of each sock top with thread of that colour. Dry socks can then be dealt into heaps by colour and the owners left to pair them as they wish.

Storing Nylon

Fitted nylon sheets must be among the worst things to fold and keep tidy. The simple way to keep them all together is to fold them and put each set into one of its pillow cases.

WORK AVOIDANCE

A great deal of work can be avoided if everything you buy for the house is thought of in terms of the work it saves or creates. For example, make sure you buy only china and cutlery which can be washed in a washing-up machine – even if you haven't got one now you may have one next year. If you like to wear pure wool, don't rush into buying a machine without a really good wool programme. A plain pale carpet up the stairs may look wonderful, but, if you have pets or children, a textured carpet could cut the vacuum-cleaning by half: try putting a muddy shoe on a sample of each before you buy. If you like the look of louvre doors, think how long they might take to dust. These are only a few examples.

WORK SURFACES

A Welsh neighbour of mine, brought up without the luxury of today's kitchen surfaces, always kept sheets of newspaper in a kitchen drawer and put one on the work top before doing messy jobs, such as vegetable peeling. It struck me as old-fashioned, until I realized how much time she saved by being able simply to roll all the mess up in the paper. Just because one CAN wipe work tops down doesn't mean it's a good use of time.

A List Of
USEFUL ADDRESSES

Alkali-resistant primer   *List of stockists available from*
Consumer Information Services
Dulux Paints,
Imperial Chemical Industries,
Slough, Bucks

Anti-static spray   Meech Static Eliminators
146–150 Clapham Manor Street
London SW4 6DA

Chewing gum spray   G.E. Holloway and Son
12 Carlisle Road
London NW9 0HL

Dyeing   *Advice available from*
Consumer Advice Bureau
Dylon International,
Worsley Bridge Road
London SE26

Easyclean   Synchemicals
44 Grange Walk
London SE1 3EN

Leather upholstery
restoration   Connolly Brothers
Wandle Bank
London SW19

Pest control
natural predators   Natural Pest Control
Watermead, Yapton Road,
Barnham, Bognor,
Sussex PO22 0BQ
(*The Royal Horticultural
Society has a list of other
companies available to
members*)

Soapfree washing bar   Shaklee (UK) Limited
                            Norfolk House,
                            92 Saxon Gate West
                            Central Milton Keynes,
                            MK9 1LS

Wiltpruf S 600   Synchemicals
                            44 Grange Walk
                            London SE1 3EN

Zebrite (and   The Stove Shop
information on   1a Beethoven Street
solid-fuel stoves)   London W10

Zinc supplement   *For nearest stockist send s.a.e. to*
                            Herbal Laboratories (UK)
                            Limited
                            Kilbane Street, Copse Road
                            Fleetwood, Lance

E45 Cream, Fullers' Earth, Glycerine, Oil of Eucalyptus
and Rose Water *are all available from most good chemists*.

INDEX